Healthy Transitions for Girls

The Essential Prevention Tool for Girls Ages 8-14

A Strength-Based Curriculum to Promote

POSTIVE BODY IMAGE

For Parents, Mentors, and Professionals

By
Peggy A McFarland, MS, LPC

Copyright Notice

Legal Notice

Author's Dedication

This book is written for my own beautiful daughters and granddaughters who are inspirational and dear to me. They are my hope, my legacy, and the joy of my heart. It is written for girls everywhere who start their lives with so much promise but lose their way in a toxic culture that robs them of their sense of inner worth. You too are the daughters of my heart. May the concepts in this program find their way into your minds and hearts and bring you safely home to a sense of your true selves.

~Peggy A McFarland
August 2011

Acknowledgements

I want to extend heartfelt gratitude to Dr. Laura Choate, Lousiana State University for her generosity in sharing her time and expertise to this project. I also received much encouragement and feedback from my Capella University mentors, including Dr. Leslie Korn, throughout my research. The expertise of Dr. Mary Pritchard, Boise State University, has been vital in moving this project forward .

My editor and long-time friend, Darla Isackson gave valuable advice, as always. I am also grateful to Kalie Chamberlain whose tireless attention to detail shaped this project in a profound way. My dear friends, Chuck and Sandi Hofmann shared invaluable wisdom and encouragement.

I thank my children for eating lots of peanut butter sandwiches while I was cloistered in my room writing, hour after hour. My son Sam shared his technical talents in numerous , vital ways. Finally, I thank my husband, Michael, for his constant support and sacrifice. He is my truest "cheerleader."

Table of Contents

Part I
Principles and Activities

Part II
Handouts, Figures, References & Index

Chapter 1: This Book Is Written for the Girls You Love

None.

Chapter 2: Building Positive Self-Talk: "I Am a Palace of Possibilities"

Chapter 3: The Mind-Body Connection: Building a Partnership with My Body

Chapter 4: Holistic Wellness: Reclaiming the WHOLE ME

Chapter 5: Building Parent Connections: Less Conflict, More Collaboration

Chapter 6: Building Supportive Connections with Other Girls

Chapter 7: Building Healthy Boy-Girl Friendships

Chapter 8: Media Literacy and Critical Thinking: Embracing the Images of REAL Beauty

Chapter 9: Coping Skills and Problem-Solving Skills

Chapter 10: Gender Role: What's So Special about Being a Girl?

Chapter 11: Physical Self-Esteem: My Body is My Best Friend for Life

Chapter 12: Curriculum and Workshop Planning

References

Index

x

Chapter 1

This Book Is Written for the Girls You Love

*I always wondered why 6th grade girls who were so lovely
and talented would say such critical things about themselves; now, I know why.*
~ School Superintendent, after a *Healthy Transitions for Girls* Presentation

As a parent, mentor, teacher, counselor, or member of clergy, you are aware that something alarming happens as girls begin to experience the changes of puberty. Girls who seem comfortable with their identity in grade school experience a crisis of confidence as they enter the middle school grades. Too often, their decreasing sense of well-being signals more trouble ahead.

As a parent, you may wonder, "What's happening to my little girl?" All of a sudden, she…
Worries more about what her friends think.
Puts herself down.
Wants to wear revealing or tight clothing.
Obsesses about her weight and appearance.
Worries about having a boyfriend.
Is embattled in girl drama (usually over boys).
Argues with family rules.

As a professional or lay-professional, you may see increased social and emotional distress in girls, at younger ages. For example, the Oregon Healthy Teens Survey (2013) of 8th grade girls revealed the following:

- 46.6% of the girls stated they were trying to lose weight.
- 25.6% have felt hopeless for longer than two weeks
- 16.1% seriously considered suicide in the last 12 months.
- 15.2% had been harassed about weight, physical appearance, acne, and/or clothes.

The Answer: Positive Body Image

If there were one single approach that could help girls resist the many frightening pitfalls of adolescence, such as substance abuse, eating disorders, depression, unhealthy dating relationships, risky sexual behavior, girl drama, bullying, and low self-esteem, what would it be? If all the money currently spent on prevention could be streamlined into one powerful effort, where would we focus? This is the answer: POSITIVE BODY IMAGE. Body image has been defined as "the greatest single predictor of self-esteem for adolescents of different ethnicities."[1] Yes, body image is a BIG deal!

---

[1] Verkuyten (1990, as cited by Wood, Becker, and Thompson, 1996), p. 86.

As girls experience the physical changes of puberty, they are unconsciously seeking belief systems to make sense of these changes. It's as if their brain is "taking snapshots" and building a photo album of "selfies" based upon what they see and experience during this critical stage. Unfortunately, because we live in the "age of image," girls experience thousands of messages daily that represent unrealistic, sexualized concepts of what it means to be a young woman in today's society. Their brain stores these images and says, "Here, this is what you are supposed to be like, even if it is impossible and unhealthy." It sounds like a powerful form of "brain washing," doesn't it?

In short, simply addressing problem behaviors, without addressing the core beliefs and emotions that motivate these behaviors, misses the *heart* of the matter. Helping girls develop positive body image is an "umbrella" solution to the many problems facing girls today. This is why *Healthy Transitions for Girls* is an ESSENTIAL PREVENTION TOOL.

How Is *Healthy Transitions for Girls* Different from Other Programs?

Healthy Transitions for Girls Includes ALL Essential Factors

Although the media plays a huge role in body image dissatisfaction, developing a positive body image requires more than addressing harmful media messages. A whole range of skills is required for girls to develop positive body image. The *Healthy Transitions for Girls* curriculum addresses all factors shown by research (Choate, 2008) to promote positive body image. This curriculum

- Reframes negative belief systems and creates positive belief systems.
- Supports the mind-body connection and a holistic view of wellness.
- Supports strong parent and peer relationships.
- Teaches media literacy and critical thinking.
- Encourages healthy concepts of femininity and challenges stereotypes (gender role).
- Supports global and physical self-esteem.
- Teaches coping skills.

Many worthwhile programs for girls address one or two of these factors; however, research shows that all these factors are *essential* for success. Efforts to develop positive body image are less effective if any of these interrelated factors are excluded. Each chapter in this book covers one of these concept areas. Because the concepts are interrelated, a concept may appear in one chapter and reappear when it correlates to a concept in another chapter. This kind of reinforcement enhances real learning and real change.

Healthy Transitions for Girls Starts Early Enough to Make a Difference

One very aware mother asked, "My daughter is only seven years old; is it too early to start?" My emphatic response is, "Absolutely not!" Incredulously, a review of research published by Common Sense Media in 2015 showed that one third of kids ages five and six years old are dissatisfied with their weight.[2]   An early study (Collins, 1991) found that 42 percent of 1st – 3rd grade girls wanted to be thinner. One merely needs to peruse the fashion section of a favorite department store to know that girls are being pounded with the "dos" and "don'ts of being cool" at younger and younger ages. The best time to address body image is BEFORE girls experience puberty. They want and need to talk about these changes. My heart tugs each time a girl admits her private fears about growing up. Whether you are a professional or a parent, it is wise to address this developmental milestone early. *Healthy Transitions for Girls* builds life-long strengths during the CRITICAL WINDOW when girls' bodies are changing and their "play dough-like," moldable brains are looking to assign meaning to those changes.

Healthy Transitions for Girls Utilizes a Strength-Based, Wellness Approach

        A wellness approach looks at the bigger picture of girls' health behaviors. "Counseling for wellness," rather than focusing on pathology, helps a girl to "improve her overall health, quality of life, and ability to cope effectively with life's demands" (Choate, 2008, p. 8). *Healthy Transitions for Girls* helps girls to feel that they have the responsibility and power to influence the outcomes in their lives. This factor, called "internal locus of control," is one of the most important single predictors of happiness based on more than 25 years of research by Myers and Sweeney (2005). In *Healthy Transitions for Girls*, the objective of each activity is an "I can" statement, such as "I can develop a working definition of femininity that is non-sexualized," or "I can recognize my support systems and learn to ask for help." *Healthy Transitions for Girls* supports the WHOLE girl!

Healthy Transitions for Girls Offers Real-Time Coping Skills

        Ideas and theories are great, but what about when a girl is having a meltdown? This curriculum not only creates resilience to unhealthy behaviors as girls transition through adolescence, but it also gives real-time solutions that can be used by professionals and parents when the girl they love or are working with is in a crisis. Chapter 9, Coping Skills and Problem-Solving Skills, provides relaxation skills and self-soothing activities that girls can use "in the heat of the moment" to cope with anxiety, grief, depressed mood, and conflict.

Healthy Transitions for Girls Uses a Values-Based Approach

        When addressing puberty in schools and counseling arenas, the role of "values" is often avoided. Mary Pipher, PhD, author of *Reviving Ophelia* and an expert in girls' issues, admonished counselors not to "check basic morality at the doors of [their] offices" (1998, p. 3). *Healthy Transitions for Girls* promotes values such as modesty in dress, sexual abstinence, and attention to spiritual needs. In *Healthy Transitions for Girls*, girls are encouraged to develop feminine traits of nurturing, empathy, compassion, and connectedness, as well as to understand the beautiful nurturing potential of breastfeeding and giving life. Girls learn to differentiate between real femininity and "sex appeal" as promoted by the media. They are encouraged to develop friendships with boys, rather than engage in steady dating. They learn how to set physical/sexual boundaries that help boy-girl relationships develop into healthy friendships. These are essential skills for developing individual identity and true intimacy,

---

[2] See this report at https://www.commonsensemedia.org/research/children-teens-media-and-body-image#

vital components of secure, life-long, marriages later on.[3] In essence, *Healthy Transitions for Girls* speaks to both the mind and the *heart* of girls.

<u>*Healthy Transitions for Girls*: A "Must Have" for Parents, Mentors, and Professionals</u>

Healthy Transitions is a "one-stop shop." Instead of going through multiple files and workbooks to find creative interventions, *Healthy Transitions for Girls* is a comprehensive intervention resource. Professionals in private practice, agencies, schools, or other settings will appreciate that *Healthy Transitions for Girls* can be used in individual or group therapy to target specific problems. It can also be used by community organizations as a prevention tool. Chapter 12, "Curriculum and Workshop Planning," provides detailed plans for promoting, planning, and conducting *Healthy Transitions for Girls* groups and workshops.

Parents will feel empowered as *Healthy Transitions for Girls* helps them to become experts in understanding the challenges and needs of their pre-adolescent and adolescent daughters. *Healthy Transitions for Girls* can be used during one-on-one time with daughters as problems arise in day to day interactions or as part of an ongoing home school program. Savvy grandmothers have had marvelous experiences using these activities with the girls they love!

Mentors in church and community groups will appreciate the fact *that Healthy Transitions for Girls* can be implemented with minimal cost and can be successfully facilitated by lay-professionals and volunteers. Instead of trying to find funding to target bullying, mental health concerns, violence prevention, and/or substance abuse prevention, this "umbrella" curriculum is economical because it addresses the core causes of multiple problems. *Healthy Transitions for Girls* is designed to help girls from diverse backgrounds discover common challenges, values, and strengths.

<u>*Healthy Transitions for Girls* Uses Creative Activities to Facilitate Real Learning</u>

Real learning requires a creative, whole body experience, especially with children and teens. Real learning needs to involve the logical left side of the brain as well as the intuitive, emotional right side of the brain. Girls need to have emotional connections to the concepts being taught for them to truly internalize new attitudes and behaviors. For that reason, art, role play, tangible objects, and movement activities are used to teach the abstract concepts in this curriculum.

Healthy Transitions for Girls tackles challenging issues in a positive way. Private, painful worries about growing up are transformed to a safe and hopeful self-concept. This program will not only increase the confidence of girls who participate, but it will also give you the tools and encouragement to know that you can truly make a difference with the girls you love.

---

[3] See *Reviving Ophelia Study Guide*. Available through the Media Education Foundation at http://www.mediaed.org/assets/products/303/studyguide_303.pdf.

This Healthy Transitions for Girls Book is Organized for Ease of Use

I am grateful for the trial and error and the feedback of professionals who have used this program. The result is a simple format that is easy to use whether you just want to know more about helping girls grow up, whether you want to choose a single activity, or whether you want to plan and carry out a *Healthy Transitions for Girls* workshop series.

Part I of the book includes a discussion of all the foundational principles required to help girls to develop positive body image. The principles discussed in Chapters 2 through 11 help the reader to understand the "big picture" of helping today's girls. Directions for all of the book's activities, which reinforce these vital principles, are also provided in Part 1 of the book.

Part I, Chapter 12, provides the details on how to organize and implement *Healthy Transitions for Girls* groups and workshops. Important ethical guidelines are provided, as well as step-by-step directions for implementing a 12-week workshop series comprised of weekly, 60-minute sessions, and a 3-week summer or after-school workshop series comprised of bi-weekly, two hour sessions. Parents, mentors, and professionals will feel confident and fully prepared to lead *Healthy Transitions for Girls* groups with the comprehensive resources included in Chapter 12.

Part II of the book includes all of the handouts which are used in the *Healthy Transitions for Girls* activities described in Part I. These handouts are grouped together in numerical order in the second part of the book for easy access. The reader will refer to these handouts repeatedly when conducting *Healthy Transitions for Girls* activities.

Figures 1 through 5 are also included in Part II. The figures provide helps for workshop preparation. For example, Figure 1 *Palace of Possibilities Display Board Template* gives directions for a visual aid that will be used throughout the workshop series. Figures 3-4 provide forms that are used for workshop promotion, parent consent, and workshop evaluation. Figure 5 provides a comprehensive list of materials that will be used in the *Healthy Transitions for Girls* activities. Even though there is a materials list at the beginning of each activity, Figure 5 helps the presenter to order materials in advance, such as books, DVD's, and a wooden castle, which are used in the book's activities.

Finally, at the conclusion of the book, the References and Index sections will assist when the reader needs to find a more information on a specific area of interest. This information can be invaluable when preparing a presentation on girls' issues, or when a parent or helping professional needs to address a specific issue with a girl they love.

It is our hope that this *Healthy Transitions for Girls* book will help parents, mentors, clergy, and professionals, with easy-to-use tools for homes, schools, churches, and agencies. Together, we can help the girls we love to have a safer place to live—in their own beautiful minds and bodies.

6

Chapter 2

Building Positive Self-Talk: I Am a "Palace of Possibilities"

Our consistent thoughts become our reality.
~Gary Craig

Imagine that deep in the center of your being there is a palace filled with an endless number of rooms, each decorated with varied colors and styles. Each of these rooms represents an emotionally-impacting experience that you have had and the beliefs and feelings you formed about that experience. Consider that you unknowingly visit the rooms of your palace constantly throughout each day. As you peek into individual rooms, you notice writing on the walls. In some rooms, the writing causes the room to feel cold and fearful, making you want to leave quickly and close the door; in other rooms, the writing is pleasant, and the mood of the room is warm and safe, inviting you to stay.

This palace is your "Palace of Possibilities," a place where you will find the beliefs that guide your self-talk, emotions, and actions every day. As stated by Gary Craig (n.d.), the originator of the Palace of Possibilities concept, "The 'writing' on our 'palace walls' contains our 'shoulds' and 'should nots'; our 'can and can't dos,' and all of our 'how-tos' " (p. 1). We literally create our lives with our beliefs. They are powerful!

Where did the beliefs that are written on "palace walls" originate? They come from the positive and negative experiences in our lives—from parents, extended family, peers, media, and cultural influences. Puberty is a time when girls are flooded with a need to formulate new belief systems that will carry them into adulthood. As girls' bodies change, their minds intently search for meaning about those changes. The beliefs they form about their changing bodies affect every area of their lives. Girls are extremely vulnerable to negative messages, and for most girls, puberty brings a crisis of self-esteem not present in earlier years. To make their "palace" a safe place to live, they must learn to challenge the constant stream of negative self-talk that bombards their minds, especially when they stand in front of the mirror.

A first step to an exploration of body image is to assess girls' current understanding of what is normal in puberty. Girls have many unspoken worries and fears about the changes that are occurring in their bodies during puberty. They need a safe place to acknowledge these concerns. The ***My Body is Changing Activity (Activity 1)*** can be used to assess fears and misinformation and teach correct information about puberty and thinness.

In the ***Palace of Possibilities Guided Imagery (or Art) Activity (Activity 2)***, girls learn firsthand how beliefs affect their emotions negatively or positively. Guided imagery is like a healthy form of daydreaming that uses the creative, right side of the brain to tune in to inner thoughts and feelings. In Activity 2, girls experience positive emotions in a room where positive statements are "written on their walls." Using the Palace of Possibilities metaphor, negative beliefs are identified as "graffiti" on the palace walls. It is not coincidence that many girls "graffiti" (cut, tattoo, pierce, or radically make up) their outer bodies based upon the inner "graffiti" that destroys their sense of inner beauty.

The following three activities can be used as a follow up to the guided imagery activity; each has the goal of increasing awareness of beliefs systems, both negative and positive, related to the body. The **My Changing Beliefs Activity (Activity 3)** allows the girls to express general beliefs about their changing body in a confidential way. The **Palace of Possibilities Body Drawing Activity (Activity 4)** can be used as a follow-up activity to Activity 2 or as a stand-alone activity to increase awareness of negative beliefs related to specific body parts. The **Who's Been Writing on My Walls? Activity (Activity 5)** helps girls identify how their beliefs have changed as they have grown up. It also helps them identify where their beliefs came from.

Girls become empowered as they learn to "erase" and re-write the messages on the "walls" of their "palace." The next set of activities and handouts in this chapter teach strategies to change or "reframe" negative beliefs and replace them with positive beliefs. **Activity 6, Mirror, Mirror Activity** raises awareness of negative self-talk and challenges it with positive self-statements or affirmations. **Handout 8, Palace of Possibilities Affirmations** can be used by the girls daily to reinforce positive self-talk in front of the mirror.

As you have undoubtedly noticed, adolescent moods are like a teeter-totter with extreme ups and downs. **Activity 7, Watch Out for the Imaginary Other Activity** addresses the emotional roller coaster caused by irrational thinking patterns that are common in teens, such as, "black and white" or "all or nothing" thinking, preoccupation with self, and obsession with "shoulds." Daniel Amen, MD, (2010) calls these beliefs the "ANTS" or "Automatic Negative Thoughts" (p. 258). **Activity 8, Be Your Own Cheerleader Activity** gives girls an opportunity to practice challenging their irrational thinking patterns with positive "cheerleading statements." Parents can gain additional understanding of common negative beliefs in **Handout 17, The Emotional Roller Coaster Starts with These Beliefs (Chapter 5).**

Make the Palace of Possibilities Metaphor Tangible

Through the creative activities in this chapter, girls can begin to see their bodies as a safe and hopeful place to live and grow. Each can discover "princess power" by being conscious of the emotions that come from negative self-talk. For the *Palace of Possibilities* activities, a model castle brings fun and concreteness to the "palace" metaphor.[4] In Part II of this book, directions are also given for a **Palace of Possibilities Display Board** (see **Figure 1**). This three-dimensional representation of "palace walls" helps girls visually compare negative and positive body image statements. It can be used throughout your implementation of this curriculum. The *Palace of Possibilities* metaphor will come alive with these valuable learning aids.

---

[4] Purchase a "Fold and Go Castle" for $49.99, plus shipping, through www.melissaanddoug.com. Or visit www.ebay.com and search for "Melissa and Doug wooden castle."

List of Activities, Handouts, & Figures Used In Chapter 2

Chapter 2: Building Positive Self-Talk: "I Am a Palace of Possibilities"

<u>List of Activities.</u>

<u>List of Handouts.</u>

<u>List of Figures.</u>

Activity 1
My Body is Changing Activity

(Time = 15 – 20 minutes)

Objectives for Each Girl.

1. I can recognize that weight gain during puberty is normal.
2. I can recognize that the "ideal thinness" presented in fashion and advertising is unrealistic for almost all women and girls.
3. I can discern that beliefs about the "ideal" body are a fad that changes with every generation.
4. I can address the worries and questions I have about my body's changes during puberty.
5. I can recognize that my friends' bodies change on a different timetable than mine.
6. I can understand how hormonal changes affect my body and my emotions.

Materials Needed.

1. Handout 1, *My Body is Changing*.
2. Pencils and paper.

Activity Steps.

1. Explain to the girls that you are going to give them a "true" or "false" pretest to see how much they know about the changes in their body. Pass out pencils and paper so the girls can record their answers. NOTE: Give the pretest before using Handout 1.

    My Body is Changing Pretest

    1) If you start putting weight on your hips and thighs, it means you need to diet and should see a doctor.
    2) It is normal for girls to put on 30 to 50 lbs. when their body changes during puberty.
    3) If you start sweating more, it means you smell gross and are probably not showering enough.
    4) Most girls and women could be as thin as models if they just exercised enough and didn't eat so much food.
    5) Only people who eat greasy food and don't wash their faces get acne.
    6) The reason models and movie stars weigh less today than when your mother was young is because they are a lot smarter about exercise and diet.
    7) If your body starts changing when you are 10 years old, something is wrong with you.
    8) If your emotions start feeling more up and down, that means you are probably depressed and need to see a doctor.
    9) Everyone's breasts should be about the same size, and if yours are not, there is something wrong with your body.
    10) If you exercise enough, no one will be able to notice that your hips are getting rounder.

2. Read Handout 1 with the girls. Ask them if they want to change any of their answers after reading the information on the handout.
3. Tell the girls that the only "true" answer on the pretest is #2. Review the pretest questions and address any misconceptions. Be sure to include the following points in your discussion:

- It is unrealistic to think that girls can look like models. Only 5 percent of girls have the body type promoted in the fashion industry; and even models who are naturally thin use drugs and poor eating to reduce weight. The other 95 percent of girls can never achieve the "ideal thin" promoted in advertising and the fashion industry. Most body types (with larger bone structure, more muscular, heavier tendencies, larger breasts and hips, etc. could NEVER look like a rail-thin model, even if they quit eating altogether.
- Standards of "beauty" change over the decades. When today's girls' mothers were teenagers, models weighed 8 percent less than the average woman; today's models weigh 23 percent less (Kilbourne, 2000). That means it is becoming less and less possible to look like a model without doing something very unhealthy. It also shows how what is "beauty" is really just a fad used to sell products.
- Weight gain in puberty is normal, between 30 to 50 pounds, with most of the gain on the hips and thighs. Exercising or dieting to keep these areas from experiencing normal weight gain will not help; it will only make them unhealthy. Most of the models we see don't look like their hips and legs have even been through puberty. Ask the girls, "Are they trying to make us feel bad about our bodies changing?" and "If they don't show what real girls look like, how can we know what normal really is?"
- Girls do not experience puberty at the same rate. Some start developing at age 9 or 10; others hardly develop at all until they are 14. Girls can start their period as late as 16 and still be normal. There is a big variation in how girls develop. That also means their breasts and bodies are going to be different sizes. It is not only the variations in timing, but variations in body type, genetics, bone structure, etc. that makes bodies different sizes. Ask the girls, "Where do we get the idea that our breasts are supposed to look a certain way?" and "Who decides what is 'normal' if my body is changing the way my genes tell it to change?"
- Sweat glands and acne are a normal part of hormonal development. Keeping faces and bodies clean helps reduce body odor and acne, but sweating and having acne does not mean something is wrong. It just means girls are having normal hormone changes.
- Explain that hormonal changes in puberty do mean they will have more emotional "ups and downs." This doesn't mean there is something wrong with them, but it does mean they are going to have to learn some new skills for dealing with their emotions.

4. Ask the girls if they have any other worries about their bodies changing. (They can put questions on a Post-it Note and then pass the notes in for the facilitator to read anonymously or they can put these notes on the walls of the palace model or the *Palace of Possibilities Display Board.*)
5. Ask: "How did this discussion help you clear up worries about growing up?" Go around the group and ask the girls to share at least one new fact she learned about how her body will change as she grows up. Encourage the girls to get help from parents or someone they trust if they have worries.

Activity 2
Palace of Possibilities Guided Imagery (or Art) Activity

(Time = 15-20 minutes)

Objectives for Each Girl.

1. I can increase awareness of beliefs that create negative body image.
2. I can increase awareness of beliefs that create positive body image.
3. I can discover that beliefs affect how I feel.

Important Note.

The purpose of this exercise is to gently examine unconscious beliefs and emotions related to puberty. The girls are NOT being asked to delve into big, private, emotional issues. Be sure to make this clear at the beginning of the activity. A guided imagery exercise may not be appropriate for girls with a history of trauma or mental illness and is suggested for use only by licensed professionals who have experience dealing with emotional abreaction and trauma. If a girl is going to have anxiety connected with this activity, it will typically surface at the beginning of the exercise as she is directed to focus inside her body. Anxiety will cause a girl to begin to breathe shallowly in her chest. Simply direct her to open her eyes, to focus on you, and to return her attention to the present moment. Redirect her attention back to the rise and fall of her abdomen. Explain that if an uncomfortable emotion arises, that she simply needs to observe it and allow it to pass like a "wave" or a "cloud." Remind her that as she is gently blowing warm sunshine into her abdomen, watching it rise and fall, she is surrounding her distress with warmth and love.

Additionally, a guided imagery activity should not be used if girls have not established a positive group connection. Emotional safety is always a top priority when dealing with the sensitive issues surrounding puberty. **If it is determined that a guided imagery activity is not ethically appropriate for the group, use this activity as an art activity by following the directions provided with the *Palace of Possibilities Art Activity Script.***

Materials Needed (when using the *Palace of Possibilities Script* for an art activity only).

1. Relaxation music CD with no words.
2. Colored markers or pencils.
3. Several sheets of blank paper for each girl.

Activity Steps.

1. It is helpful to use this script with some relaxing music that has no lyrics. Make sure the room is free of distractions. Create an atmosphere where girls can truly relax. If using the *Palace of Possibilities*

Script as an art activity, provide drawing materials for the girls. They may each need several sheets of paper to draw the elements described in the script.

2. It is important that everyone feels safe from ridicule during this experience. If a girl does not feel comfortable closing her eyes doing the guided imagery, explain that she should not giggle or make noise that will distract the others. Similarly, if doing an art activity, assure them that they will not be judged on their art ability and are not required to show their drawings to the rest of the group. Girls should be instructed not to ridicule each other's drawings if the script is used as an art activity.

3. Explain to the girls that they will be using their right brain, which is the imaginative part of their brains. Explain that they are most familiar with the cognitive or left part of their brains, which they use for school and homework. Tell them that it is important that their right brain gets exercise as well, although it may feel a bit strange as they begin to practice using their imagination and let go of their "logical" mind.[5] Tell the girls that you want them to pay attention to what they feel as they visualize [or draw] the elements you describe. Explain that when girls are visualizing [or drawing] the elements of the script, they may visualize [or draw] dark vivid colors and even "scribbles" to reflect strong feelings. Or they may visualize [or draw] pastels and soft lines to express calm emotions.

4. Use a slow, deliberate voice as you read the script. Avoid high-pitched inflections; try to keep your voice lower-pitched and soothing.

Palace of Possibilities Guided Imagery Script

First, begin to pay attention to your breathing. Don't change it or make it faster or slower. Just notice it. Notice how it feels to breathe in through your nostrils, allowing your nose to cleanse and warm the air. Breathe out through your mouth. Feel the air pass through your lips, allowing the air to gently push against your lips, puffing them out slightly. Continue to breathe in through your nose and out through your lips. Inhale and exhale completely in this manner five times. Do not feel rushed.

Feel your shoulders droop slightly as you become more relaxed. Uncross your legs if they are crossed. Allow your arms to droop at your sides.

Now, close your eyes or focus your eyes on the end of your nose as you breathe. Allow your mind to drift. Now place your hands on your stomach. Imagine as you breathe, that you have a balloon inside of your tummy. As you inhale, the balloon in your tummy grows round and full; as you exhale, the balloon in your tummy lets the air out and gets floppy. Do this five times, or until you feel you have a rhythm with your breathing and you can feel your tummy going up and down as you breathe. Blow and release air in and out of your "balloon" for five breaths.

As you breathe in this relaxed state, pretend that you are traveling into the center of your being, where you have your very own palace. If you start to feel nervous, simply place your hand on your tummy and once again feel the rise and fall of your breath. In your mind, send warmth and sunshine into your body with each breath. Feel the peace that comes over you. Look as your palace comes into your view.

---

[5] My good friend, Sandi Hofmann, a Master Rapid Eye Therapist and Certified Personal Coach, suggests using an eye patch over the dominant eye (usually the right eye) as the girls draw their art activity. This helps to quiet the mind, relieve stress, and enhance self-expression.

Visualize your palace. For some of you, this view will be vivid and colorful. For others it will be pastel and fuzzy. What your palace looks like isn't important. Only continue to feel relaxed and have fun on this inner adventure. Allow your mind to stay focused on this palace. If your mind wanders, simply notice that it is happening and gently pull your focus back to your palace.

You are very curious about this palace; it is big and has long halls and many rooms. As you look down one of the halls, you see a room that feels very safe. You feel at home in this room. Notice where this room is located. The door is slightly ajar, inviting you to come in. Touch the location on the outside of your body where you think this room might be located, giving yourself a gentle reminder that your body can be a safe home for you.

When you look inside your safe "Comfort Room," notice the furniture and how it is decorated. Just the way you like it! [Pause.] You may see words written on the walls. These words are messages that make this a comforting place to be. Do any words stand out to you? They may be written in letters that are "cloud" letters. What are the "cloud words" that you see written on the walls of your room? Notice the emotions you feel as you read these words.

Spend a few seconds enjoying the feeling of your "Comfort Room." [Pause.] Although you are grateful for the peaceful feelings you have in your "Comfort Room," you are ready for more adventure. Once again, imagine that you are looking down the long hall to find other doors which are open.

Imagine that you are entering another room that has an open door. Let your imagination guide the décor, the colors, and the mood, that you experience as you enter this second room. You can make it any kind of room you desire.

Again, look to see the writing that is on the walls. Look at the letters in the words which are written on the walls. Do the letters have a color? Is the color pleasant? Is it scribbled? What words are written on the walls of this second room? The writing on the walls will determine the mood that you feel in the room. Even if you cannot read the words, you may notice a feeling in your body as you stand in that room. Can you identify the feeling? [Pause.]

You are now ready to leave the second room and walk down the hall. As you walk down the hall, you realize that you go in some of these rooms many, many times a day and read the writing on the walls. [For art activity, ask the girls to draw some footsteps showing how they go in and out of the rooms many times a day.]

Look down the hall and find a room that says, "Changes in My Body" on the door. You may get a feeling like, "I don't want to go in there," and you may want slam the door. Or you may be curious but a little nervous. Notice how you feel. It can be different for everyone. As you carefully peek inside the open door of this "Changes Room," you may see some graffiti written on the walls. It may look like blotchy spots of paint. It may be dark and scribbled. You may see some very mean words written on the walls. You may have a nervous feeling in your tummy or a lump in your throat. Just gently breathe as you notice these feelings. The feelings will pass like a little wave rolling over your body.

Imagine yourself taking a few steps backward and stepping out the door of the "Changes in my Body Room." Imagine that you close the door and walk once again into the hall. Look down the hall. Walk back to the door of the first room you visited, your "Comfort Room."

As you are ready, slowly turn your thoughts back to your breathing. You feel a little sleepy and relaxed. You are curious how your mind could create such an adventure. As you prepare to come back to participate with the group, thank your mind for this imaginative experience. Gently count your breaths... 1... 2... 3... 4... 5. You are now ready to open your eyes and look around. Shake out your arms and hands. Wiggle your fingers and toes. Thank your body and mind for this interesting experience.

Palace of Possibilities Art Activity Script

First, begin to pay attention to your breathing. Don't change it or make it faster or slower. Just notice it. Notice how it feels to breathe in through your nostrils, allowing your nose to cleanse and warm the air. Breathe out through your mouth. Feel the air pass through your lips, allowing the air to gently push against your lips, puffing them out slightly. Continue to breathe in through your nose and out through your lips. Inhale and exhale completely in this manner five times. Do not feel rushed.

Feel your shoulders droop slightly as you become more relaxed. Uncross your legs if they are crossed. Allow your arms to droop at your sides.

Now, close your eyes or focus your eyes on the end of your nose as you breathe. Allow your mind to drift. Now place your hands on your stomach. Imagine as you breathe, that you have a balloon inside of your tummy. As you inhale, the balloon in your tummy grows round and full; as you exhale, the balloon in your tummy lets the air out and gets floppy. Do this five times, or until you feel you have a rhythm with your breathing and you can feel your tummy going up and down as you breathe. Blow and release air in and out of your "balloon" for five breaths.

As you breathe in this relaxed state, pretend that you are traveling into the center of your being, where you have your very own palace. If you start to feel nervous, simply place your hand on your tummy and once again feel the rise and fall of your breath. In your mind, send warmth and sunshine into your body with each breath. Feel the peace that comes over you. Look as your palace comes into your view.

Draw your palace. For some of you, this drawing will be vivid and colorful. For others it will be pastel and fuzzy. What your palace looks like isn't important. Only continue to feel relaxed and have fun on this inner adventure. Allow your mind to stay focused on this palace. If your mind wanders, simply notice that it is happening and gently pull your focus back to your palace.

Imagine that your palace has a long hall with several doors. Draw a long hall with doors on each side of the hall. [Pause while the girls draw these elements.] One of these doors is slightly ajar, inviting you to come in. Draw footsteps leading to this room. Draw this room, which you may call your "Comfort Room." This may require another sheet of paper. Draw furniture and choose colors that make this room comfortable for you. [Pause to allow the girls to draw their "Comfort Room."]

There are words written on the walls of your "Comfort Room." These words are messages that make this a comforting place to be. These words may be written as puffy "cloud words" or some other style of lettering. Draw the colors, writing style, and words that are written on the walls of your "Comfort Room." [Pause while the girls draw the writing on the walls.]

Spend a few seconds enjoying the feeling of your "Comfort Room." [Pause.] Although you are grateful for the peaceful feelings you have in your "Comfort Room," you are ready for more adventure. Once again, imagine that you are looking down the long hall to find other doors which are open.

Draw footsteps leading to another room that has an open door. Let your imagination guide you as you draw the décor and the furniture of this second room. You may use a separate piece of paper for this room. Use colors to express the mood you want to experience in this second room. You can make it any kind of room you desire.

Like the first room, this room also has writing on the walls. Choose messages that match the mood you want to create in this room. Draw these messages on the walls of this second room. [Pause.] Spend a few seconds to observe the mood you have created in this room. [Pause.]

You are now ready to leave the second room and walk down the hall. As you walk down the hall, you realize that you go in some of these rooms many, many times a day and read the writing on the walls. [For art activity, ask the girls to draw some footsteps showing how they go in and out of the rooms many times a day.]

Draw footsteps leading to another room that has "Changes in My Body" written on the door. As you start to draw this room, you may get a feeling like, "I want to draw a locked door on this room." Or you may be curious but a little nervous about drawing this room. As you draw the "Changes in My Body Room," imagine what kinds of colors and furniture are in this room. Draw the writing that is written on the walls. Is there graffiti? Are there blotchy spots of paint? What colors are used? Draw the words you think may be written in this room. You may have a nervous feeling in your tummy or a lump in your throat. Just gently breathe as you notice these feelings. The feelings will pass like a little wave rolling over your body.

Draw footsteps that show you taking a few steps backward and walking out the door of the "Changes in My Body Room." Imagine that you close the door and walk once again into the hall. Draw footsteps that show you walking back to the door of the first room you visited, your "Comfort Room." These drawings can be on several sheets of paper. Show that you are very happy to be back in your "Comfort Room." [Pause.]

Now draw footsteps to show that you are leaving your "Comfort Room," walking back down the long hall of your palace and back out through the palace doors. You may draw the big palace doors if you wish. When you are finished drawing, slowly turn your thoughts back to your breathing. Think about all the things you have drawn and the different feelings you had during this experience. Gently count your breaths... 1... 2... 3... 4... 5. Shake out your arms and hands. Wiggle your fingers and toes. Thank your body and mind for this amazing experience.

The girls are now ready to process this guided imagery or art activity. Give them a few minutes to stretch before proceeding. Use My Changing Beliefs Activity (Activity 3) or My Palace of Possibilities Body Drawing Exercise (Activity 4). The Mirror, Mirror Activity (Activity 6) can be used as an additional follow-up.

Activity 3
My Changing Beliefs Activity[6]

(Time = 10 minutes)

Objectives for Each Girl.

1. I can understand the beliefs I have about my changing body.
2. I can feel more comfortable about the changes in my body.
3. I can develop positive beliefs about the changes in my body.

Important Note.

1. In the *Palace of Possibilities Guided Imagery (or Art) Activity*, the girls visited a "Changes Room" to examine the beliefs they had about the changes happening in their bodies. One of the goals of *Healthy Transitions for Girls* is to help girls become more comfortable with the changes they are experiencing in their lives and to help girls to recognize that they can change the distressing beliefs that they might currently have about puberty.
2. The statements the girls write in this activity can help the facilitator know how many girls are currently experiencing serious distress and how much resistance there is to the subject of puberty. If girls are not comfortable writing down these private thoughts, it may indicate that they feel a low level of safety in the group—an important fact for the facilitator to recognize. Assure the girls this activity is voluntary and they if they do participate anything they write will be kept confidential.
3. It is helpful to keep the Post-it Notes and repeat the exercise at the end of the *Healthy Transitions for Girls* workshop series. The facilitator can compare the thoughts written in the first weeks with how the girls felt in subsequent weeks.
4. Be careful to protect the anonymity of the notes by not revealing the handwriting on the notes to the group. Note where the girls place their notes. For example, in my castle model, there is a prison room with a barred door. It is not uncommon for girls to place their notes in the prison room where they can be "locked up" from view.

Materials Needed.

1. For this activity, you will need a model castle with blank walls.[7] An alternative to using a castle is to use scrapbook paper that looks like wallpaper. Tell the girls that they are going to write on the "walls" of their castle. They can either write directly on the scrapbook paper or stick Post-it Notes to the blank walls on the model castle.
2. Handout 8, *Palace of Possibilities Affirmations*.

Activity Steps.

---

[6] This activity is used as a follow-up to the *Palace of Possibilities Guided Imagery (or Art) Activity* (Activity 2) .

[7] Purchase a "Fold and Go Castle" for $49.99, plus shipping, through www.melissaanddoug.com. Or visit www.ebay.com and search for "Melissa and Doug wooden castle."

1. To initiate the activity, review the Palace of Possibilities metaphor explained in the introduction of this chapter and experienced in the *Palace of Possibilities Guided Imagery (or Art) Activity* (Activity 2).

2. Tell the girls you are going to ask them some questions which they will answer on Post-it Notes or squares of scrapbook paper. They will not be asked to share what they have written with anyone else. They are not asked to put their names on their notes.

3. Read the following questions, pausing after each question to allow time for the girls to write their answers.

> Question 1: You have begun to notice or have experienced changes in your body. List 3 words that describe how you feel about these changes. These can be the emotions words or "writing on your walls" you experienced in the *Palace of Possibilities Guided Imagery (or Art) Activity*.

> Question 2: Complete this sentence. "What I want to change about my body is _____."

> Question 3: Complete this sentence. "The scariest thing about my body changing is_____."

> Question 4: Who makes the rules about what my body is supposed to look like?

4. Tell the girls to fold and post their Post-it Notes directly on the wall of the palace model. If they have written on the scrapbook "wall" paper, they can pass their notes to the facilitator or keep them for use with Palace of Possibilities Drawing Activity (Activity 4). They can fold their notes to protect their privacy.

5. Explain to the girls that it is healthy to get their thoughts and worries "out" of their body. It will make the process of changing less scary. Explain that it is not necessary to talk about these things with everyone, only with people they trust. Invite those who wish to share what they wrote. Reassure them that no matter what worries or negative feelings they have, they will be able to resolve their worries as they participate in *Healthy Transitions for Girls* workshops and activities. Say, "You can erase the negative beliefs on your palace walls and write new beliefs."

6. (Optional.) Follow up with Activity 4, Palace of Possibilities Body Drawing Activity.

7. Follow the instructions on Handout 8, *Palace of Possibilities Affirmations*, to help the girls begin to "write" new beliefs about their changing bodies on their walls.

Activity 4
Palace of Possibilities Body Drawing Activity[8]

(Time = 10 minutes)

Objectives for Each Girl.

1. I can identify what I feel about my changing body.
2. I can recognize fears I have about growing up.
3. I can recognize social rules that determine how I feel about my body.

Materials Needed.

1. Handout 2, *Healthy Transitions for Girls* Body Drawing.[9]
2. Post-it Notes or squares of scrapbook paper and pencils.

Activity Steps.

1. Complete Steps 1-4 in Activity 3, *Palace of Possibilities Drawing Activity*. In addition to their answers to the questions in Step 3, ask the girls to write any words they experienced or drew on their "palace walls" in Activity 2, *Palace of Possibilities Guided Imagery (or Art) Activity.* Have them write their words on a Post-it Note or a square of scrapbook paper which is used to represent "wallpaper".
2. Have the girls to write the words from their Post-it Note onto Handout 2, *Healthy Transitions for Girls* Body Drawing, *labeling each part of the body with a word that describes how they feel about it.* For example, by the thighs, they might write "fat" or "embarrassed."
3. If they cannot remember any specific words from Activity 2, *Palace of Possibilities Guided Imagery (or Art) Activity*, or if they did not do Activity 2, simply ask them to pick out a few parts of the body and write words or emotions that describe how they feel about those parts of the body. Remind them that what they put on their drawing is private and will be known only by them.
4. Tell the girls that while criticism and embarrassment about their bodies is common, their bodies need to hear positive messages. Tell them they can send loving messages to the parts of the body that are embarrassing to them. Have the girls draw hearts or flowers on any part of their bodies they think needs extra love.
5. Note any embarrassment observed as the girls work on their body drawings. Explain that this kind of embarrassment is normal because of the many messages they have received about their bodies. Reassure them that no matter what worries or negative feelings they have, they will be able to resolve their worries as they participate in *Healthy Transitions for Girls* workshops and activities. Say, "You can erase the negative beliefs on your palace walls and write new beliefs."
6. Follow the instructions on Handout 8, *Palace of Possibilities Affirmations.*

---

[8] Use after the *Palace of Possibilities Guided Imagery (or Art) Activity* (Activity 2).
[9] Girls are welcome to change the hair or draw clothing on the body drawing. They can personalize the drawing to look like themselves if they wish.

Activity 5
Who's Been Writing on My Walls? Activity

(Time = 15 – 20 minutes)

Objectives for Each Girl.

1. I can recognize past experiences and people that have influenced how I feel about my body today.
2. I can recognize how my beliefs about my body have changed as I have grown older.
3. I can recognize "social rules" that determine how I feel about my body.

Explanation.

Parents and therapists can both benefit from using Handout 3, *Who's Been Writing on My Walls*, to discover the effect of girls' early experiences on beliefs related to their bodies. A parent may assume that a girl has not been affected by comments she has heard from family members, only to discover that she has been much affected. Comments which were well-meaning or unintended as criticism can linger in the mind of a sensitive girl.

This activity can also help to assess other influences, such as the influence of peers, magazines, or celebrities. Helping girls to identify how their beliefs were formed helps them become an "observer" of their own experience, more conscious of beliefs that are harmful and more able to challenge those beliefs. Similarly, girls will benefit from seeing how their beliefs have changed as they have grown older. Some girls will discover that while they felt great about their bodies as young girls, growing older has made them more self-conscious.

Materials Needed.

1. Chapter 9, Handout 42, *The Butterfly Hug Self-Soothing Technique.*
2. Handout 3, *Who's Been Writing on My Walls?*
3. Handout 8, *Palace of Possibilities Affirmations.*
4. Pens or pencils.

Activity Steps.

1. Use Handout 3. Ask the girls to pretend that they are traveling to different time periods in their life. At each time period, they are going to get a picture in their mind of what they looked like and then try to remember how they felt about their appearance. They will write down their thoughts on the handout.
2. Start at the first time period, "Early Childhood." Say, "Close your eyes and travel back to the time when you were between the ages of 0 and 8 years old. Can you see what you looked like when you were that age? What were you wearing? In the picture you see in your mind, how old were you?

When you look at yourself, what do you feel? Are you excited? Are you were cute and fun? Do you like what you see? Do you have critical thoughts about yourself?"

3. Ask the girls if they can remember a particular conversation, movie, magazine, or person that influenced how they felt about their looks at that early age. "Do you remember a relative commenting on how you looked?" "Do you remember a movie star you want to look like?"

4. For each time period, repeat Steps 2 and 3. (If the girls are younger the latter time periods may not apply.) The goal is for the girls to identify WHAT they felt and WHERE that belief came from during each stage of their lives.

5. Explain to the girls that these beliefs (or "writing on the walls," when applying the *Palace of Possibilities* metaphor), are an important part of what they feel today. Explain that sometimes a girl will have a negative experience that harms how she feels about her body. Urge the girls that you do not want them to dwell on any negative beliefs, you only want them to understand their negative beliefs so they can begin to change them.

6. When the girls are done remembering and recording each age period, invite them to share specific influences they discovered. These influences can be negative or positive.

7. Ask the girls if the beliefs they had about their body have changed as they have grown older. Ask them to compare how they feel now with how they felt as very young children. Ask, "Have your feelings about your body become more complicated?"

8. As a follow up, use Handout 8, *The Palace of Possibilities Affirmations.*

9. Have the girls follow the steps on Handout 42, *The Butterfly Hug Self-Soothing Technique* (Chapter 9) and "butterfly hug" any negative feelings they discovered. Then, following Steps 1 and 2 on Handout 8, have them "write positive messages in their hearts" using the affirmations listed in Handout 8.

Activity 6
Mirror, Mirror Activity

(Time = 45 minutes)

Objectives for Each Girl.

1. I can recognize and challenge negative self-talk.
2. I can use self-care when I have negative beliefs about my body.
3. I can use self-care techniques for relaxation and stress management.

Explanation.

Remember the movie *Snow White*? In the movie, the villainess went to the mirror and asked, "Mirror, Mirror, on the wall, who is the fairest of them all?" The *Mirror, Mirror Activity* gives girls an opportunity to play both the part of the villainess and the heroine as they go to the mirror.

The girls love dressing up but will benefit from some privacy as they complete their worksheets in front of the mirror. The mirror should be placed in a corner of the room where the girls will not be observed as they stand in front of the mirror.

Materials Needed.

1. A full length mirror.
2. A black hat and black cape (villainess).
3. A tiara and wand (princess).
4. Handout 4, *Mirror, Mirror Activity Part 1*.
5. Handout 5, *Mirror, Mirror Activity Part 2*.
6. An orange or raisin (for use with Chapter 3, Activity 9).
7. Handout 42, *The Butterfly Hug Self-Soothing Technique* or Activity 29, *EFT: Self-Help for Anxiety and Negative Beliefs* (Chapter 9).
8. Pencils or pens.

Activity Steps.

1. (Optional). To prepare them to use the skill of "mindfulness" to recognize their self-talk as they stand in front of the mirror, first do Activity 9, *A Simple Mindfulness and Acceptance Activity* in Chapter 3.
2. Pose the following questions to the group.

    Question 1: When you see someone do you find yourself noticing their flaws first?

Question 2: Do you pick apart their hair, clothes, or skin, rather than notice the positive things about them?

Question 3: Do you find yourself comparing others to how you look?
Question 4: What kinds of critical things do you notice about others?

3. Explain that the critical things girls notice about others is a good indicator that they have negative beliefs about themselves as well. There is an old saying that when you have your (index) finger pointed at others, there are three fingers pointing back at *you!* Looking for negative traits in oneself and others can become a habit that affects mood and contributes to unhealthy behaviors such a peer bullying, dieting, purging, substance abuse, and cutting.

4. Explain that each girl will stand in front of a full-length mirror two different times. The first time, they will wear a black hat and/or a black cape. The second time, they will wear a tiara or princess crown.[10]

5. The first time the girls go to the mirror wearing a black hat and/or cape, they will be asked to complete Handout 4, *Mirror, Mirror Activity Part 1*. In their villainess costume, ask the girls to write down the first negative thought that comes to their mind after reading each of the affirmations. They will read each affirmation and then write the "yes, but…" statements that discount their belief in the affirmation. For example, the first affirmation says, "My body is a miraculous creation." A "yes, but…" that might come up is, "YES, my body is a miraculous creation, BUT…I have all these zits and I hate them" or "My body is a miraculous creation…BUT I am too short compared to all my friends." After the girls have gone to the mirror for the first time, ask them to do a self-soothing exercise as they repeat each of their negative statements. Two simple and effective self-soothing exercises are discussed in *Handout 42, The Butterfly Hug Self-Soothing Technique* and Activity 29, *EFT: Self-Help for Anxiety and Negative Beliefs* (Chapter 9).

6. The second time the girls go to the mirror wearing a tiara, they will be asked to complete Handout 5, *Mirror, Mirror Activity Part 2*. They should each read the affirmations and then write down one or two positive things they observe about themselves--**without negative judgment**. (These mindfulness and acceptance are explained more specifically in Activity 9). As they observe the "miraculous creation" of their bodies, they might observe, "My eyes have many colors inside of them" or I have many different little colors in the strands of my hair."

7. After each girl completes the exercise, explain to the group that since they are the "princesses of their castles," they can learn to protect their castles from negative self-talk that causes emotional distress and harmful behaviors.

---

[10] Most girls will love the opportunity to dress up. For the rare girl that is not comfortable, dressing up can be an option.

Activity 7
Watch Out for the "Imaginary Other"

(Time = 15 – 20 minutes)

Objectives for Each Girl.

1. I can recognize when I am listening to negative self-talk.
2. I can recognize when I am "mind reading" other's thoughts.

Explanation.

Handout 6 addresses a common thought pattern in which girls think "someone" is focusing on them, picking apart their appearance or behaviors. This imaginary person is a harsh judge that creates self-consciousness and worry. The "imaginary other" is related to one of Dr. Daniel Amen's (2010) "ANTS" or "automatic negative thoughts" called "mind reading" (p. 262). In the mind reading distortion, girls assume that others are judging them or thinking harshly of them. For example, if someone looks at her but doesn't smile, a girl will think, "I know she thinks I look stupid. That's why she didn't smile." This activity raises awareness of this thought pattern.

Materials Needed.

1. Handout 6, *Watch Out for the "Imaginary Other."*
2. Pens or pencils.
3. A hand mirror or a full-length mirror.

Activity Steps.

1. As an introduction, ask the girls to think about their experience getting ready in the morning. Say, "What kind of thoughts went through your mind when you got ready this morning? When you looked in the mirror and fixed your hair, did you worry about what someone might say about you? Did you worry that someone might notice something that you felt uncomfortable about, such as a zit, the way your hair was styled, or the way your nose is shaped?"
2. Use Handout 6. Read the handout together. Ask the girls to complete the exercise by filling in things the "imaginary other" says to them that are not included on the handout list.
3. When the girls have completed the handout, invite one girl to pretend she is the "imaginary other." Invite another girl to stand in front of a mirror. While she is looking in the mirror, invite the "imaginary other" to whisper things in the mirror which make her feel self-conscious. The girl playing the "imaginary other" can refer to her handout for ideas of what to whisper. Ask the girl standing at the mirror to describe how she feels as she listens to the "imaginary other." Give other girls a chance to be at the mirror or play the role of the "imaginary other."

4. Now, repeat the exercise, but this time, instruct the "imaginary other" to say only positive things to the girl at the mirror. Ask, "How does that feel different from when the 'imaginary other' made negative statements?" Emphasize that negative self-talks perpetuates negative emotions.

| **Activity 8** |
| Be Your Own Cheerleader |

(Time = 20 minutes)

Objectives for Each Girl.

1. I can learn to challenge unrealistic or irrational beliefs.
2. I can support myself with balanced thoughts.

Explanation.

In this activity, girls are asked to challenge irrational, negative beliefs and write positive statements. The ability to recognize irrational thoughts and then to challenge them is a valuable strategy for improving mood and self-image. Common irrational beliefs of teens are listed in Handout 17, *The Emotional Roller Coaster Starts with These Beliefs* (Chapter 5) and in Handout 6, *Watch Out for the "Imaginary Other."*

Materials Needed.

1. Handout 7, *Be Your Own Cheerleader*.
2. Handout 8, *Palace of Possibilities Affirmations*.
3. Pencils or pens.

Activity Steps.

1. Take a moment and review some of the following common irrational beliefs with the girls.[11] Explain that irrational beliefs cause most of our distress in life. You may want to include the following concepts in your discussion.

   - **Black and White Thinking or "Awfulizing"**: Life is either "awesome" or "awful."
   - **Stereotyping**: People are either "cool," "geeks," or "preps."
   - **Over-Generalized Thinking**: Exaggerated statements begin with "nobody" or "everybody."
   - **Imaginary Audience Syndrome**: Someone is watching every little detail of her life.
   - **Egocentric Thought**: Preoccupation with self, such as "I am the only one who does work around here."
   - **Emotional Reasoning**: If she feels it, it has to be true. "I feel lonely, so I am."
   - **Preoccupation with Fairness and Justice**: High expectations of others' performance, especially their parents, even when their own is poor.
   - **Immediate Gratification**: "I need it now, regardless of the long-term consequences."

---

[11] Pipher (1998) gives several examples in the *Reviving Ophelia Study Guide*. Available through the Media Education Foundation http://www.mediaed.org/assets/products/303/studyguide_303.pdf.

2. Distribute Handout 7. Explain that some of these irrational beliefs are listed on their handout. Read the statements listed on the handout. Tell them their job is to "be their own cheerleader" by challenging these irrational thought patterns with positive thoughts.

3. Use the hints listed at the top of the handout to help girls write their cheerleading statements. The goal is to make the statements less exaggerated and emotional, to make the statements more realistic, and to normalize uncomfortable feelings. The following examples are given to assist the girls in writing their cheerleading statements.

    Start with "It's okay if….."

    - It's okay if I feel sad.
    - It's okay if I have problems.
    - It's okay if there is not a perfect solution.

    Replace "I can't" with "I can."

    - I can face this situation one step at a time.
    - When I am unhappy, there are some things I can do.

    Challenge words like "everyone," "no one," "never," and "always."

    - I know some people think _____ about me, but not necessarily everyone.
    - I feel good about myself sometimes.
    - I am not the only one who has problems.

    Challenge exaggerations. Make the statement more accurate.

    - I don't have to believe others' criticism of me.
    - I don't really know why my parents fight.
    - My problems bother me, but I have good things happening too.

4. Challenge the girls to be more conscious of their irrational beliefs by noticing what they were thinking as soon as they begin to feel "down" emotionally. Invite them to bring a list of three irrational beliefs and three cheerleading statements to the next session or workshop. Tell them that when they get stuck on a belief and can't think of a cheerleading statement, they can seek out a parent or friend to help them. Remind them that their beliefs are very powerful! Being their own cheerleader will help them handle the inevitable ups and downs of life.

5. Challenge the girls to follow the three steps on Handout 8, *The Palace of Possibilities Affirmations*[12] for one week. Ask them to report back to the group what they experienced.

---

[12] Another suggestion is to use Handout 42, *The Butterfly Hug Self-Soothing Technique* or Activity 29, *EFT: Self-Help for Anxiety and Negative Beliefs* and "tap" on these affirmations at the beginning or end of each group. Keep a dialogue open for girls to discover what messages keep them from truly feeling these positive beliefs in their bodies.

Chapter 3

The Mind-Body Connection: Building a Partnership with My Body

*Allowing my emotions to surface into awareness
and to be able to name my emotions is the beginning of emotional exploration.
I am moving forward, trying to find my position within the family, within the community, and in life.*
*~Candace Pert, PhD. Author, Molecules of Emotion:
The Science behind Mind-Body Medicine*

Amazing things happen when we "tune in" to our bodies! Early in my career, I had the rewarding experience of working with a group of severely traumatized women who taught me in obvious ways the value of the mind-body connection. The common problem with these women was the disconnection (or "dissociation") they felt with their bodies. They viewed their bodies as a source of shame and emotional discomfort. They chronically used drugs and alcohol to numb this pain and escape from their body messages. As much as they resisted it, reconnecting with their bodies was a primary factor in helping them to heal emotionally.

One day, a member of this group came to me, very distraught over the death of a family member with whom she had a very conflictive relationship. She was experiencing symptoms of a panic attack. I used **Activity 28, *"Blowing Balloons" Relaxation Activity** (Chapter 9) to help her breathing become slower and less centered in her chest. I directed her to feel the comforting warmth of her breath and to send it more deeply into her abdomen. As she began to calm down, I grabbed a picture of a body diagram, similar to **Handout 2, *Healthy Transitions for Girls Body Drawing*** (Chapter 2). I asked her to take some crayons and to begin drawing the sensations she felt in her body onto the diagram. She drew swirls up and down her arms and described the rush of emotional energy she felt there. She described the thoughts and feelings that became clearer as she tuned in to this part of her body.

Then she moved her focus to her abdomen which she described as sick and nauseous. She drew a figure that looked like a swirling hurricane and listed many conflicting emotions such as "love," "want forgiveness," "angry," and "weird." She was able to discuss the "love-hate" relationship she had with the deceased and accept that both grief and anger could co-exist within her.

As a final step, I asked her to draw something comforting on the parts of her body that felt turmoil or pain. She drew flowers on her stomach and arms. Then she wrote a positive affirmation across her head, to guide her in having a positive focus as she experienced the grieving process. After this exercise, she no longer felt panic, but instead she had a sense of comfort that carried her through the day.

The profound lesson of this experience and later clinical experiences is that the body and the emotions are holistically interconnected. Girls need to recognize that they are in a partnership with their bodies. Even before a girl is mentally aware of her emotional reactions, her body is sending signals or "body signs," such as a clenched jaw, a tightening in the stomach, a raised eyebrow, or slumped shoulders.

At the heart of girls' unhealthy behaviors is not just dissatisfaction with their bodies, but a psychological "disconnection" with their bodies. Girls become so worried about what they look like on the outside that they have no idea what they need or feel on the inside. Rather than learning to tune inward, they lose touch with their own inner voices; instead they develop a nagging obsession to meet the standards of others. This limits their ability to manage emotional distress, which often leads to harmful ways of coping.

Anecdotes to these challenges are mindfulness skills, body awareness, and self-soothing skills, which are taught in this chapter and in Chapter 9, "Coping Skills and Problem-Solving Skills." **Activity 9, A Simple Mindfulness and Acceptance Activity**, introduces the skills of basic mindfulness. Mindfulness benefits girls in three important ways:

1. It increases awareness of distressing, unconscious beliefs and body messages.
2. It promotes the body as a source of wisdom, comfort, and strength. This is a paradigm shift from the constant "war" girls tend to wage with their bodies.
3. It helps girls recognize their need for healthy self-soothing skills and problem-solving skills, which can supplant unhealthy patterns of acting out.

Girls are introduced to the concept of body awareness in **Activity 10, Body Talk Activity.** They learn to recognize that emotions have a positive purpose and to recognize how their body is their partner in helping them to recognize and manage emotions. They also learn that they need to use positive tools for soothing emotions and meeting emotional needs.

Activity 11, My Feelings Meter Activity helps girls to recognize the varying degrees of intensity they feel. This challenges girls' natural tendency to feel like every problem is a "five alarm fire." This skill gives girls another effective tool to manage emotions effectively.

The ideas in this chapter are simple, yet profound. Connecting to the body and learning self-soothing skills as a way to cope with distress and even heal from painful experiences will help girls to bond with a loyal partner that will carry them through life.

List of Activities, Handouts, & Figures Used in Chapter 3

Chapter 3: The Mind-Body Connection: Building a Partnership with My Body

List of Activities.

List of Handouts.

List of Figures.

None.

Activity 9
A Simple Mindfulness and Acceptance Activity[13]

(Time = 10 minutes)

Objectives for Each Girl.

1. I can learn skills to increase my inner awareness.
2. I can learn to reduce negative judgments about what I see and feel.

Materials Needed.

1. Obtain a simple object for the girls to examine, such as an orange or raisin.
2. A mirror

Explanation.

Linehan (1993) teaches three "how-to" steps to achieve mindfulness:

- **Observe**. Just notice the experience. Have a "Teflon mind," letting thoughts and feelings pass through the mind without getting stuck. Step inside yourself and feel thoughts as they come and go.
- **Describe**. Assign words to your experience, and talk to yourself as an observer of your own experience. Do this without judging your experience.
- **Participate**. Enter into your own experience wholly. Become one with it.

Activity Steps.

1. Ask the girls to pay attention to a simple object, such as an orange or a raisin. Ask them to observe and list details about the object, to stay focused on the present state of the object and the sensory experiences they are having with the object. Give example responses. "The orange smells pungent." "It makes my mouth water." "It feels bumpy against my skin." "It feels like sunshine in my tummy." Ask them to resist making any judgments about the bumps or flaws in the orange or raisin. Tell them to just observe, but not judge.
2. Now take this exercise one step further. Invite the girls to practice looking at themselves in a mirror, just like they do every morning when they wake up. Invite them to use the same steps they used when looking at the orange. Ask them to note all the things they observe about themselves *without making any critical comments.* For some girls with severe body image dissatisfaction, this is very difficult because they have become so conditioned to critical self-talk. Tell the girls that learning to make non-judgmental observations in the mirror is the start of a new relationship with their body.

---

[13] This exercise is a helpful precursor to the Activity 6, *Mirror, Mirror Activity* (Chapter 2). In the *Mirror, Mirror Activity*, the girls practice mindfulness and acceptance in front of a real mirror.

Activity 10
Body Talk Activity

(Time = 20 minutes)

Objectives for Each Girl.

1. I can learn the purpose of emotions.
2. I can learn to recognize emotional body signs.
3. I can use self-care when I feel distressing emotions.
4. I can listen to the messages my body gives me and care for my body.

Materials Needed.

1. Handout 9, *My Body Talks*, and Handout 10, *Emotional Body Talk*.

Activity Steps.

1. This activity will be more effective if you have done Activity 9, A Simple Mindfulness and Acceptance Activity or Activity 28, *"Blowing Balloons" Relaxation Activity* (Chapter 9) to help them tune in to their bodies. Read the handouts. Give the girls time to ponder the questions on the handouts.
2. Explain that emotions have a function, that they "urge" us to do something. For example, if you are in a dark alley and hear footsteps, you feel fear. What is the function of fear? (It tells you to take action to protect yourself.) When people are kind, you may have the urge to express your gratitude. How would you do that? (Give them hugs or squeeze their hands, or write little notes to them.) Explain that emotions drive behaviors. Explain that although girls sometimes struggle with emotions, they would not be able to survive or have a meaningful life without them.
3. Ask the following questions.

   Question 1: Can you remember a time when your body gave you a message that caused you to act in some way?

   Question 2: What was the emotion?

   Question 3: What did it urge you to do? (This can be a positive or negative experience.)

4. Introduce the concept of "body talk" with Handout 9. After reading the handout together, ask girls to tune in to their bodies right now. "What kind of messages or emotions do you feel?" "Is your tummy growling?" "Are you thirsty?" "Do you feel worry somewhere in your body?" "Do you feel happiness somewhere in the body?" Ask the girls to observe and describe these sensations, but not to judge them.
5. Follow the instructions on Handout 10. Read together.

6. Emphasize that the body is a partner in life and an important source of information. Encourage the girls to listen to body messages which "urge" them to get rest, eat well, and exercise. Tell them that listening to emotional "body talk" is a great way to take control of their lives and really learn who they are inside.
7. Follow up with Activity 11, *My Feelings Meter Activity*, which helps girls recognize the intensity of the emotions they feel in their bodies or Activity 14, *The Wise Place Inside of Me Activity* (Chapter 4), *which helps girls to develop their intuitive warning system or "gut" feelings.*

Activity 11
My Feelings Meter Activity

(Time = 15 minutes)

Objectives for Each Girl.

1. I can learn to recognize the intensity of emotions I feel in my body.

Materials Needed.

1. A ruler for each girl (optional).
2. Handout 11, *My Feelings Meter*

Activity Steps.

1. This activity is a follow-up to Activity 10, *Body Talk Activity*. While Activity 10 helps girls to identify the various emotional body signs and gain an appreciation of the role of emotions in their lives, this activity specifically helps them to measure the intensity of their emotions. Since teens have a tendency to "awfulize" their experiences, all negative emotions feel like they are at the high end of the intensity scale; therefore, this is an important step to emotional regulation.
2. Use Handout 11, *My Feelings Meter*. Explain to the girls that not only do they feel different emotions in their bodies, but that they feel these emotions at different levels of intensity. Explain, "Emotions can be intensely happy or intensely sad or somewhere in between. I am going to ask them to measure emotions in various situations using the Feeling Meter. As I describe a specific scenario, identify the emotion you would feel, and place your finger on the number that indicates how strongly you would feel that emotion."
3. You may use scenarios shared by the girls in the previous activity, *Body Talk Activity*, since this is a follow-up, or you can use ideas from the following list:

    *   You are just falling asleep late at night and hear a tapping at your bedroom window.
    *   You are taking a Math Test and can't remember anything you studied.
    *   Your "best" friend tells an important secret to another not-so-good friend.
    *   You hear your parents arguing.
    *   You get an anonymous note on your locker describing why you are such a neat person.
    *   You wake up feeling "blah" and wish you could stay home and do nothing.
    *   You wake up in the morning and smell smoke.
    *   Your mom tells you that your family is having financial problems and she is going to have to work more hours; she needs you to take more responsibility around the house.
    *   You find the perfect shoes to match your new outfit.
    *   Your name is announced over the school intercom as being selected for the week's "most valuable student."

4. Have the girls share their responses. Explain how different circumstances can change the intensity of what they might feel. Also emphasize that each girl may interpret the same situation differently. Emphasize that not every situation requires a high emotional response; some situations are better handled if they are not feeling overly-emotional, such as dealing with a friend, versus seeing if the house is on fire.

Chapter 4

Holistic Wellness: Reclaiming the "Whole Me"

A girl needs holistic wellness and balance in her life in order to thrive.
~ Laura H. Choate, PhD., Author of Adolescent Girls in Distress:
A Guide for Mental Health Treatment and Prevention

Consider the consequences if a mysterious ailment restricted vital circulation of blood to only the visible, external parts of our body. We would look at the healthy pinkness of our outward body parts and marvel at how our body is thriving. "Yes," we would say, "I'm doing all the right things for my body's success." We are yet unaware that the unseen, inner parts of our body are literally starving to death. It is only when the healthy parts of our body start to lose their healthy pink color that we discover the need for a solution.

We decide to pump even *more* blood to the outward parts to help them regain their healthy pinkness. "Yes, that is the solution," we say, "I will give more attention to the outward parts." But sadly, because we are unaware that we have inward parts that need care, our efforts to revive the outward parts are futile. For the whole body to thrive, all the parts must receive care and nourishment.

Sadly, today's culture emphasizes physical appearance to the exclusion of the other aspects of self—social, emotional, intellectual, and spiritual. Girls are often pressured to spend so much time on appearance and performance-related aspects of self they neglect developing an appreciation of their "inner world." In this strength-based, wellness approach, girls are encouraged to acknowledge, balance, and fully develop each aspect of the self.

In her *Reviving Ophelia Study Guide*, Mary Pipher, PhD, stated that some of the biggest mistakes of counselors are to "pathologize ordinary experience" and "focus on weakness rather than resilience" (1998, p. 7). Girls already focus so much on what is wrong with themselves; they need us to focus on what is strong about them! A conscious focus on strength-building, as implemented in this course, can help girls adapt to a rapidly changing and very stressful world.

While each chapter in this book helps develop strengths in one or more of the holistic areas, this chapter specifically helps girls gain awareness of their holistic natures and develop a desire to increase skills in each area. **Activity 12,** ***The Whole Me Activity*** increases self-understanding and goal-setting in each area of their personalities.

Research overwhelmingly validates the benefit of spiritual practices in reducing at-risk behaviors and depression in adolescent girls. Since spirituality is an often-neglected aspect of girls' natures, **Activity 13,** ***My Spiritual Self Activity*** encourages girls to recognize their spiritual natures and their need for an inner guidance system and values. This activity presents spirituality as a universal and essential aspect of personality. The concept of looking inward for spiritual guidance honors universal beliefs of many cultures and religions. The Bible instructs that "the kingdom of God is within you,"[14] and religions around the world urge a turning inward to this metaphysical "kingdom" for guidance and strength. (This is not to be confused with a hedonistic "worship" of the body.) In this activity, girls are encouraged to support the religious and cultural traditions of their families.

Activity 14, *The Wise Place Inside of Me Activity* builds upon this principle and reinforces the need to rely on "gut feelings" or intuition as a source of guidance and protection. Women through the ages have been honored for their "women's intuition," a gift the girls of today need to reclaim as they also work to reclaim a reverence and appreciation for their bodies. In her book, *The Wise Child*, intuitive counselor, Sonia Choquette, PhD, invites parents and mentors to teach their children what intuition feels like. She defines it as "a subtle, vibrating energy that center[s] in the heart and move[s] outward to the stomach, the gut, the chest, the throat." (See **Handout 15, The Wise Place Inside of Me**.) She also suggests that we develop a vocabulary to describe these feelings, such as the word "vibes" (Choquette, 1999, p. 6). One very sensitive girl I know felt little vibrations deep in her tummy when she sensed potential danger; she described her inner warning system as her "tail wagging." Children naturally have intuitive abilities that diminish as they grow older if they are not cultivated.

Feeding the physical self in an attempt to decrease the hunger in the spiritual or emotional self simply doesn't satisfy. An excellent complement to the activities in this chapter is found in **Activity 30, *What To Do When I'm Blue Card File Activity* (Chapter 9).** This art activity teaches girls how to identify which parts need care and choose an activity that will effectively feed the "hungry" part.

In an interesting way, girls who learn to value each part of themselves also learn to value their whole bodies. Balancing the needs of the "whole" girl is a key to thriving in a stressful world.

---

[14] Luke 17:21.

List of Activities, Handouts, & Figures Used in Chapter 4

Chapter 4: Holistic Wellness: Reclaiming the "Whole Me"

<u>List of Activities.</u>

<u>List of Handouts.</u>

<u>List of Figures.</u>

None.

Activity 12
The WHOLE Me Activity

(Time = 30 – 40 minutes)

Objectives for Each Girl.

1. I can recognize that many parts that make up the whole me.
2. I can rely on parts of me that are strong.
3. I can set goals in areas where I need to become stronger.

Explanation.

As you help the girls identify their strengths and set goals for becoming stronger in specific ways, encourage the skills you feel are most needed in an increasingly challenging world. What traits will help them adapt to unexpected change? What traits will help them manage emotional distress? What traits will help them stay focused on goals in the face of adversity? Use your knowledge of each girl to emphasize existing strengths as well. Many girls "discount" or devalue their strengths with self-criticism. Most important, challenge them to resist "victim-thinking." One of the most important traits of people who are happy is that they take responsibility for their thoughts and actions.

Materials Needed.

1. Handout 12, *The WHOLE ME: Discovering My WHOLE Self*.
2. Handout 13, *The WHOLE ME: Blossom into the WHOLE You*.
3. Pens or pencils.

Activity Steps.

1. Use Handout 12 to introduce the girls to the concept that each part of them has to be developed in order to have balance and well-being. Ask, "How many different parts do you have?" (They may say that they have many different body parts.) Explain that just like they have different parts to their bodies, they have many different parts of their personality and "whole self." Explain that advertisers and other people often only emphasize one part of them: their physical appearance. However, every part is important.
2. Tell the girls that they will deal with many problems in their lives, and they will need skills in each of these areas to handle problems. Explain that developing skills in each of these areas will help them to have more balanced lives. No one can be truly happy if she worries only about her physical appearance.
3. Have the girls fill out two or three strengths they have in each of the areas listed on Handout 12. Tell them this is a great chance to know themselves better. They may find that they know a lot about themselves in one area but not very much about themselves in another area. Be attentive to

specific "survival" skills that will help them cope with the difficulties of a changing world. Emphasize these skills.

4. Girls may struggle to identify strengths in some of the areas. A goal of the exercise is not only to help them identify strengths, but also to discover areas that need further development. Help them brainstorm to discover skills in areas they may have left blank. Again, emphasize skills that are important for daily coping.

5. Use Handout 13 to help the girls identify the goals they want to achieve in each area. Focus on areas where they need to build strengths and areas where they already have strengths. A common thinking pattern of girls is "all or nothing" thinking. It is helpful for them to see that they can have both areas of strength and areas of weakness at the same time. Explain that there will always be a need to develop strengths. This is called "personal growth." Individuals can always "grow" their skills. At the same time, they can value their strengths. Everyone has strengths! The strengths they have in each area are tools they can use to solve problems.

6. Invite the girls to share their goals. Ask them to work on one goal and report back next week to describe their efforts.

Activity 13
My Spiritual Self Activity

(Time = 30 minutes)

Objectives for Each Girl.

1. I can rely on my spiritual self to help me stay true to my values.
2. I can write down spiritual thoughts and impressions.
3. I can ask for spiritual help when I need it.

Explanation.

The spiritual aspect of girls deserves special attention in our highly secular society. Addressing spirituality does not mean advocating a specific religious philosophy; nor does it mean minimizing religious practice. Spirituality, an important part of every human being, needs to be nourished. Girls need to know that they have an all-knowing, all-loving "Higher Power" or God to guide them. They need to feel that their experiences have a purpose.

In *Be Who You Want to Be: Dealing with Life's Ups & Downs*, author Karen Casey (2007) offers spiritual definitions that can be used in school- or agency-based settings.[15] Excerpts from her book can be used to illustrate the concepts presented Handout 14, *The Spiritual Part of ME: Discovering My Authentic Self* and Activity 13, *My Spiritual Self Activity*.

Materials Needed.

1. Handout 14, *The Spiritual Part of ME: Discovering My Authentic Self*.
2. Scrapbook paper.
3. Markers and other journal-making supplies.
5. Stapler or hole punch and ribbon.

Activity Steps.

1. Tell the girls they are going to make a journal to record their "spiritual" thoughts and impressions. Girls may not understand what "spiritual" thoughts are compared to any other thoughts. Explain that the focus of this activity is to help them become more acquainted with the spiritual part of themselves. Read the following Karen Casey quote to help them understand what spirituality means.

   There is something very special inside of all of us. Maybe you already know what it is. Have you ever heard of Spirit...? Do you wonder what Spirit does? I've heard that it helps us to be kind to others. It helps me to remember that I am special. (p. 297)

---

[15] For more information, see Karen's website: www.womens-spirituality.com

2. Give the girls time to make their journals using the art supplies at hand. A suggested format is to use 8 ½ x 11 white copy paper and fold it in half. Then, fold a large piece of scrapbook paper over the white copy paper to make the journal cover. Staple the journal together on the folded edges. Allow the girls time to trim and decorate the cover. Encourage them to personalize it. Say, "I want this to be a book that you feel very special about, a place where you can put spiritual thoughts and feelings."

3. Read Handout 14 together. As you read the questions, have the girls record their answers in their journals. Give them time to process their answers. Girls may struggle to understand what it means to have a "purpose" for their lives since this is a very abstract concept and since the media culture presents such confusing ideas. Read the following quote by Karen Casey to help them understand what it means to have a purpose.

    > Everybody has a purpose, or she would not have been born. Everything that happens has a purpose too. Do you know what that means? It is a pretty difficult idea, but here is what it means. Nobody is in this world by accident… Everything that happens around us can teach us something… I like thinking this way. It makes me feel like my life is important… It helps me look for lessons in what happens at home, at school, and in my neighborhood. (p. 293)

4. After the girls have completed the activity, invite them share some something they recorded in their spiritual journal.

5. Summarize the activity by explaining that every person has a spiritual self that needs care. Explain that each girl needs to connect to a higher spiritual power. Say, "How a person defines the spiritual power in her life is different depending upon culture and religious beliefs. Some people call the spiritual power in their life 'God' of 'Jesus Christ;' others call this power the 'Great Spirit,' 'Mother Earth,' the 'Creator,' or some other name." Encourage them to recognize and embrace their family traditions.

6. Read the following quote from Karen Casey.

    > What counts is asking God for help when I am scared or lonely. Talking to someone who I can't really see may sound silly, but I don't have to talk out loud. I can talk just in my mind. God will hear me, and I will feel so much better. (p. 297)

7. Tell them that their journal is a place where they can write the questions they want to ask God and write the spiritual answers they feel. They can also discuss these questions with clergy and parents.

Activity 14
The Wise Place Inside of Me Activity

(Time = 40 – 45 minutes)

Objectives for Each Girl.

1. I can recognize my intuitive warning systems or "gut feelings."
2. I can learn to act upon my "gut feelings" even when they don't seem logical.
3. I can recognize that "stay away" feeling and act on it.
4. I can trust my body wisdom and "turn inward" when I need important answers rather than relying on "the crowd."
5. I can set personal boundaries to keep me safe from harm and encourage healthy friendships.

Explanation.

Many experts in child safety have moved away from the "stranger danger" message. This has occurred for two reasons: 1) harmful people are often acquaintances or family members; and 2) being afraid of strangers keeps children from seeking help from law enforcement or others in a position to help them. A most important focus is for girls to learn to trust "gut" feelings or intuition and to recognize and assert personal boundaries.[16] This activity urges girls to "look inward" and to reconnect to their body wisdom as a source of guidance and protection.

Materials Needed.

1. Handout 15, *The Wise Place Inside of Me*.
2. Activity 17, *My Space, Your Space Activity, Part 1* (Chapter 6).

Activity Steps.

1. Use Activity 28, *"Blowing Balloons" Relaxation Activity* (Chapter 9) or Activity 9, *A Simple Mindfulness and Acceptance Activity* (Chapter 3) to help the girls quiet their minds and become more in tune with their bodies. You can also adapt Activity 2, *Palace of Possibilities Guided Imagery (or Art) Activity* script (Chapter 2) for this exercise. When reading the guided imagery script, simply invite the girls to visit a "Wisdom Room" rather than a "Changes" Room. The Wisdom Room will be a room where they will feel peace and guidance.
2. Read Handout 15 together with the girls. Tell them you are going to share some examples of girls who tuned in to the "wise place" inside. Tell them you will give them a chance to share their thoughts after each example.
3. Read Example 1. Then ask the questions and read the discussion statement.

---

[16] One such program is *GirlStrength*, sponsored by the Portland, Oregon Police Bureau. For more information contact GirlStrength@portlandpolice.org or visit http://www.portlandonline.com/police/index.cfm?c=49818.

Example 1. Mari was standing in line at Burger King waiting for to order some lunch with her younger friend, Sara. A man walked in the door and got in line behind her. He was dressed nice and looked like a nice man, but she had a funny feeling inside that made her want to pull Sara close. The feeling got stronger so she took Sara and went out to the car to wait until the man left.

Example 1 Questions.

Question 1: Do you think Mari did the right thing by going back to the car with her friend?

Question 2: Could the man really have hurt her or Sara standing in the middle of Burger King? Was her decision "logical?"

Example 1 Discussion. Mari did the right thing by going to the car. Even if it was not *logical* to be afraid of the man because they were in a public place where he could not kidnap them or hurt them without getting caught, it is still important to get away from situations that make us feel "icky" or uncomfortable whenever possible. Mari never knew why she had those feelings, but by honoring those feelings, she took a step toward learning to trust herself.

4. Read Example 2. Then ask the questions and read the discussion statement.

Example 2. Jessica was excited to get into middle school so she could make new friends. Two girls sat by her in the lunchroom on the second day of school, so she started hanging around with them. At first they seemed nice, but every day when she went home from school, she felt irritated and "crummy." Before she began hanging out with these girls she came home from school hungry for a snack, not feeling irritable. She wondered if the "crummy" feeling was because her new friends spent so much time gossiping and making fun of other girls.

Example 2 Questions.

Question 1: Does the wise place inside give people warning signs about what kind of friends are going to lift them up or tear them down emotionally?

Question 2: Is Jessica a snob if she stops hanging out with these two girls?

Question 3: What suggestions do you have for Jessica?

Question 4: Would this situation cause you to feel "crummy"?

Question 5: Are these the kind of friends that you would trust in your "personal space"?

Question 6: How can Jessica, or anyone, set boundaries about situations that cause them to have "crummy" feelings inside?

Example 2 Discussion. Every girl is different in her ability to handle negative situations. Even in the same family, what bothers one child and causes them to feel tired or down inside will be brushed off as "no big deal" by another child. Girls who are especially sensitive to negative messages or situations must be encouraged to rely on the wise place inside, even if others don't have the same feelings.

Jessica is wise to listen to her feelings. She may not have the experience to understand the warning signs of bullying. People who continually talk mean about others eventually start doing mean things. Jessica could be labeled as a bully if she keeps hanging out with these girls. She could even end up getting in trouble with school authorities. The wise place inside of us protects us, even when we do not have enough facts or experience to understand why we should follow our warning feelings.

5. Read Example 3. Then ask the questions and read the discussion statement. Then, share the follow-up statement.

Example 3. Jennifer was downtown walking through the stores when she saw a boy from her school. He seemed very lonely, and she felt sorry for him. At the same time, she had a little "stay away" feeling inside that made her feel cautious.

Example 3 Questions.

Question 1: Jennifer had two feelings, feeling sorry and feeling cautious. How does she know which feeling is really coming from the wise place inside?

Question 2: Is Jennifer being mean if she decides not to make friends with this boy?

Question 3: If she does decide to be friendly, what precautions can she take to honor her feeling of cautiousness?

Question 4: Do you ever meet people and get a "stay away" feeling, but you don't understand why?

Example 3 Discussion. Many times we will have conflicting feelings when we sense a message from the wise place inside our bodies. Sometimes our mind will argue with us: "Why do you feel that way? You are just being judgmental." OR "You are just being a worrier; everyone else says he is nice." Thoughts from our head often judge us for the messages we feel from our wise place inside. We must learn to trust our wise place inside even when we may not logically understand our feelings. Learning to listen to our inner guidance system takes practice.

Situations also dictate how we handle the feelings we have from our wise place inside. If we are alone with someone and get a "stay away" feeling, we need to get away fast. If we are in a crowd of people and get a "stay away" feeling about someone, we know that we do not want to put ourselves in a situation where we might be alone with that person. We may not be in danger of immediate harm, but we know that we should protect our personal space from that person.

Example 3 Follow-Up. In this true story, Jennifer did not talk to the boy while she was alone with him downtown. She did not want to encourage a relationship where he might think that they could hang out alone together. When they were at school, she was kind to him, but she still did not feel she should encourage a friendship. She still felt sorry for him but decided that it was more important to choose friends who made her feel safe and comfortable. Later, Jennifer confided in one of her teachers that this boy had been following her. The teacher told Jennifer she should stay away and to report to him if the boy followed her any more. Jennifer felt confused because he just seemed like a very lonely boy, but she followed the teacher's advice, and she followed her "stay away" feeling. One night, Jennifer's mother got a call from the police. The boy had been arrested for breaking into girls' homes and stealing their underwear. Jennifer's name was on a list that the police found on the boy. Fortunately, since Jennifer lived several miles from town, the boy had not come to her home yet.

6. Explain, "You may not know why you have warning feelings from the wise place inside in certain situations. Rather than telling yourself that you are 'crazy' or just being a 'chicken,' it is better to listen to your feelings. If you have conflicting feelings, continue to tune in to your wise place and ask for help from your parents and those you trust, as you figure out what you should do."
7. An excellent companion to this exercise is Activity 17, My *Space, Your Space, Part 1 Activity* (see Chapter 6) which introduces the concepts of "personal space" and "setting boundaries."

Special Caution for Parents and Mentors

Parents and mentors, anxious for their children to please and respect adults, may unknowingly diminish their children's intuitive sense. It is valuable to listen to the things our young people feel about other people. For example, if a child says he or she gets the "creeps" around someone we revere, we would do well to "tune in" to those feelings, rather than scolding, "You are supposed to respect your elders." We are not encouraging disrespect; we are nurturing the ability to operate by an inner guidance system. Similarly, we should not require our children to hug people they have not developed a natural affection for; it is better to teach them to have "personal space" and allow them to decide when they have developed enough trust to display affection.

Chapter 5

Building Parent Connections: Less Conflict, More Collaboration

At the very time when a girl needs guidance most from her mother
regarding the things she will need to know in life, she's too busy
rejecting her mother to listen. It makes me worried for my daughters.
~ Shelley Blake, mother of four daughters

Television portrayals of the "generation gap" often show bumbling, out-of-touch parents trying to be "hip" pals with their sophisticated, all-knowing teens. Coupling this with a girl's increasing demands for independence can make parents doubt their influence. Why would media advertisers want to discourage strong parenting? Parents who minimize their leadership role and give in to children's demands for material things they think will make them popular keep those who target teens well-funded. Peddling cosmetics, fashions, music, electronics, and snack food to kids is big business! Yet, parents need to disregard false portrayals of an inevitable generation gap and believe that girls want and need structure and support. One research project (Dove, 2008) showed that the *top wish* of girls is for their parents to communicate better with them.[17] Yet this media barrage makes most parents less sure of what to say and doubtful that anything they say can really make a difference.

Even parents who have had great relationships with their daughters may feel unprepared for role changes when girls move into adolescence where the normal psychological task is to achieve more autonomy. Parents need help to navigate the mixed messages they receive from their daughters. Sometimes girls want input; sometimes they resent it and wonder why they are being treated like babies. Parents may "keep the peace" by trying to be their child's "peer" or they may intensify their authority by arguing, accusing, and punishing their child. When a girl moves through puberty, the effective parent becomes more collaborative, rather than authoritarian; at the same time, effective parents provide consistent structure, clearly stated expectations and consequences, daily hugs, and constant loving encouragement.

Healthy Transitions for Girls recognizes the challenges of parenting and the essential contribution of parents in the development of positive body image; therefore, parent homework and handouts, are included throughout this book. This chapter highlights parent resources and specific activities that require parent participation with their daughters.

As daughters move through a new life stage, the handouts from Chapter 5 have a specific goal to help parents re-negotiate the parent-child relationship. These handouts can also be used by professionals who work with parents in family therapy. Many parents yearn to know what is normal and what is not normal when they see erratic emotions and new independence in their girls **Chapter 5, Handout 16, *What's Happening to My Little Girl?*** helps parents to recognize changes that are typical in

---

[17] This project, commissioned by the Dove Self-Esteem Fund in 2008, studied girls in Denver, CO ages 8 through 17. 84% of girls ages 8-12 turn to their mothers as a resource when they feel badly compared to 60% of girls ages 13-17. Key findings of the report are available at http://content.dove.us/makeadiff/pdf/SelfEsteem_Report.pdf.

pre-adolescent and adolescent girls. (Handout 16 could also be coupled with a discussion on warning signs of depression and what is *not* normal for adolescents).

Chapter 5, Handout 17, *The Emotional Roller Coaster Starts with These Beliefs* helps parents to understand common irrational thought patterns of pre-teens and teens. Irrational beliefs exist in children too, but when coupled with hormonal changes of puberty, they are more apparent and more challenging. Knowing that these irrational beliefs are part of teen thinking can help a parent recognize why teens have roller coaster emotions and why they still need parents to help them with problem solving.

Even parents who know the value of communication may still need help with communication skills. As girls grow from grade school children to preteens and young women, the parent-child dialogue must reflect that change. **Chapter 5, Handout 18, *Open the Door to Better Talk*** teaches basic active listening skills. In my *Healthy Transitions for Girls Parent Workshops* (*See **Chapter 12, Activity 45, Parent Workshop Activity***), I use this handout in a role-playing activity for mothers (or mentors and grandmothers) and daughters. I ask the girls and adults to pretend their roles are reversed: "Pretend that you are the mom and your daughter is …" It is fun to see the girls assuming an adult role and feeling the kind of responsibility their mothers carry. I have also used this handout as a guide for role-playing between mothers and daughters in therapy sessions. Active listening skills are so simple, but they take practice to become a tool that is used daily.

Since increased independence is an important psychological task of adolescence, parents can use collaborative problem solving in which the child is given more responsibility and accountability for making and keeping the rules. **Chapter 5, Handout 19, *Create a Safe Space for Problem Solving*** offers strategies to help girls feel more autonomous and understood without diminishing the parent's authority. The *Let's Play Four Square Activity* included on this handout teaches a collaborative problem-solving approach that will create more "teaching moments" and less combat moments when girls disagree with parental boundaries.

It has been said that the best gift a mother can give a child is the gift of her own well-being. Since adult women face the same body image pressures as their daughters, they need to do a "fearless moral inventory" of what they say about their own bodies in front of the mirror and of the comments they make about their daughters' bodies. It is easy to unknowingly pass our own insecurities on to our daughters. Girls are so sensitive about the changes going on in their bodies during puberty that even innocent comments create self-consciousness and negative beliefs. Notably, the daughter's perception of family approval of her appearance was the critical factor in the McKinley (1999) study of girls' body image. Mothers can hang **Chapter 2, Handout 8, *Palace of Possibilities Affirmations*** on every mirror in the house to support positive self talk for themselves and their daughters.

Similarly, **Chapter 10, Handout 55, *What's So Special about Being a Girl? Parent Letter,*** helps mothers to create positive values within their daughters about the physical changes of puberty. It allows mothers to reaffirm their love for their daughters and to reaffirm the joy of their child's birth. Using this handout, mothers and grandmothers can pass on a legacy of positive messages about womanhood to their daughters.

Ferron (1997) not only confirmed the correlation between mothers' attitudes about body image and daughters' attitudes, but also noted that without understanding their influence, mothers can contribute to the problem by encouraging early dating and popularity through over-emphasis of appearance. **Chapter 7, Activity 23,** *Heart Healthy Relationships Activity,* and **Activity 24,** *Relationship Timeline,* are designed to parents, mentors, clergy and professionals set clear boundaries to help girls resist the pressure for early, steady dating and sexual experimentation and instead, focus on appropriate age-related goals, such as friendship skills and educational goals.

Mother, mentors, and grandmothers are the "gatekeepers" of the home who can set boundaries about TV, music, movies, magazines and fashions that promote sexualized images of young girls and unrealistic standards of beauty. **Chapter 5, Handout 20,** *Be a Media Conscious Parent* lists resources to help parents evaluate what media is safe for their child. **Chapter 10, Activity 35,** *Be Your Own Fashion Designer Activity,* includes a parent letter (**Handout 52**) with modest fashion guidelines to help you protect your daughter from today's sexualization of girls. Use this handout and its guidelines each time you go shopping with your daughter. Setting these kinds of limits sends a powerful message to the girls we love: we want them to feel valued and beautiful for who they are inside.

As girls value their bodies more, they will want to care for them better; but, they need parent help. Parents need to be very vigilant (Should I say "militant?") about making nutritious food choices available because "junk food" is the norm of our culture. **Chapter 11, Activity 63,** *Turn Over a New Leaf,* invites mothers and daughters to partner up and start some new health habits. If parents haven't yet joined the "green smoothie" craze, they will be amazed how delicious it can be to "go green" with **Chapter 11, Handout 59,** *"Go Green" Hulk Smoothie Recipe.* **Chapter 11, Handout 62,** *Healthy Transitions for Girls Healthy Snacks,* offers quick recipes that parents can encourage girls to make at home. Parents can help by keeping ingredients on hand for healthy snacks that nourish the body and the emotions as discussed in **Chapter 11, Activity 40, The Food Mood Connection Activity**. If parents familiarize themselves with the principles in this activity and help their daughters keep a food log (**Chapter 11, Handout 61, Take the Food Mood Challenge Log**), they can help their daughters to experience fewer emotional "melt-downs."

Along with the **References** section, **Figure 5, Comprehensive Materials List**, will help parents to find additional resources and to obtain materials for conducting Healthy Transitions for Girls activities with their daughters. Finally, **Figure 3, Parent Consent Form**, will help parents to understand more about the objectives of *Healthy Transitions for Girls*. Parents will reaffirm their commitment to actively support the essential concepts their daughters are learning through *Healthy Transitions for Girls*.

List of Activities, Handouts, & Figures Discussed in Chapter 5
Which Require Parent Collaboration

Chapter 5: Building Parent Connections: Less Conflict, More Collaboration

<u>List of Activities.</u>

<u>List of Handouts.</u>

<u>List of Figures.</u>

Chapter 6

Building Supportive Connections with Other Girls

Our teacher told us that we were so awful to each other
she would not want to be friends with any of us!
That started us thinking that we had better make some changes.
~6th Grade Girls in a Healthy Transitions for Girls Workshop

One of my therapist friends received an "SOS" call from her brother-in-law, a middle school principal. With the immature and aggressive behaviors that typify boys at that age, she figured he called to request intervention for dealing with the middle school boys he supervised. "It's the girl drama," he said. "It's driving me crazy." My own brother, also a former middle school principal said, "The boys get mad and get it over with. But the drama between the girls never stops."

Considering that girls, by nature, thrive on social connections, why does girl drama seem to dominate so much of the interaction between girls today? Why do you hear so frequently, "I don't have any friends," "No one really likes me," and "All my friends are gossiping about me." Or worse, maybe the girl you love has been involved in bullying in its many forms.

Girls' lack of maturity in setting boundaries, hormonal ups and downs, decreased sense of confidence, and the media-fueled competition for boys and popularity all contribute to friendships that come and go, much to the chagrin of girls who long for loyal friends. Girls who want to avoid high-risk behaviors will inevitably lose friendships as some friends descend into the abyss of harmful choices. Be prepared that even in the best circumstances, adolescence is a challenging time to build loyal friendships.

Girls are rarely aware of their competitive behaviors, yet in a world that puts so much emphasis on status and popularity, it is an unspoken "rule" that some girls will measure up and some girls won't. This contributes to a sense of isolation, even among girls who seem to have a lot of friends.[18] Faer, Hendriks, Abed, and Figueredo (2005) found that competition for male partners significantly influences body dissatisfaction and a drive for thinness which cause women to adopt "highly competitive behaviors, in which they seek achievement, to win at all costs, and to achieve high status among their female peers" (p. 406). In short, in the appearance-oriented world of girls today, there is not room for everyone at the top. Sadly, these superficial judgments create a lack of nurturing and support between girls, one of the inherent capacities of their sex.

Healthy Transitions for Girls helps girls to recognize their need for connection and support from each other as well as the unhealthy beliefs and behaviors that harm true friendships. **Activity 15, Measure Your Friendship IQ** *(for older girls)* offers a quiz to help girls evaluate the competitive nature

---

[18] This concept is discussed in more detail in Chapter 8, "Media Literacy and Critical Thinking."

of their current relationships with other girls. Helping girls increase awareness of harmful, competitive behaviors, such as spreading gossip, is also the objective of **Activity 16,** *Identity Theft Activity—Taking Steps to End "Girl Drama*." Although *Healthy Transitions for Girls* does not directly focus on bullying behaviors, it can be an important solution for bullying problems.

Boundaries! Boundaries! Boundaries!

Social media (such as MySpace, Snapchat, Twitter, Facebook, WhatsApp, Ask.fm, Instagram, or Tumblr)[19] has caused appropriate boundaries to disintegrate among adolescents! Not only have sexual boundaries disintegrated, but personal boundaries of all kinds have eroded. With their natural tendency toward an egocentric view, they live in their own "mini-planet"; they do not truly understand that when they share a status update or a risqué photo, they are posting personal information for hundreds of others to see. Not only is this naïveté dangerous, but it does not establish a sense of personal privacy that is essential to respecting self and others. Boundaries are a vital element in developing mutually respectful relationships. If every girl knew to how to respect personal space, most peer conflicts would be easily resolved!

The sad truth is that girls who have been abused or girls who have low self-esteem may already have very loose boundaries, such as an inability to set limits on physical affection or inability to say "no" to requests made by others. The lure of the social media culture, with its promise of social acceptance, causes girls to follow the crowd into a media-driven, sexualized culture. Teaching boundaries builds strength to resist unhealthy peer influences.

The activities in this section help girls set boundaries in the following areas:

- appropriate self-disclosure;
- appropriate limits for physical touching;
- the ability to have mutually beneficial friendships; and
- the ability to recognize when boundaries are too loose or too rigid.

The **My Space, Your Space Activities** (**Activities 17-19**) use several approaches to create real learning, such as open discussion, art, journaling, and role-play. Parents and professionals are encouraged to present this material in multiple sessions to allow time for reinforcement after each concept is presented.

Healthy boundaries are established with good communication skills. There are two activities in this chapter to increase accurate and assertive (not aggressive) communication. **Handout 26,** *Listening: Rules That Work* helps girls avoid some of the misinterpretation that occurs in girls' dialogue due to their over-sensitive natures. **Handout 27,** *Speaking Up: Rules That Work* teaches girls how to ask for their needs to be met, an important life skill in today's world.

---

[19] A good resource for learning about the risks of each popular social media tool is www.commonsensemedia.org. Visit the section on "Parent Concerns."

The Power of a Safe Group

Finally, just being in a Healthy Transitions for Girls group increases these skills. In groups, girls connect on a deeper level and discover that others experience the same problems they think only they experience. **Activity 47, *One Body Activity*** (Chapter 12) helps girls recognize the unique talents each girl brings to the group. It helps girls begin to express themselves as individuals rather than trying to be so focused on fitting in to a mold.

In one of my workshops, a 5th grade girl frequently complained that she had no friends. She described herself as lonely, even though her teacher said she was always with friends on the playground. During one of the groups, another older girl, who was perceived as being popular, shared that she often felt she did not have true friends. The 5th grade girl was visibly shocked! She said, "I thought you had tons of friends. I thought I was the only one that was lonely." It was a great opportunity to help the 5th grade girl reframe her perceptions and to recognize that all girls feel lonely at times.

In another group of 6th grade girls, one girl was so painfully shy that she did not say a word unless all the other girls were gone. It was interesting to watch her eyes light up and her eyebrows raise as the other girls made comments. Seeing that other girls shared her concerns increased her confidence. In one of our activities, she was able to role-play in front of the other girls. Her confidence increased again as she stepped out of her comfort zone and received encouragement from the group. Through a group experience, this girl did make strides in her ability to reach out and trust others. Working in a *Healthy Transition for Girls* group speaks to girls' inherent need to build connections with each other.

List of Activities, Handouts, & Figures Used in Chapter 6

Chapter 6: Building Supportive Connections with Other Girls

List of Activities.

List of Handouts.

List of Figures.

None.

Activity 15
Measure Your Friendship IQ Activity

(Time = 15 minutes)

Objectives for Each Girl.

1. I can recognize my need for supportive girl friends.
2. I can identify attitudes that hurt my friendships with girls.
3. I can resist competing for boys with my friends.

Explanation.

There are several kinds of harmful actions which keep girls from experiencing true friendships. These are some of the most common.

Indirect bullying can occur when a girl doesn't directly say mean things to another girl, but participates in spreading rumors behind her back. These rumors can be very malicious and cause emotional harm and even "bullycide" (suicide that occurs because an individual is bullied.)

Cyberbullying occurs when the internet is used to spread malicious stories or make harmful threats. Often cyberbullying is done anonymously.

Social alienation occurs when a group of girls decide to deliberately exclude another girl from the group because they want to make her feel bad or because they are jealous.

Other behaviors that hurt friendships may not be considered "bullying," but they are nonetheless harmful: not keeping confidences when a friend has told you a secret, constantly putting a friend down to help you feel better, and hanging out with a friend only because you think she can help you to become popular.

Materials Needed.

1. Handout 21, *Friend or Competition?*
2. Pencil or pen.

Activity Steps.

1. Ask each girl to privately consider if she feels she has close friendships: "Do you feel you have loyal friends?" "Do you ever feel lonely?" "Do you feel you can trust girls your age?" "Do you feel you are a trustworthy friend?"
2. Share the case study of Monica. Ask the case study questions and then give the explanation that follows.

Case Study: Monica had long blond hair that was highlighted and a nice tan. She had long thin legs and was very athletic. Monica was a cheerleader in a very large school. She had received a lot of votes and passed through many hurdles to win the title of cheerleader.

Question 1: Would you want to be friends with Monica?

Question 2: Do you think she would be the kind of girl who would be a good friend?

Question 3: Would you feel too inferior to Monica to be her friend?

Question 4: Would you look for faults in Monica to make yourself feel better?

Case Study Explanation: The truth about Monica is that she was very lonely. Even though popular boys asked her to dances and gave her attention, she had the nagging feeling that she only got dates because of her appearance. Girls her age disliked her out of jealousy. Monica has many acquaintances, but few real friends. People voted for her because she was thin and pretty, not because they knew anything about her personality.

Follow-Up Question: Can you think of situation where you have judged someone from the outside and resisted offering friendship?

3. Share the case study of Katrina. Ask the case study questions that follow.

Case Study: Katrina and her sixth grade friends had all been "besties" (best friends) since kindergarten. They took dance lessons together and had birthday parties together. They had a big group of friends, about 13 girls. Something strange happened in 6th grade, however. All of a sudden, the girls started to pair up into little cliques of two or three girls. These little cliques began to fight and pick on each other.

Katrina was pressured to choose a clique to join and to be mad at the other cliques. She liked it much better when the girls were just one big group of friends and when they were not jealous if she hung out with one friend one day and another friend another day. She told the girls she didn't like these new social rules. All of the girls got mad at her, and for two weeks, she did not have one friend at school. Finally, Katrina got help from her teacher. She explained what was going on and how lonely she felt at school. The teacher explained that every year in 6th grade, girls start to have "girl drama," the kind that was happening to Katrina and her friends.

Katrina decided to take a stand against girl drama. Even though she was lonely for a while, she told her friends that she refused to get involved in choosing one friend over the other. Eventually, some of the girls' parents found out what was going on, and they helped their daughters apologize to Katrina. Because she took a stand, other girls decided that they like have a big group instead of a bunch of little cliques that fought. Even though the girls had different interests, they remained friends for many years. Katrina learned to have one or two very close friends, but found that she could be friends with many different girls, too.

Question 1: Have you ever had a similar experience?

Question 2: What would you have done if you were Katrina?

Question 3: How do you feel about having just one or two friends?

Question 4: Can you benefit from learning to be kind to many different girls?

4. Use Handout 21. Tell the girls that they are going to measure their "Friendship IQ"; in other words, they are going to measure attitudes that might keep them from being a supportive friend to someone else.
5. Have the girls complete the quiz on the handout. Invite the girls to share what they learned from the quiz. Ask if they discovered any warning signs about their competitive attitudes.
6. Explain that in one real-life situation, a group of 6th graders friends found that they were constantly fighting over boys. They would gossip about each other and pick at each others' faults. After a few miserable months, their teacher told them that they needed to take a hard look at how they treated each other. They realized that they were putting boys ahead of friendship and that life would be much happier if they stopped being jealous. The rest of the school year went much better once this group of friends decided that they wanted to support each other, rather than compete against each other.
7. Emphasize that in real friendships, each girl has someone unique to offer. It is more important for girls to share their personalities and talents with each other than to compete. They can learn to appreciate many different kinds of friends. They can find common interests, offer support and kindness, and learn from their friends' differences when they put friendship ahead of competition.

Activity 16
Identity Theft Activity—Taking Steps to End "Girl Drama"

(Time = 15 minutes)

Objectives for Each Girl.

1. I can recognize how gossip and criticism causes harm.
2. I can resist passing on negative information about other girls.
3. I can be a friend who is emotionally safe and trustworthy.
4. I can avoid making critical statements about others' appearance.

Explanation.

This activity raises awareness of the behaviors that fuel "girl drama" and helps girls commit to eliminate gossip. Gossip is so common among pre-adolescent and adolescent girls that they may not even consider it a problem. However, gossip is a form of serious bullying when it causes a girl to suffer a loss of reputation and become isolated from her peers. Gossip creates an emotionally unsafe atmosphere where girls continually worry that if they don't do and say just the right thing, then "Everyone will be talking behind my back." Gossip and criticism of girls' bodies and appearance really sticks, and it increases the body shame already fueled by the media. With social and electronic media, gossip can spread faster than ever, making it even more threatening to girls.

At times, it seems girls can almost be compulsive in their need to keep stirring up drama. If girls experience constant conflict in their families, they may not conceive that harmonious friendships are even possible. I asked my level-headed eleven-year-old granddaughter, "How do you handle girl drama at your school?" She replied matter-of-factly, "I stay away from the girls that cause it." This activity teaches boundary skills and gets girls thinking about what kind of relationships they want in their lives.

Materials Needed.

1. Handout 22, *Don't Be an Identity Thief.*

Activity Steps.

1. Ask the following questions and discuss the answers as a group.

   Question 1: How have your girlfriend relationships changed as you have grown older? (Most likely, they will readily identify that "girl drama" has become a big part of their lives.)

   Question 2: Can you describe examples of "girl drama" that are going on right now?

   Question 3: What do you think causes "girl drama?"

Question 4: How has "drama" and conflict with your friends affected you?

Question 5: Have you ever felt left out or lonely because of "drama" with girls your age?

Question 6: Have you seen girls lose friends and reputations when rumors were spread around? Has this happened to you?

Question 7: What are things you can do to be an emotionally safe and loyal friend?

Question 8: When girls are continually wrapped up in fighting with their friends, they miss out on positive experiences and positive relationships. What can you do to avoid situations that get you involved in "girl drama"?

2. Use Handout 22. Read the handout together and give the girls time to complete the questions.
3. Role-play examples of how to resist hearing and spreading gossip.
4. Emphasize that by signing the NO GOSSIP PLEDGE, they are making an important commitment to be better friends and to attract better friends.

Activity 17
My Space, Your Space Part 1

(Time = 30 – 45 minutes)

Objectives for Each Girl.

1. I can recognize my need for "personal space."
2. I can recognize the need for boundaries to protect my personal space.
3. I can make careful choices about what I share with people I don't know well.
4. I can choose the kind of physical touch I want to allow.

Explanation.

This lesson introduces the concept of personal space. It presents the idea that personal space is different for each person and for each situation. The need for boundaries in personal disclosure is discussed, particularly in relation to social media. Girls have the right to set limits about the kind of physical affection or touch they will allow from others.

Materials Needed.

1. A long piece of yarn, at least 36 inches, for each girl.
2. Handout 23, *My Space, Your Space.*
3. Handout 27, *Speaking Up: Rules that Work.*
4. A rural-type mailbox with a lid/door that opens and closes (optional).

Activity Steps.

1. Give each girl a piece of yarn. Have the girls tie the ends together to create a circle that represents "My Personal Space." Have them lay the yarn circle on the ground and stand in the center of their yarn circle. Have girls adjust the size of their yarn circle to indicate how close a stranger can get before they feel uncomfortable. Have them adjust the yarn circle again to indicate how close their parents or a trusted friend can get. Explain that every girl has a "personal space" that is an important part of who she is.
2. Read Handout 23 together. Emphasize that every girl needs to develop a sense of personal space. Ask the girls to share what kind of rules their parents have about what they should post on social media. Discuss why following their parents rules is a good idea. For girls who don't have rules about social media, discuss why rules would be a good idea. Explain that having personal space means that personal information is only for those you know and trust; it is not healthy to be revealing personal emotions to people who are only acquaintances. Explain that an important part of having self-respect and self-confidence is having personal boundaries.
3. Girls can decide what they want to allow in their personal space in many ways. Discuss that girls should set the following boundaries in their lives:

- How close they want someone to be to their body.
- What kind of language (profanity) or jokes they will tolerate.
- What kind of physical affection they want.
- What they want to share or what they want others to share about them.

4. Ask the girls to describe situations where they felt someone else violated their personal space. Examples might be: sharing a secret, calling too late at night, sending a bunch of email forwards that you didn't request, posting your picture on the internet without permission, snapping your bra, hugging you aggressively, telling a crude joke and getting mad when you don't laugh, asking to copy from homework, or borrowing things without permission.

5. Role-play how to set personal boundaries using examples given by the girls in Step 3. Use Handout 27 to help girls practice communicating their boundaries to others.

6. Remind girls that being a true friend means you respect others' boundaries. Tell them to watch for non-verbal cues that they have "violated" another's space. Say, "What kind of non-verbal clues let you know when someone doesn't like what you did?" Remind them that a good friend readily apologizes and is not defensive. Explain, "When someone tells you that you have disrespected their personal space, tell them you are sorry and resolve not to do it again."

7. Encourage the girls that learning to have healthy boundaries is a life-long process, but they need a healthy start now.

8. If desired, complete the following optional mailbox activity. I have a rural mailbox which has a hinged door. It is spray-painted and decorated so that it is a fun addition to *Healthy Transitions for Girls* activities. The hinged door can be opened to varying degrees. I use this to demonstrate that girls can choose how much they want to open up their "personal space" to others. When discussing social situations (such as those listed in Step 3), I let the girls open or close the door to demonstrate how much they want to "open the door" and share, or how much they want to "close the door" in order to protect their personal space. Girls will vary in how much privacy they desire and they can indicate this by moving the mailbox door. Use the mailbox to demonstrate "loose" or "rigid" boundaries by opening and closing the door tightly or flinging it open all the way. The mailbox activity teaches girls that having balanced boundaries means they know how to open and close their "mailbox" when necessary.

Activity 18
My Space, Your Space Part 2

(Time = 30 – 45 minutes)

Objectives for Each Girl.

1. I can distinguish between rigid boundaries and loose boundaries.
2. I can recognize healthy, balanced boundaries.
3. I can establish mutual friendships by knowing when to say "yes" or "no" to requests.
4. I can improve my friendship by understanding healthy boundaries.

Materials Needed.

1. Handout 24, *My Space, Your Space: Find the Balance*
2. Handout 25, *My Space, Your Space: Good Boundaries Make Good Friendships Better*
3. Handout 27, *Speaking Up: Rules that Work*

Activity Steps.

1. Ask the following discussion questions:

   Question 1: Do you have trouble knowing when to say "yes" or "no" when a friend makes a request?

   Question 2: Do you worry that your friends are always taking advantage of you?

   Question 3: Do you find yourself always being the one that compromises what you want to do?

   Question 4: Do you find yourself saying "yes" to things you know are wrong so others won't be mad at you?

   Question 5: Do you believe that being a good friend means you should always say "yes"?

   Question 6: Do you protect yourself from being hurt by never sharing feelings?

   Question 7: Do you have a hard time knowing how much to trust others?

   Question 8: Do you trust everyone and then feel angry when they burn you?

   Question 9: What would you describe as your biggest problem in relationships?

2. Explain that all these problems can be improved by knowing how to set boundaries or, in other words, create healthy "personal space."

3. Explain that Handout 24 can be used as a guide to measure what healthy boundaries look like.[20] Use the items on the list to generate more discussion. Ask each girl to circle at least 3 items on the "loose" or "rigid" boundaries list that she thinks cause problems for her.

4. Read Handout 25 as a group. After you have read the guidelines for helping girls to know when to say "yes" or "no," ask the girls if they now know how to solve the boundary issues they circled on Handout 24 in Step 2. Invite them to share their dilemmas. Discuss solutions using guidelines from the handouts.

5. Using the items the girls circled in Step 2 on Handout 24, role-play how they could become stronger in those areas and have more balanced boundaries. Use Handout 27 to provide guidelines on how to communicate wants and needs.

6. Summarize the activity by explaining that the goal of balanced boundaries is to help girls protect themselves from harmful situations and yet still keep themselves open to the kind of support and friendship that every girl needs. Remind them that setting honest boundaries with friends and communicating honestly with friends will make their friendships more sincere and loyal in the long run. Encourage them to have mutual give-and-take friendships.

7. Ask each girl to choose one "take-away" idea from the activity. Ask, "How will you take what you learned today and use it to solve a friendship problem you have right now?" Tell them you want them to report back to the group to discuss their progress with the problem they identify.

---

[20] This list is a great reference and can be referred to often when discussing relationship and behavior problems in family discussion or therapy settings.

Activity 19
My Space, Your Space Part 3

(Time = 20 – 30 minutes)

Objectives for Each Girl.

1. I can develop awareness of my personal boundaries.
2. I can recognize when I need to strengthen my boundaries.
3. I can recognize when rigid boundaries limit friendships and growth.
4. I can develop awareness of steps that will allow more joy in my life.

Explanation.

This lesson is an art activity that helps girls become aware of unconscious beliefs they may have about boundaries. This activity can actually be used as a discovery lesson before any of the other lessons, or as a stand-alone activity. Before conducting this activity, make sure the girls understand definitions for "personal space" and "boundaries," as explained in Handout 23.

Materials Needed.

1. Handout 23, *My Space, Your Space*.
2. Handout 24, *My Space, Your Space: Find the Balance*.
3. Crayons, markers, and white paper.

Activity Steps.

1. Distribute the art supplies. Tell the girls, "You are about to draw a picture of a house that represents your life. You can call the project 'My Life as a House' or 'If My Life Were a House.' Don't worry about getting the project 'right' or meeting someone else's expectations. Don't worry if your house is very different than someone else's. Just let your creative self take over and have fun! Be sure to include a yard and fence around your house."
2. Allow 15 minutes drawing time, or as much time is needed for girls not to feel rushed.
3. After the girls complete their houses, discuss the following questions with the girls.

   Question 1: How many colors have you used? Are they bright or dark? Is there a message in the colors you chose?

   Question 2: Are there flowers? Are there no flowers at all? If there are no flowers in your yard, does it mean you need to add more beauty to your life?

Question 3: What season have you drawn? Is it winter? Are things dying? (This is not a "bad" thing; it just means you are preparing for new things in your life.) Are new things planted? Are there any plants at all? What do you think the season you chose to draw represents about your life?

Question 4: What does your fence look like? Is the fence really close to or tight around the house? Is your yard big or small?

Question 5: What size is your fence in relation to your house? Is it high? Can you see through it? Is it toppled down? Does your fence have barbed wire? Can a person get through your fence easily? Do you have a gate? Is it locked? Is it wide open? Can anyone get through, or just some people? How do you decide who gets to come through your fence?

Question 6: What might your fence tell you about the boundaries you currently have in your life? Are you giving yourself space to grow? Are you keeping others completely out? Are you letting too many people in? Do you need to hang "No Trespassing" signs or "Welcome" signs on your fence?

Question 7: Do you have windows? Can others see in? Is there light coming in or out? Are the shades drawn? Are there lots of windows or just a few? Do you feel there is any particular message about the windows? (There is no right or wrong answer. Just take your best guess.)

Question 8: Take a quick scan of your house and yard overall. What do you notice? Does it feel cluttered? Does it feel empty? Are you comfortable in this house? What would make it feel more pleasant?

Question 9: If this drawing represents "personal space," what message have you learned about boundaries in your life?

4. Allow the girls to discuss insights they may have gleaned from this activity. Remind the girls that the purpose of boundaries is to help them develop friendships that protect them from harm, yet still experience the supportive social connections they need. Challenge them to take one thing they learned from this activity about their boundaries and set a personal goal. Use Handout 24 to help them set their goals.

Chapter 7

Building Healthy Boy-Girl Friendships

*Peder. Normally she would shout hello, but the past year a strange
feeling had come inching into Miri... she had begun noticing things about him,
like the pale hair on his tanned arm and the line between his brows that deepened
when he was perplexed. She liked those things. It made Miri wonder if he noticed her, too.*
~ from *Princess Academy* by Shannon Hale

It is an understatement to say that something "strange" happens to girls' feelings about boys as they enter puberty. The boy she's known since kindergarten all of sudden makes her self-conscious and tongue-tied. Girls handle this hormonally-driven dilemma in different ways. For some girls, "drama" about boys may occupy a major portion of their waking hours. Girls may go to great lengths to attract male attention—evidenced by constant worry about physical appearance and constant focus on wondering, "Does he love me?" or "Love me not?" Still other girls decide they will deal with their developmental discomfort by competing with the boys in their lives, continually trying to "one-up" them in sports or academics or criticizing them but never learning to build mutual friendships.

Pressure and More Pressure

As girls' bodies change and they develop natural feelings of sexual attraction, they face a huge new set of pressures. These pressures may be largely unconscious, but they are nonetheless real:

Pressure to have a steady boyfriend as a measure of self-worth.
Pressure to experiment with newly-discovered sexual urges.
Pressure to be sexually attractive based upon pop culture standards.

Since this curriculum targets girls ages 8 to 14, it may seem too early to explore attitudes about sex; but consider that in the Oregon Healthy Teens Survey (2013), 10.4 percent of girls had experienced sexual intercourse by 8th grade. This percentage escalated to 45.2 percent by 11th grade. The pressure is on! Although discussions about sex with 8-9 year olds is going to be different than the discussions with more mature, more experienced 13-14 year olds, it is nonetheless important to address how to handle developing sexual attraction early. Even as young as age 8, girls are forming attitudes about sex and relationships that will affect the choices they make in the next few years. Just peruse the beginner bra section of your favorite department store and you will find leopard prints, underwire, and an inch of padding. The pressure starts early and girls' interests are being derailed by a focus on appearance!

Where does all this pressure come from? It comes from

- Social media interactions that erode personal boundaries.
- TV and movie portrayals that glamorize sex between teens.
- Sexual education programs that support sexual exploration.

- Peers who are influenced by pop culture images.
- Parents who want their children to be popular with peers.

Are you a parent who can't wait for your daughter to have a date to the middle school dance or to have her first romance? Take a moment and reconsider the consequences of encouraging girls to "pair up." Unknowingly, parents who want their kids to be popular and who are excited when their daughter has a boyfriend are feeding the problem, rather than the solution. JeaNette G. Smith, LMFT, a private practice marriage and family counselor, counters the notion that steady dating is just inevitable, harmless fun. In her book, *Unsteady: What Every Parent Absolutely Must Know about Teenage Romance* (2008), she explains that the inevitable fate of teen romance is to either end in heartbreak or continue to become more intensely committed and sexually involved. As pointed out in the book, *steady dating relationships ...*

- limit growth experiences critical to development of self.
- limit choices in opposite-sex friends.
- narrow their focus away from future goals.
- isolate them from same-sex friends.
- isolate them from their parents.

Keep Girls Safe from the "Safe Sex" Message

Girls (ages 12-18) are simply not prepared with the maturity or skills to handle the intensity of romantic sexual relationships. Dr. James Fowler (2004), emeritus faculty of the Center for Ethics at Emory University in Georgia, points out that an important goal in early adolescence is to develop identity, which is defined as "having values and purpose, self-knowledge and judgment." Girls at this age must learn how they are unique or similar to others; they have a great need to learn their own likes and dislikes, identify talents, and begin to see that they have something valuable to offer to the world. It is vital that they learn to set the kind of personal boundaries that protect their individual uniqueness and identity. Setting personal boundaries requires self-knowledge and self-respect.[21] As girls develop a sense of self, they are ready to move into the later stage of adolescence where, as explained by Dr. Fowler, the goal is to learn how to form close relationships. Kyle N. Weir, PhD, LMFT (2015) summarizes, "The process of development mandates that an adolescent must first master [her] identify development before they can be successful at intimacy" (p. 25).

Longing for attention and approval from boys is natural, but being "boy crazy" and having premature physical encounters harm both a girl's ability to establish her clear identity and her ability to have healthy intimacy in adult relationships. Consider the following real-life examples that show the harm that occurs when girls believe that their *self-worth* depends on whether they have a boyfriend, or when getting and keeping a boyfriend becomes a primary focus:

- A 6th grade girl in one of my workshops stated that she was not eating that day because she had just had a "bad breakup" with her boyfriend.

---

[21] Personal boundaries are addressed in **Activities 17-19, *My Space, Your Space*** (Chapter 6).

- Another girl had to visit the doctor because of insomnia and weight loss when her boyfriend started dating another girl.
- Still another girl became ostracized from her family because her steady boyfriend told her they were too "controlling." Simultaneously, he sexually exploited her, which caused her to become further alienated from family and religious support.

Without the maturity to form a healthy friendship, and pressured by the need to fit in and feel worthwhile, a girl's giddiness over a boyfriend soon becomes a focus on the thrill of kissing. The intense passions that arise from kissing are like a drug high that invite more and more experimentation, until the young pair is wholly involved in a whirlwind of sexual intimacy that overshadows all other aspects of their relationship. Sexual intimacy floods a girl's brain with oxytocin, a hormone that creates trust and bonding. A brain that is "drenched" in this hormone naturally wants to receive love and commitment (Grossman, 2008). She longs for commitment and care that he is too immature to offer. Instead of fulfillment, she is plagued with insecurity about the relationship, an insatiable sense of longing that is unrequited. Needless to say, when the break up happens, as it typically does, she feels "hurt, shame, and self-loathing" (Fowler, 2004).

With each new relationship, the pattern repeats. This culture of casual sex "invites self-deception and the denial of negative emotions [which] often leads to medical and mental health issues with significant consequences" (Fowler, 2004). Tragically, teens become young adults who are unable to establish truly intimate relationships, the kind which involve "bringing the selfhood of partners into emotional, intellectual, and moral intimacy with each other" (Fowler, 2004). Girls may develop life-long patterns of codependency or chronic people- pleasing, compromising personal values and true feelings for the need to please others. Codependent relationships can put girls at risk for sexual exploitation, psychological manipulation, and physical abuse.

Research supports an abstinence approach to sexual experimentation as a protection for girls' mental and physical health. First, consider that there is an extremely high correlation between sexual experimentation and depression among teen girls.

- A 2006 study of 19,000 teens conducted by the National Institute of Mental Health (NIH) found that girls who experimented sexually were four times more likely to develop depression than girls who were abstinent.[22]
- In a study of 6,500 adolescents, sexually active teenage girls were more than three times more likely to be depressed, and nearly three times as likely to have had a suicide attempt, than girls who were not sexually active (Grossman, 2007, p. 4).
- Another report, titled "You Don't Bring Me Anything but Down: Adolescent Romance and Depression," analyzed data on 8,000 teens. The two researchers concluded that "females experience a larger increase in depression than males in response to romantic involvement," and "females' greater vulnerability to romantic involvement may explain the higher rates of depression in female teens" (Grossman, 2007, p. 4).

---

[22] See a summary of this study at http://www.nih.gov/news/pr/may2006/nida-15.htm. Full report is published in the May 15, 2006 issue of the *Archives of Women's Mental Health.*

- 91 percent of girls experience regret after casual sex and report "feeling used" (Grossman, 2008).

Second, science demonstrates the physical health risk of sexual experimentation. Young girls are more vulnerable to sexually transmitted diseases (STD's) than adults, and there is an extremely high rate of STD's among teen and college-age girls.

- The cervix (entrance to the uterus) has an area called the "transformation" zone that is very vulnerable to HPV (human papillomavirus, which causes genital warts) and other sexually transmitted diseases when girls are young. This area thickens in adult women and is less vulnerable to disease than when girls are young. Because of this immature transformation zone, it is common for girls to become infected with a sexually transmitted disease from one of their first sexual partners (Grossman, 2009, p. 77).
- In 2008, one out of four sexually active girls was infected with a sexually transmitted disease by the time she was college age (Grossman, 2009, p.4).
- HPV is so common and so contagious, especially in the college population, that most young women are infected within a few years of becoming sexually active (Grossman, 2007, p. 17).
- There are fifteen million new cases of STDs a year (Grossman, 2007, p. 29).

Additionally, research supports the fact that casual sex harms the ability of girls to build life-long intimate relationships when they become adults. In their study of 2035 married individuals, Busby, Carroll, and Willoughby (2010) found that even though most of the couples in the study had sex within three months of meeting each other, participants who delayed sex until after marriage reported the highest rate of sexual satisfaction and the highest satisfaction in their overall relationships. The conclusion was that couples who had developed communication and intimacy in all the other aspects of their relationship prior to becoming sexual intimate had built the best foundation for happiness.

My own clinical experience and that of many other couples therapists demonstrates the frequency of couples who jump into sex and then into cohabitation or marriage, only to discover that they have little foundation for building a long term relationship together. Busby, Carroll, and Willoughby (2010) discuss this phenomenon called "relationship inertia." "Relationship inertia" is like a slippery slide, where the emotions of sex early in a relationship rush girls to emotionally bond with a partner who may not be a good match at all.

In light of these facts, is there something surreal about the glamorized media depictions of no consequences sex and romance? Does it seem irresponsible that sexual education programs portray sex among teens and condom use as a responsible choice with little or no consequences? Girls are paying a very high price for these myths. *Healthy Transitions for Girls* wants to arm parents and professionals with the facts they need to take a strong stand to protect girls' bodies and emotions.

The Goal is Healthy Friendship

Contrast the codependent examples described earlier with the case of Suzy, age 16, who shares a mutual interest in literature with Preston, also age 16, which is cited by Dr. Weir (2015). After their date, which does not include physical affection other than a brief hug, Suzy ponders her interest in plays and symbols and discovers that she want to be a drama critic. She learns that she can talk with a boy about her interests and be respected for her opinions. Suzy's sense of identity and confidence increases as a result of her date with Preston. Clearly, Suzy is successfully navigating the essential milestones of adolescence that will lead to healthy relationships later in life.

Healthy Transitions for Girls puts the focus back where it belongs—on building non-sexual, healthy friendships based upon self-control, mutual respect, good boundaries, and good communication skills. **Activity 20, "Conversations & Diplomacy Rules" Role Play Activity** is a first step in teaching friendship skills. This activity borrows some help from the award-winning book *Princess Academy* by Shannon Hale. In this favorite role-play activity, girls learn very specific skills for talking to boys that can be applied in a variety of social situations. Girls of all ages enjoy this role play.

The themes of songs, television programs, and movies continually promote codependent relationships: "I'm lost without you"; "I can't live without you"; and "I'll do anything if you'll be mine." Romeo and Juliet had a classic case of codependency! **Activity 21, *Codependency Versus Healthy Relationships Activity*** specifically discusses codependent boy-girl relationships. **Handout 29, *I Can't Live Without Him and Other Lies You Hear in Country Songs*** helps girls to differentiate between healthy and unhealthy boy-girl relationships. (Both of these activities are designed for older girls.)

To combat the fact that both boys and girls are being socialized to look for a steady dating partner that can improve their social status and fulfill sexual drives, *Healthy Transitions for Girls* encourages girls to build friendships based upon common interests.[23] Girls look at their "Prince Charming" and think, "Oh, he is so cool" or "He is so popular." "Cool" and "popular" are defined by unspoken, superficial rules that rarely have anything to do with values, character, skills, or potential for success. **Activity 22, Cinder Edna *Bibliotherapy Activity*** (for younger girls) is a humorous learning activity that teaches girls how to build relationships based upon accurate self-knowledge and the ability to discern between superficial attractions and the deeper qualities that build trusting friendships.

Healthy Transitions for Girls Offers Healthy Guardrails

Healthy Transitions for Girls helps parents, mentors, and counselors provide the guardrails that will keep girls from jumping off the cliff of teen romance and sexual experimentation like a bunch of pop culture lemmings. Although *Healthy Transitions for Girls* specifically discusses boy-girl relationships, the message to abstain from sexual experimentation and instead focus on identity development and other goals during adolescence also applies to girls who experience same-sex attraction or to girls who feel ambiguous about their sexual identity. Girls who have parents that are lesbian or gay, or girls who presently experience same-sex attraction should not feel excluded from this discussion of boy-girl relationships; but, they should be encouraged to learn the universal skills that are essential to all healthy relationships: 1) Self-control; 2) Mutual respect; 3) Good boundaries; and 4) Communication skills.

---

[23] See also the discussion of "objectification" in Activity 25, Media Detectives Activity (Chapter 8).

For older girls, **Activity 23, *Heart Healthy Relationships*** and the **Activity 24, *Relationship Timeline Activity*** work together to help girls recognize that, 1) sexual boundaries are necessary and possible, and 2) they have more important things to do at this time in their lives than develop drama-filled, emotionally-entangling romantic relationships. **Activity 23, *Heart Healthy Relationships*** gives specific limits for physical affection in relationships; it supports an abstinence approach and gives parents and counselors a hands-on tool for helping girls set healthy limits. **Activity 24, *Relationship Timeline Activity*** helps girls to identify the important goals they need to accomplish during this amazing time in their lives. It helps them broaden their perspective and begin to view adolescence as a time of preparation for adulthood.

Healthy Transitions for Girls invites girls ages 8 to 14 to build a healthy respect for the role of sexual intimacy in their lives. Sex is not "bad," but it is powerful and can cause serious, long-term harm when misused. To be "safe," sexual intimacy must be accompanied by the ability to be safely intimate in other ways. "Intimacy means the capacity to engage in closeness with others, including sexual closeness, without needing to use or manipulate the other, and without allowing or fearing a loss of the self" (Fowler, 2004).

This kind of sharing, a sharing of the whole self, can't be taken lightly and needs to be protected by exclusive, life-long commitment. "To be physically intimate outside of the covenant of marriage is to be so deeply vulnerable without any promise of safety, security, permanence, or exclusivity in return. That's just too great a risk for our youth to make when their identities have yet to be fully formed" (Weir, 2015, p. 24). This program advocates that girls wait until marriage to have sexual intimacy because this is the "safest" and most responsible position for a program that wants to support overall wellness in girls. Dr. Miriam Grossman, a nationally recognized psychiatrist and specialist in women's health summarizes, "The only people who are completely safe are those who, along with their spouses, waited for marriage, and once married, remain faithful" (Grossman, p. 2007, p. 30).

List of Activities, Handouts, & Figures Used in Chapter 7

Chapter 7: Building Healthy Boy-Girl Friendships

<u>List of Activities.</u>

<u>List of Handouts.</u>

<u>List of Figures.</u>

None.

Activity 20
"Conversation & Diplomacy Rules" Role-Play Activity

Time = 45 minutes

Objective for Each Girl.

1. I can increase my confidence and skills in talking to boys.[24]

Materials Needed.

1. A tennis ball.
2. Handout 28, *How to Build Friendships with Guys.*
3. A copy of the book *Princess Academy* by Shannon Hale.

Activity Steps.

1. Although many girls may have read the book *Princess Academy*, some may need a brief summary of the story. *Princess Academy* is a valuable "coming of age" resource for girls ages 8 to 14. The title, *Princess Academy*, may make the book sound like a fairy tale, but the characters and plot are exciting and inspiring. Explain that in the story, the girls of Mount Eskel have all been given the task, by royal decree, to prepare to be the crowned princess of the Danlanders. They leave their village in the highlands and travel to the Princess Academy to receive training for this daunting responsibility. Although only one girl will eventually qualify and be selected as the princess, the *Princess Academy* storyline reinforces the concept that girls can choose friendship over competition.
2. In the process of qualifying to be chosen as the princess, all the girls are tutored in social skills, or "Conversation and Diplomacy Rules." These skills are especially timely for the main character of the story, Miri, whose relationship with her childhood friend, Peder, has suddenly become more awkward. Miri wants her friendship with Peder to continue, but her new grown-up feelings make it seem more complicated. Read page 84 and discuss with the girls how Miri's relationship with Peder is changing. Ask the girls if they are having similar experiences.
3. Read pages 167-169 and ask the girls to notice how Miri feels about touching Peder. Explain that feelings of attraction are normal and caused by biological changes in the body that occur during puberty.
4. Explain that having feelings of attraction requires them to learn some new skills so that they can handle these feelings responsibly. The most important goal they can learn is to build positive friendships with boys, despite these feelings of attraction. Read pages 42-43, 53, 63. Ask the girls to identify something that tells them that Miri is learning to build a relationship with Peder based upon friendship, respect, mutual trust, and emotional safety.
5. Explain that Miri used the "Conversation and Diplomacy Rules" she learned at the Princess Academy to help her talk to Peder. Review the rules with the girls.

---

[24] In previous workshop evaluations, girls have indicated that this was one of the most helpful skill sets they learned during *Healthy Transitions for Girls* workshops.

     ✓ Say his name.
     ✓ Make observations, not judgments.
     ✓ Return the conversation to him.
     ✓ Recognize strengths, give compliments.[25]
     ✓ Build upon common ground.

6.   Discuss in more detail what each of these rules means.

To *repeat his name* means to look someone in the eyes and use their name, rather than calling them, "Hey You," or some other term. People like to hear their names; it shows you have a personal interest.

Making observations, not judgments helps girls resist criticism or sarcasm as a way to start conversation. It requires them to notice what is going on with another person and demonstrate friendly acceptance: "Hi, John, I noticed that you were really concentrating during that science test."

Having a conversation is like tossing a tennis ball back and forth. It isn't one-sided, where only you talk or where only he talks. It isn't about only one person's point of view. When you have a made a comment or asked a question, *return the conversation* or "toss the ball" back to him so that both of you are able to express your thoughts and ideas.

Recognize strengths and give compliments. We don't want girls to act as if someone is better or worse than they are or more or less than they are. We want to *encourage* reciprocal relationships. The rule invites girls to 1) recognize the strengths in others; 2) feel comfortable giving compliments; 3) learn from the strengths of others; and 4) resist thinking they need to be better than others to be important. In this fantasy book, Miri was taught conversation to help her talk to a prince; it was important that she remained confident as she acknowledged his title as Prince.

To *build upon common ground* is to find things you have in common. Ask about things he is interested in. Show that you are interested. Volunteer information about what you are interested in as well. Offer information about what you like and ask more questions to keep the conversation going.

7.   In this role-play, they will find that the girl who is role-playing a boy will truly get into her role and will not have much to say, which is commonly the case with a middle school-age boy. Encourage the girls to use Handout 28 to encourage more verbalization. The facilitator observes the girls and

---

[25] In the book, this rule is described as "act as if someone is your better." Acting as if someone is your "better," as described in the story, does not mean girls should put themselves down, act passively, or feel inadequate. It is asking girls to resist using "put-downs" or being competitive with boys to get attention.

elicits understanding about why a conversation stalls and what rule can be used when they run out of things to say. After the girls have role-played, ask the following questions.

Question 1: What was the most difficult part of the role-play?

Question 2: Did the Conversation Rules help?

Question 3: What rule was most helpful?

8. Invite the girls to get into pairs to practice the rules of conversation. They will take turns pretending that they are using the rules to initiate a conversation with a boy. Ask them to be good actors and to capture the feelings they have whenever they are around a boy who makes them nervous.

9. To help emphasize the idea that conversations are a two-way process, have the girls throw a tennis ball back and forth to their role-play partner each time they finish saying something. The girl who is holding the ball may stammer and not be sure what to say, but holding the ball is a reminder that she needs to make an effort to keep the conversation going and "throw the ball back."

10. Encourage the girls to practice these skills during the week and to report their experiences during the next workshop.

Activity 21
Codependency Versus Healthy Relationships Activity[26]

(Time = 45 minutes)

Objectives for Each Girl.

1. I can become aware of the codependent messages that are pervasive in music, television, and movies.
2. I can recognize the warning signs of unhealthy relationships.
3. I can recognize the negative emotions created by unhealthy relationships.
4. I can get help when I am in a negative relationship.
5. I can end relationships that are unhealthy.
6. I can identify the qualities of healthy relationships.
7. I can build healthy friendships rather than serious dating relationships with boys.

Explanation.

The objective of this activity is 1) to raise awareness of codependent relationships; and 2) to help prevent codependent relationships with boys by teaching girls the early warning signs.

Materials Needed.

1. Handout 29, *I Can't Live Without Him ... and Other Lies You Hear in Country Songs.*

Activity Steps.

1. Begin the discussion by asking the girls how they feel about having a boyfriend. Are having boyfriends a condition of being popular? Do they feel weird if they don't have a boyfriend? Are they someone who always needs to have a boyfriend to feel good?
2. Ask the girls to think of some popular songs that talk about boy-girl relationships and breaking up. Allow them to share these lyrics with the group. Discuss whether or not these lyrics describe relationships that are codependent. Ask the girls to challenge the messages in music and other forms of entertainment: "Is it really healthy to stop being happy or to want to die because a guy stops liking you?"
3. Have the girls read the signs of Healthy Friendship vs. Codependency, shown in Handout 29. Ask them to describe movies where they have seen the signs of codependency. (If a movie depicts people being miserable in a relationship, or a lot of relationship drama, it is a good sign the

---

[26] The Cinder Edna *Bibliotherapy Activity* (Activity 22) is a good follow-up activity to demonstrate what a healthy relationship looks like. The *Heart Healthy Relationships Activity* (Activity 23) and *Relationship Timeline Activity* (Activity 24) teach girls how to set boundaries on physical affection and put boy-girl relationships in perspective with the other goals in their lives.

relationship is codependent.) Have they seen signs of codependency in people they know? What would they do if they knew someone who was in an unhealthy relationship?

4. Explain that a serious warning sign of codependency is when a girl believes she can't say no to sex without losing her boyfriend. Girls can be pressured into sex and then feel so shameful about it that they continue in a bad relationship. One of the reasons it is important not to steady date is that girls do not have the skills to handle sexual pressures until they are older.

5. Another serious warning sign of codependency is if a girl is slapped, has her arms squeezed, or is ridiculed by a guy but continues to see him. Anytime a guy puts a girl down to make her feel she has to stay in the relationship, she is being psychologically manipulated. Girls will also lie for guys who are doing drugs, alcohol, stealing, or cheating, even when they know these things are wrong. They don't tell anyone because they believe telling would be disloyal or not loving.

6. Make sure girls know that they need to tell an adult if they believe a friend is in a harmful boy-girl relationship. Staying in an unhealthy relationship will only cause more heartache. The longer a girl stays in a codependent relationship, the more she loses her ability to know that she is being harmed. **Role-play** the following scenarios:

    Scenario 1: End an unhealthy relationship with a boy.

    Scenario 2: Confront a friend who is at risk in an unhealthy relationship with a boy.

    Scenario 3: Get help from an adult because a friend is in an abusive relationship.

7. Emphasize again the value of building healthy friendships with guys, rather than steady dating.

Activity 22
Cinder Edna Bibliotherapy Activity[27]

(Time = 45 minutes)

Objectives for Each Girl.

1. I can challenge stereotypes that limit my friendships.
2. I can build friendships based upon common interests, rather than appearance and popularity or superficial "social rules."

Explanation.

Cinder Edna is a comical and memorable picture book by Ellen Jackson.[28] It is a spoof of the traditional Cinderella story that also sends a profound message about the unrealistic, idealistic notions the media perpetuates about boy-girl relationships. This book introduces the idea that the best relationships are built upon common interests and friendship, not romance, and challenges popular stereotypes in a humorous way. An emphasis on being oneself and having wholesome fun—and a de-emphasis on physical appearance and dating drama—make this a delightfully rich and timely story.

This activity teaches the following principles.

- Girls need to resist media pressure which says they have to have a boyfriend to be popular.
- Stereotypes of what is "cool" or "popular" cause people to be labeled and judged by who they are on the outside, not the inside.
- It is important to identify and challenge stereotypes and "rules" about who is cool and who isn't and select friends based upon internal personal attributes.
- The goal of boy/girl relationships should be learning to develop friendships, not going steady or sexual experimentation.
- It takes new skills to learn how to develop boy/girl friendships. These skills will help girls to build healthier relationships as they grow into adulthood and choose a marriage partner.

Materials Needed.

1. *Cinder Edna*, a picture book by Ellen Jackson.
2. A lunch tray with various sections for food.
3. Lima beans or some other sortable object.
4. Post-it Notes and a pen.

Activity Steps.

---

[27] This activity teaches Boy/Girl Friendship Skills and Peer Relationship Skills.
[28] Purchase a copy at www.amazon.com.

1. Using the lima beans and the lunch tray, ask the girls to describe the different social groups they observe at school (i.e., geeks, nerds, preps, Goths, brainiacs, etc.) Write these labels on the sticky notes. Place one note in each section of the lunch tray.

2. Give each girl a lima bean and ask her to put her bean in the slot where she fits in according to her peers. Place the reminder of the lima beans in various slots.

3. Ask the following discussion questions.

   Question 1: How does it feel to be judged based upon social rules?

   Question 2: Do you judge others by these social rules?

   Question 3: Who makes up the social rules?

   Question 4: What are the rules for being cool or popular in your school?

   Question 5: Do these rules describe the inside of a person?

   Question 6: What rules does the media give you about the boys you choose as friends?

   Question 7: Do you have to follow these rules? What rules define how you choose your friends?

4. Explain the definition of "stereotypes." Tell the girls you are going to read a book that teaches about stereotypes. Ask them to notice when people like each other based upon a "stereotype" or outer appearance and when they like each other based upon real friendship. Then, read the book.

5. After the story, ask the following questions.

   Question 1: Does this story give you a new idea about what kind of boy-girl relationship is really the healthiest? How?

   Question 2: What do you learn about building friendships with boys from this story?

   Question 3: What are some of the things that Rupert and Edna did to build their friendship?

   Question 4: What are some things you can do to build friendships with boys?

   Question 5: Are there boys you would like to know better, but don't try because of labels?

6. Challenge the girls to pick one boy they want to know better, not because he is "cute," "cool," or "popular," but because they think he might be a kind friend with common interests.

Activity 23
Heart Healthy Relationships Activity

(Time = 30 minutes)

Objectives for Each Girl.

1. I can challenge the pressure to have a steady boyfriend.
2. I can challenge unrealistic media portrayals of love and relationships.
3. I can set physical boundaries that support healthy friendships with boys.
4. I can build friendships rather than serious dating relationships with boys.
5. I can avoid the harm of sexual experimentation by setting boundaries for physical affection.

Materials Needed.

1. Handout 30, *Heart Healthy Relationships.*
2. Paper and pencils.
3. Thoroughly read the introduction to this chapter as a preparation for this activity.

Activity Steps.

1. Ask questions to help girls recognize that most media portrayals of relationships are unrealistic. The media makes it seem that young people can meet and immediately become physically affectionate (passionate kissing, sexual experimentation) without any consequences.

    Question 1: What kind of rules about physical affection and sex do you see portrayed in the movies and on television?

    Question 2: What messages do movies send about the purpose of sex in a relationship?

    Question 3: If a couple becomes physically affectionate or sexually active, how does that influence their relationship—based upon what you see in the movies?

2. Explain that the movies portray that couples who are attracted to each other physically are "in love."

    Question 1: In the movies, the more passionate people are, the more that means they truly love each other. Do you think that is realistic?

    Question 2: Do you think couples who become sexually involved really have relationships that last longer?

Question 3: Do you think it hurts a relationship if a couple gets sexually involved early in their relationship? What does the media portray?

3. The media shows that what makes people loveable is whether they are physically attractive enough. In reality TV shows, girls often compete to see who can look the best so they can get the guy.

   Question 1: Would you want a relationship where a guy only liked you for your looks?

   Question 2: Would you want to worry that a guy might not care for you anymore if you didn't look as good as someone else?

4. Explain that scientific research (Busby, Carroll, &Willoughby, 2010) does not support the messages of the media. Getting involved sexually hurts relationships. Even though the media shows couples having sex on their first date, or within just a few weeks of meeting each other, and living "happily ever after," research shows that relationships where couples have sex before marriage do not last as long and are less happy.

   Question 1: Is building a relationship on physical attraction a good idea?

   Question 2: What do you think is most important when building a relationship with boys?

5. Ask the following questions.

   Question 1: What do you think are qualities of a healthy boy-girl relationship at your age?

   Question 2: Do you feel a lot of pressure to have a boyfriend?

   Question 3: Do most kids your age think having a boyfriend is a good idea?

6. Read the following statement.

   "Most girls your age are influenced by the media and think they have to have a boyfriend to be popular. They are not shown the consequences of steady dating. They do not learn about the benefits of building friendships with guys rather than steady dating with one guy."

7. Tell the girls you want to help them make a "pros and cons list" about steady dating. Help them know that being attracted is completely normal at their age, but they can choose how they want to handle attraction. Explain, "The media makes it seem like attraction is uncontrollable, but this is not true."

8. Use the paper and pencils and make the pros and cons list. In the "cons list," be sure to have the girls include these factors below that which make steady dating unwise. Early steady dating:

   - Introduces the drama and heartache of break-ups.

- Leads to sexual experimentation.
- Distracts from developing their own sense of who they are.
- Narrows their chance to get to know lots of guys.
- Narrows their focus away from future goals.
- Isolates them from their girlfriends.
- Isolates them from their parents.

Ask the girls to compare which list shows a more realistic picture about serious romantic relationships. Do the "pros" out weight the "cons"? For girls who commit to build friendships and avoid steady dating, tell them you have some ideas to help them. One of the best ways to keep a relationship from getting too intense and distracting from friendship is to set boundaries about physical affection. Explain the concept of "relationship inertia."[29] Relationship inertia is like a "slippery slide"—you climbed to the top but didn't realize that once you were at the top, the slide would take you down without being able to stop. Physical affection early in a relationship moves the relationship "down a slide" of getting emotionally serious but not building a healthy friendship foundation.

9. Introduce Handout 30. Explain that each stage of a relationship has an appropriate, emotionally safe level of physical affection.

   - What level of affection is appropriate for married people?
   - What level of affection is appropriate for people who have just met?
   - What level of affection is appropriate for the relationships you want to have right now?
   - What kinds of relationships do you see portrayed in the media? Are they "heart healthy" or not?

   Explain that when couples push their physical relationship fast, they are moving their relationship to be more serious and committed, even if it is not a relationship that will last or make them happy in the long term. Invite them to set a goal about what kind of physical affection they are going to allow and to set boundaries to maintain friendships.

10. Tell the girls that they are going to do an activity which shows that they have some very important things to accomplish in the next few years. Tell them that getting into a serious relationship with boys needs to happen AFTER they have accomplished some other very important things. (See Activity 24.)

11. Ask the girls to take Handout 30 home to their parents. Ask them to discuss what kind of boundaries their parents feel are most appropriate for building friendships and to ask their parents for help in learning to build healthy friendships with guys.[30]

---

[29] Busby, Carroll, and Willoughby (2010) expounded upon a theory called "relationship inertia." This theory states that when a couple becomes sexually involved, they become emotionally connected and make a decision to commit to each other, even though they may not be compatible in other important ways. Even when warning signs and conflicts signal long-term trouble ahead, the couple is so emotionally "entangled" that they continue into marriage with a shaky relationship foundation.

[30] Many parents are not aware of the risks associated with sexual experimentation since, unfortunately, sexual education materials promoting "safe sex" tend to be more "politically correct" than physiologically accurate. I highly recommend parents visit www.drmiriamgrossmanmd.com for accurate resources on the serious health risks of pre-marital sex.

Activity 24
Relationship Timeline Activity[31]

(Time = 20 – 30 minutes)

Objectives for Each Girl.

1. I can focus on the goals that are important right now.
2. I can recognize how the decisions I make now will affect my future.
3. I can wait until I am older to pursue serious boy/girl relationships.

Explanation.

In the minds of pre-teens and teens, life is only about the "moment." This activity seeks to expand girls' consideration of the "bigger picture." They need to know that each season of their lives has priority goals. Learning to focus on goals is an important life skill. Girls who become goal-oriented and learn to delay immediate gratification are establishing a pattern that will lead to success throughout their lives. Specifically, girls will identify that serious relationships with boys are best reserved for a later stage of young adulthood when they have had time to mature and have more self-knowledge.

Materials Needed.

1. Handout 31, *My Timeline*, and Handout 32, *My Timeline Events*.
2. Scissors & glue sticks

Activity Steps.

1. Have the girls lay Handout 31 flat in front of them so they can view the columns: "Now," "High School/College," and "Building a Family/Marriage/Children." Have them cut, along the dashed lines, each of the "milestones" from Handout 32.
2. Ask the girls to sort the milestones by placing them in the column or time period when that goal should be accomplished. For example, they will place the "improving my GPA" milestone in the "Now" or "High School/College" column.
3. After the girls have finished placing all their milestones, invite them to share what they placed in each column. Allow girls to share how they prioritized their goals and what kind of goals they have for the future. Explain that focusing on goals at each stage of their lives puts them in the driver's seat to a happier life. Tell them that if they don't set goals, their lives will just drift along, and they will not like the outcome.
4. Discuss where the girls put the "steady dating" and "gain sexual experience" milestones. Remind them that even though the media pressures them to experience these things now, that is just because they media wants to erode their boundaries and fuel impulsive, out-of-control behaviors.

---

[31] This activity is a follow-up activity to Activity 23.

People who don't have boundaries will spend money irresponsibly on products. The media also displays unhealthy sexual relationships because they believe more people will watch that kind of "drama." Even though the media teaches girls that they have to sexually experiment to choose the right guy, the truth is that people who wait until they marry have much better relationships. Say, "Make choices based on what is real, not on media myths or politically correct lies."

5. Have the girls make any adjustment of where they want to place their milestones based upon the discussion and then glue them down to finish the activity.

Chapter 8

Media Literacy and Critical Thinking:
Embracing the Images of Real Beauty

The beauty of a woman is not in the clothes she wears, the figure that she carries,
or the way she combs her hair. The beauty of a woman is seen in her eyes,
because that is the doorway to her heart, the place where love resides.
True beauty in a woman is reflected in her soul. It's the caring that she lovingly gives,
the passion that she shows, and the beauty of a woman only grows with passing years.
~ Audrey Hepburn

We live in the "age of image." Hundreds of visual images flashed on billboards, computer monitors, televisions, movies screens, magazines, smartphones, and iPods influence our minds every day! In previous decades, we had the age of books, when what people read was most influential; we had the age of radio, when what people heard was most influential. Today, we have the age of the glitzy image coupled with the power of musical beat and computer-generated photo enhancement. Today's images give advertisers more power over the minds of girls than ever before.

> When adolescents are struggling to achieve an autonomous adult identity and are exploring their emerging sexual awakenings, they are undoubtedly more vulnerable to the combined influence of high-impact visual and auditory messages. (Strouse and Buerkel-Rothfuss, 1995, p. 505)

The PBS documentary, *The Merchants of Cool*, documents what could be described as the "predatory nature" of advertisers who knowingly encourage harmful behaviors to sell products.[32] Corporate marketing giants fool teens into believing they care about their well-being, while they seek out the "edgiest" kids they can find and flash these images again and again to create new definitions of what is "cool." They don't look for trendsetters who are positive role models, but they look instead for charismatic deviants who erode moral and social norms.

The astounding intent of advertisers is to fuel impulsive behaviors and *create emotional distress* in teens. At the heart of advertising, as summarized by Kupelian (2005), is not concern for the welfare of teens, but the desire to exploit. They do this by creating greater levels of *need*, especially in the areas of base, innate human desires, such as the need for acceptance and sexual gratification. A distressed teen without moral and social restraints will buy, buy, buy trying to satisfy her unmet needs.

I constantly hear the angst of parents and grandparents who describe their girls' anxiety and panic symptoms, chronic low self-esteem, obsession with appearance, and heart-wrenching peer

---

[32] This resource can be purchased through www.amazon.com.

conflicts. As professionals, we must not treat depressed or anxious women and girls without recognizing the major role of the media culture. In my clinical work, I frequently use materials from the **Media Detectives Activity (Activity 25)** to help clients understand the influence of the media culture.[33] The **Media Detectives Activity (Activity 25)** prepares girls with the tools to "decode" the **Media Mind Games (Handout 34)** of advertisers and pop culture gurus. Girls can build skills to resist:

- The persuasive influence of media.
- The unrealistic expectations of media.
- The insatiable and subconscious sense of need created by media.

These activities will have much more impact if parents are media savvy and actively engaged in helping their daughters to make wise media choices. A parent handout is included in Chapter 5 to help parents protect their girls (**See Handout 20, Be a Media Conscious Parent**).

A crowning concept of this chapter is the need to embrace a holistic definition of beauty. In 2004, the Dove complexion bar company began a worldwide promotion called the "Campaign for Real Beauty," which showcased the beauty of real, ordinary women.[34] The **My Image Activity (Activity 26)** invites girls to develop an image that is consistent with their values and personality. Helping girls develop a holistic definition of beauty is the focus of **What is Real Beauty? Activity (Activity 27)**.

Embracing realistic and intrinsic definitions of real beauty eases the paralyzing struggle with body image. It brings a feeling of overall well-being, an "I am enough" kind of feeling. The anxiety subsides and girls are set free to make meaningful contributions to the world around them. The culture paints for them the impossible goal of being "Barbie" (see **Handout 38, The Truth about Barbie**); in *Healthy Transitions for Girls*, we ask them to connect to their hearts.

---

[33] Further excellent resources for parents and professionals are found at www.mediaed.org and www.medialit.org.
[34] Dove has videos which can be used with girls and/or parents and are available for viewing at http://www.campaignforrealbeauty.com.au.

List of Activities, Handouts, & Figures Used in Chapter 8

Chapter 8: Media Literacy and Critical Thinking:
Embracing the Images of Real Beauty

<u>List of Activities.</u>

<u>List of Handouts.</u>

<u>List of Figures.</u>

None.

Activity 25
Media Detectives Activity

(Time = 45 – 50 minutes)[35]

Objectives for Each Girl.

1. I can "decode" harmful media messages.
2. I can challenge harmful media messages.
3. I can challenge unrealistic portrayals of beauty and perfection.
4. I can recognize distressing thoughts and feelings that come from media messages.

Important Note.

The *Killing us Softly 3* Handouts show photos of advertising that may not be appropriate for young girls, even though they are not more risqué than the magazines at the grocery store checkout stand. You may select alternative advertising photos or you may use Post-it Notes to conceal aspects of the *Killing us Softly 3* Handouts that you do not feel are appropriate for younger girls.

Materials Needed.

1. *Killing Us Softly 3* Handouts.[36]
2. Handout 33, *Media Words You Should Know.*
3. Handout 34, *Media Mind Games.*
4. Handout 35, *Be a Media Detective.*
5. Handout 36, *Media Detective: Case Solving Score Sheet.*
6. Optional: Handout 37, *Media Detectives: Sleuthing for More Hidden Messages* and Handout 38, *The Truth About Barbie.*
7. Choose at least 10–12 advertisements clipped from magazines that target teen girls and women.
8. Poster paper and markers (for optional workshop follow-up activities).
9. Optional. A good resource to demonstrate how makeup and photo tricks are used to create unrealistic perfection is the Dove Real Beauty Project.[37] The STAR Magazine's "Stars without Makeup" issues also show how stars look in real life when their looks have not been enhanced with makeup and photo tricks. Not only do these pictures show what famous stars really look like without their makeup, but the text also criticizes stars' physical features and why they lost their last boyfriend based upon their physical "flaws." This demonstrates how the media encourages unhealthy competition between girls.

---

[35] Additional art and role-play activities are included for an additional 60 minute workshop.

[36] These can be obtained free on the Internet from the Media Education Foundation (MEF). To download this free resource, go to www.mediaed.org. Click on "Materials & Resources." Then, click "Handouts & Articles." Scroll down the page. Under "Handouts," you will see the "Killing Us Softly 3 Study Guide Handouts." Click on the link to download the .pdf file. Print off the pictures provided in this packet to use with this activity. The web address for the handouts at the time of this printing: http://www.mediaed.org/assets/products/206/studyguidehandout_206.pdf.

[37] See http://www.campaignforrealbeauty.com.au.

10. Use a palace model or *Palace of Possibilities Display Board* as described in Chapter 1 to keep positive beliefs in the forefront of the discussion.

Activity Steps.

1. Explain: "Every advertiser persuades through pictures, music, and/or slogans. Advertisers create emotional messages. These messages are often subliminal—not consciously understood. Your subconscious mind will pick up the messages, even if you are not aware of the message. It is as though you are being brainwashed with ideas and emotions but don't know it is happening."

2. Explain: "Although it may appear that advertisers relate to teens and care about them, the truth is that they want to create emotional distress. If you are distressed, you buy products to make yourself feel better. This distress can happen and you don't realize it; you just have a little nagging feeling inside that says you need to buy a product to look prettier, to be more popular, or to be happier."

3. Give the girls the following hint. HINT: THE BEST WAY TO IDENTIFY A MEDIA MESSAGE IS TO PAY ATTENTION TO WHAT YOU FEEL INSIDE.

4. Use Handout 33, *Media Words You Should Know*. Have the girls write the word definitions on the handout as you present the activity. Say, "In this activity, you are going to be a Media Detective and discover the hidden messages of several different advertisements. First, you will view pictures that show some of the common themes of the media. As we discuss these themes, use your handout to write notes about these themes. You need to understand them to be a Media Sleuth."

Theme 1: Objectification

Show: Handout 2A and 2B.[38]

Ask: What has happened to the woman's body in these ads? Is this a normal way to use a woman's body? What kind of feeling do you get about you body when you see these pictures?

Summarize: A common theme in advertising is "objectification." When a girl or woman is seen as an object and not a person, what happens? Boys are being taught they can treat girls and women as though they were just objects and not real people with feelings. Girls learn to treat each other without being empathetic to each other's feelings.

Theme 2: Dismemberment

Show: Handout 3C, 3D, 3E, and 3F.

Ask: Why do you think advertisers would only show pictures of legs? Are there certain body parts that are emphasized in advertising besides legs? (Yes. Breasts, thighs, midriff, buttocks, and face.) What about the other parts of the body? Aren't they important, too?

---

[38] The handouts in this section of the activity come from the *Killing Us Softly 3* handouts. See Footnote 5.

Summarize: This is called "dismemberment." Advertisers do not focus on your whole body as a miraculous creation; they tell you that you are just a collection of body parts and that only certain body parts are valuable. "Dismembering" is something you would do to an animal as you cut it up to eat desirable parts, such as chicken thighs or chicken breasts. You are not a chicken! You are a real person with feelings! It is demeaning to only value certain body parts. Often in advertising, girls are shown as mere shadows or shapes, but not as real people valued for who they are. You see pictures like this again and again, without realizing how they make you feel.

Theme 3: Thinness

Show: Handout 4A.

Ask: What message do you get from this ad about how your body should look? Is this a common message that you see today?

Summarize: Thinness is a big message of advertisers. They have all kinds of photo tricks to make a person look skinnier than she really is. This push for thinness is actually dangerous. It creates a lot of distress, especially when your body begins to change in puberty. You need to know the facts about thinness.

- Only 5 out of every 100 women can look as skinny as a model without unhealthy dieting. Many of the models you see use drugs to stay thin. Their full-time job is to keep their bodies looking thin and tanned. Who wants to spend their full time worrying about how they look? You have more important things to do than that!
- 1 out of every 5 women in America today has an eating disorder because they believe they need to be thin in order to be valued.
- Advertisers use models that look like they have not been through puberty. Their bodies are straight and skinny with no curves. In other words, they are telling you that your body should not change and grow up. It is normal for your body to put on 30-50 lbs during puberty. When girls start to put on this normal weight, they think something is wrong with them and start to diet.
- In one study of 4th graders, 80 percent of the girls were on diets.
- What is defined as "beauty" changes from one decade to another and from one culture to another. In the 1950s, a beautiful woman who weighed 145 pounds would now be considered fat; the same woman would need to weight 125 pounds today to be considered beautiful. On the other hand, in some cultures, such as in Polynesia, if a woman is thin, it means she is not well cared for by her husband or family.

Theme 4: Sexualization of Girls

Show: Handout 9A, 9B, 9C.

Ask: What message do you get from these ads? What feeling is the ad trying to create? What messages are these ads trying to tell girls about their changing bodies?

Summarize: The media wants you to believe that the only reason your body is changing is so that you can be "sexy." You may not realize that this message is bombarding you, but it is. This is a very distressing message for many girls that makes them not want to grow up at all. Many girls believe all that matters is getting a boyfriend who will be sexually attracted to them. Girls get pressured into doing things they really don't want to in order to feel valued by boys. You don't have to believe these messages! They don't tell the truth about boy-girl relationships.

Theme 5: Isolation (Competition vs. Support between Girls)

Show: Handout 6A, 6B.

Ask: What is the message of these ads? How do you think these women feel about each other? Why is there conflict? How often do you experience "girl drama" in your relationships? Have you ever thought that this "girl drama" was happening because you were being "brainwashed" by the media?

Summarize: One of the messages of the media is that girls have to compete for boys and popularity rather than support each other. Girls whose bodies are changing can begin to feel very lonely. Fifth and sixth grade is a time when "girl drama" tends to heat up, unlike the earlier grades when girls didn't feel competitive.

Theme 6: Victimization

Show: Handout 11A, 11B, 11C.

Ask: What is going on with the women in these pictures? Do they look confident and happy? How are advertisers trying to create distress with these pictures?

Summarize: Remember, advertisers sell products by creating distress! They want you to feel helpless. They want you to feel that you do not deserve to be treated well by boys or others in your life. They want you to believe that you have no power to make good choices. Many girls allow themselves to be in unhealthy dating relationship where boys slap them, squeeze their arms, and scare them to get control. The media promotes unhealthy relationships that keep you feeling lousy about yourself.

Theme 7: Unrealistic Perfection

Ask: Did you notice in these pictures that the girls did not have acne? Did you notice that their skin was unnaturally shiny and all one skin tone?

Summarize: Many of the women and girls in these pictures do not even have pores in their skin because the photos have been "doctored." It is important that you recognize that photos tricks are used in advertising. Your mind thinks these pictures are real and tells you that you need to look like that; but it is impossible to look like a "photo trick!" You have to tell your mind, "Hey, that's not real. Don't buy the lie."

5. Use Handout 34, *Media Mind Games*. Explain: "This handout shows some of the messages that are "written" on your "palace walls" by the media.[39] If you learn about media tricks and messages, you can begin to control what is being written in your mind or your palace walls. Remember: If the media can get you to do risky, unhealthy behaviors, you will be distressed, and you will buy more products."

6. Pass out an advertisement (clipped from a magazine) for every girl or every two girls. Use Handout 35, *Be a Media Detective*. Read the clues aloud. Tell the girls they are going to use these clues to find the hidden message of their ad. Remind them to pay attention to the emotions created by the ad.

7. Use Handout 36, *Media Detective Case Solving Score Sheet*. Give them 7-10 minutes to complete the score sheet on this handout. After the girls have completed Handout 36, go around the group and allow the girls to share what they discovered. If there is time, have the girls evaluate another advertisement.

8. Assess girls' understanding of the concepts presented by asking the following questions.

    Question 1: What media message do you think has been written on your walls about your body?

    Question 2: What message would you like to change?

    Question 3: Who or what influences your ideas about how you should look?

    Note: Girls can write the answers to these questions on Post-it Notes and add to the "Palace Walls" of the *Palace of Possibilities Display Board* or the palace model.

9. Follow Up Art Activity. (20 minutes) Provide markers, legal size white paper, or poster board. Ask the girls to make their own advertisements to persuade other girls about the harmful messages of the media. They can choose to focus on one specific theme or on the concept that impacted them most. Explain that other girls need to know how to challenge unhealthy media messages when they are watching television or viewing magazines.

10. Follow Up Role-Play Activity. (20 minutes) Ask the girls to pretend they are Media Detectives and News Reporters who work for station KMDR. They can use their posters and role-play how they would persuade others to be critical thinkers of media messages. Have them work together to create their own news documentary.

---

[39]Review Chapter 2 to understand this metaphor.

Activity 26
My IMAGE Activity[40]

(Time = 20 – 30 minutes)[41]

Objectives for Each Girl.

1. I can recognize how celebrities and models influence my ideas about appearance.
2. I can recognize when I try to change myself to make others like me.
3. I can seek to know the real person inside of me throughout my life.

Materials Needed.

1. Handout 39, *My Image*.
2. Scrapbook paper (scrapbook paper will continue the Palace of Possibilities theme from Chapter 2).
3. Pencils.
4. Poster paper, colored markers (for optional follow-up art activity)

Activity Steps.

1. Ask the girls to close their eyes and imagine in their minds what they think they should look like. Have them visualize their ideal self with all the attributes that would make them "pretty." Ask, "Where did you get your idea of what your ideal self should look like?" Ask, "Did you think of a celebrity you want to look like, or someone else you know?" Tell them to visualize themselves acting and looking like the person they want to be like. Have them draw on scrapbook paper some of the attributes they visualized, such as hair, dress, make-up, smile, mannerisms. Then ask, "When you think about what you 'should' look like, does it feel real?"
2. Explain that we live in the "age of image." The media imprints images on our minds about what girls "should" look and how popular girls "should" act. They see hundreds of images every day that help them decide what they want to be as they grow up. Celebrities pay people to help them create an "image." An "image" is the kind of message they want people to believe about them: "edgy," "glamorous," "super confident," "all together," or "flawless." The images we see in movies and magazines are media creations manipulated with lighting and photo tricks, even though our minds tell us these images are real and possible. Whenever our mind views any image, even the image of our friends, we see the outer image and make assumptions about the whole person: "If they look good on the outside, then that means they have it all together on the inside." OR "Celebrities are glamorous; therefore they are confident and happy."
3. Explain to the girls that they are not expected to understand everything about their personalities right now, but they will increase self-confidence as they learn to act from their inner guidance

---

[41] An optional follow-up art activity is included, which will increase the time by approximately 20 minutes.
[41] An optional follow-up art activity is included, which will increase the time by approximately 20 minutes.

system rather than trying to be some kind of "image." You may want to read the following explanation:

> *You grow in self-understanding throughout your life. However, you do have an inner guidance system that can help you understand what is real and right for you. When you do something that is not right for you, or when you try to be an "image" of what you think others want, you are going to feel a little tug in your tummy. You are going to have a sense that you have lost a bit of your self-confidence. Whenever we compromise our real self to please others, we hurt our self-confidence.*

4. Read Handout 39 with the girls. "Image" is an abstract concept that will become more concrete as they consider their own experience. After they have answered the questions, ask them if they would like to share their responses. Were there questions they could not answer? Were there questions they didn't understand? Explain that promoting a different "image" of themselves with different people is not the same as having different moods; it is not the same as being more serious and respectful with teachers, but being fun and lively with friends. Trying to promote an "image" of yourself that is different with different people means you are trying to "be" someone else and not your true self. You are trying to please people in a way that feels "phony" to you.

5. Ask the girls to share a time when they did something just to please someone else and ended up feeling a loss of self-respect or confidence. Ask them what kind of "images" they think people their age are pressured to have.

6. Referring back to the Palace of Possibilities metaphor from Chapter 2, remind them that they can choose what is written on the walls of their palace. They can challenge media images, which are unrealistic. They can challenge thoughts that tell them that a person who looks good on the outside has it "all together" on the inside. Happiness comes from the inside out.

7. Follow-up Art Activity. (10-15 minutes) Ask them to draw a billboard of the kind of image they want to have based upon inner qualities and values. Use this poster in each workshop session and in future parent workshops.

Activity 27
What Is Real Beauty? Activity

(Time = 30 minutes)

Objectives for Each Girl.

1. I can develop realistic ideas about physical appearance.
2. I can understand real beauty is more than just physical appearance.
3. I can recognize the beautiful women in my life who "warm my heart."
4. I can learn to be beautiful on the inside by nurturing each part of myself.
5. I can learn that happiness comes from feeling good on the inside, not from looking "perfect" on the outside.

Explanation.

This activity offers an important definition of "REAL" beauty—when we experience REAL beauty, it is something that warms our hearts. That is the message of Handout 40, *Let's Celebrate REAL Beauty* and Handout 41, *REAL Beauty Is…* . Real beauty is something that is sensed and felt by other women, not just something we look at on the outside.

Special Note to Mothers, Grandmothers, and Mentors.

Every woman, not just girls and teenagers, is surrounded with images of what women are "supposed" to look like. In our minds, we may feel a nagging, discouraging sense that whatever we look like, it is not what we "should" look like. The "shoulds" that women and girls impose upon themselves harm their emotional health and their relationships. The quest for an unattainable beauty causes girls and women to miss what we all need the most from each other: genuine acceptance, encouragement, intuition, discernment, and wisdom. Getting in touch with our own definitions of beauty and our own sense of inadequacy helps us to be more authentic with the girls we love. It helps us connect by being fully present with our hearts and not worrying so much about whether we are measuring up.

Materials Needed.

1. Handout 40, *Let's Celebrate REAL Beauty*.
2. Handout 41, *REAL Beauty Is…*
3. Pens or pencils.

Activity Steps.

1. Use Handouts 40 and 41. Tell the girls that it's time for them to "Get REAL." Ask, "When someone tells you to 'get real,' what does that mean?"

2. Explain that because they live in an age with ready access to media images of women and girls, the girls are exposed to many unrealistic ideas of what real women look like. Tell them instead of watching TV to see what normal girls look like, they would be happier if they sat outside Wal-Mart and observed the first 100 women who walk into the store. That's what real people look like!

3. Explain to the girls that our society not only offers a definition of beauty that is based on lots of make-up and photo tricks, but it offers a definition of beauty that is only based upon physical appearances. Explain that they can learn to discover the real beauty in the women that influence their lives in a positive way every day. Read the qualities of "real" beauty on Handout 41.

4. Emphasize the question again, "What do real women look like?" Explain, "'Real' women look like you. They look like your grandmother, your neighbor, your aunt. They look like the clerk at the grocery store. They look like what we all look like if we camped in the woods for a week without any makeup or hair care products (as scary as that might sound)."

5. Tell the girls to think about women who "warm their hearts," since women who warm our hearts are beautiful! Women who "warm our hearts" inspire us to be our best. They help us feel valued and loved. Explain that being beautiful involves all parts of ourselves, not just how we look. "Recognizing that beauty comes from all parts of us helps us 'get REAL.'" Ask, "Is there a woman who influences your life every day in a positive way?" Have them record their thoughts on Handout 41.

6. Ask the girls to express how they would feel if they received a note telling them they were beautiful inside. Explain, "We all want to feel beautiful! It's something we feel from the inside out." Invite them to take the "Real Beauty Challenge," explained in Handout 40. Encourage them to report the response they receive back to the group.

Chapter 9

Coping Skills and Problem-Solving Skills

The best protection against unsafe, worrisome behaviors
may be a wide repertoire of positive, adaptive coping strategies.
~ Dr. Kenneth Ginsburg, Pediatric Specialist in Adolescent Medicine

How often have you thought or heard, "Girls are so EMOTIONAL!" Melt-downs, drama, crying, slamming doors, brooding for hours—sound familiar? Is there a girl in your life who is fueled by anxiety and worry, who drives herself from one accomplishment to the next, but rarely feels satisfied? On the flip side, girls can be bouncing off the wall with happiness that's so contagious it seems to light up the whole world! Those are the moments we wish would last forever.

In my practice, I teach my clients that emotional energy is a resource that can be harnessed and channeled as "fuel" for positive change. Resilience expert, Christian Moore, LCSW (2014), author of groundbreaking book, *The Resilience Breakthrough*, describes a quality called "street resilience." Street resilience is channeling your emotions, guiding them, directing them, and using them for a productive purpose, instead of letting your emotions use you. (p. 103) In the midst of "meltdowns," Moore invites us to "Flip the Switch," and ask:

How can I use this emotional pain, challenge, or situation to better my circumstances and make me more resilient—today, this hour, this moment, this second? (p. 36).

Just knowing that adversity can be a catalyst for something positive instead of an inevitable disaster creates a more positive mood.

To help girls to regulate their emotional ups and downs and to be more resilient in the face of daily challenges, this chapter offers two categories of skills: 1) coping skills, "emotional first aid" to soothe the emotional distress that is being experienced in the body; and 2) problem-solving skills to help girls find solutions to their dilemmas.

Coping Skills

A common pattern in girls and women is to employ judgmental, negative self-talk at the first sign of emotional distress. "You shouldn't be feeling that way." "Only babies want to cry." "It's not normal to feel this way." Girls can also feel that they have to believe and act upon every emotion. "If I feel distressed, that means life must really be awful." "I'm really mad, so I have to yell at someone." "I don't feel happy today; that means I am depressed and life is terrible." Learning to turn "inward" and observe distress without judgment helps girls learn that when they feel distress, it is time to implement "self-soothing," rather than over-thinking or acting out. This kind of response to distress is called "mindfulness." Mindfulness skills are taught in Chapter 3, **A Simple Mindfulness and Acceptance**

Activity (**Activity 9**). As they gain more emotional regulation skills, they become more resilient in finding solutions to problems.

Coping or "self-soothing" activities in this chapter can be used as "emotional first aid" to calm the body's natural response to stress. **Handout 42, *The Butterfly Hug Self-Soothing Technique*** is a simple self-soothing activity that is easy to teach and can be used in any kind of stressful situation. **Activity 28, *"Blowing Balloons" Relaxation Activity*** is another commonly-used exercise which dissipates overwhelming worries. Both of these exercises are playful, yet supportive.

Emotional Freedom Technique (EFT) is another highly effective self-help tool for addressing stress and anxiety. (See **Activity 29, *EFT: Self-Help for Anxiety and Negative Beliefs*.**) Not only has it been shown to reduce the "fight or flight" response in the brain, but it is an excellent tool for reframing negative belief patterns.[42] While we don't completely know *why* EFT works, it is backed up with a large body of growing research.[43] EFT is being used worldwide for trauma and many other issues. Because it is easy to learn, it is not only a remarkable therapeutic tool for use by professionals, but also a self-help tool that adults and children can easily learn.

In **Activity 30, *What to Do When I Am Blue Card File Activity***, girls learn that each part of them (social, emotional, intellectual, spiritual, or physical) needs care and nurturing. Rather than trying to "feed" social, intellectual, emotional or spiritual needs through over-eating or obsessing about the physical self, they can learn to use a variety of self-care skills that acknowledge the many aspects of their personalities. This is a favorite art activity of girls. When they are finished, they will have their very own card file of emotional first aid skills to use whenever they need them.

Problem-Solving Skills

Activity 31, *My Ecomap Activity* specifically teaches girls to identify resources that can help them in times of distress. For many girls, asking for help is something they resist because of an irrational belief that asking for help is a sign of weakness or means they are not grown up. When girls are emotionally overwhelmed, they may not even be aware of or consider the resources available to them. Instead they ruminate on thoughts, such as, "Nobody can understand my problem" or "I don't know who I can trust to help with my problems."

Activity 32, *A 5-Step Problem-Solving Model Activity* breaks problems down into small increments that do not seem so overwhelming. It considers the old adage, "How do you eat an elephant? One bite at a time!" Developing a step-by-step approach to finding solutions will help girls to make more rational, less impulsive choices.

Activity 33, *Make an Energy Circle Activity* is a creative way to help girls develop positive goals and affirmations. This activity, which is based upon principles of quantum science or energy vibration,

---

[42] A favorite four minute You Tube instructional EFT " tapping" video featuring EFT expert, Jessica Ortner, is found at https://www.youtube.com/watch?v=pAclBdj2oZU

[43] See www.energypsych.org or http://www.eftuniverse.com/research/ for the latest EFT research.

can help girls to more clearly identify what they want to create in their lives. It can help them recognize the "e-motion" or "energy-in-motion" that comes from their positive beliefs, and it can help those beliefs become more tangible.

The final activity in this chapter, which focuses on making assertive requests, is **Activity 34, *Using Assertiveness Skills to Resolve Problems*. Handout 27, *Speaking Up: Rules That Work,*** was used to build relationships in Chapter 6; it is used in this activity to help girls gain confidence in using verbal skills to solve problems. This activity provides role play ideas for a variety of common problems.

Think of the difference having a tool belt full of coping and problem solving skills can make for a teen girl. As her mind fusses over her problem, she can say, "Which of these tools should I use?" instead of, "My whole life is a total disaster!"

List of Activities, Handouts, & Figures Used in Chapter 9

Chapter 9: Coping Skills and Problem-Solving Skills

Activity 28
"Blowing Balloons" Relaxation Activity

(Time = 10 – 15 minutes)

Objectives for Each Girl.

1.   I can use skills to manage worry and anxiety.

Important Note.

This is a great exercise often used by counselors to help calm clients' anxieties and worries. Girls can do it throughout the day whenever they feel nervous or feel worries popping up. Remind the girls that this exercise is to relieve small worries that pile up each day; it is not meant to address big problems that might require professional help. Also, remind the girls to respect each other's experience and not to laugh and tease each other during the exercise.

Activity Steps.

1.   Read the following script.

Blowing Balloons Script

First, begin to pay attention to your breathing. Don't change it or make it faster or slower. Just notice it. Notice how it feels to breathe in through your nostrils, allowing your nose to cleanse and warm the air. Breathe out through your mouth. Feel the air pass through your lips, allowing the air to gently push against your lips, puffing them out slightly. Continue to breathe in through your nose and out through your lips. Inhale and exhale completely in this manner five times. Do not feel rushed.

Feel your shoulders droop slightly as you become more relaxed. Uncross your legs if they are crossed. Allow your arms to droop at your sides.

Now, close your eyes or focus your eyes on the end of your nose as you breathe. Allow your mind to drift. Now place your hands on your stomach. Imagine as you breathe, that you have a balloon inside of your tummy. As you inhale, the balloon in your tummy grows round and full; as you exhale, the balloon in your tummy lets the air out and gets floppy. Do this five times or until you feel you have a rhythm with your breathing and you can feel your tummy going up and down as you breathe. Blow and release air in and out of your "balloon" for five breaths.

Imagine that each time you exhale you are blowing your balloon gently into the air. Each breath makes the balloon go higher. What color is your balloon? Puff warm air onto your balloon until you see it float away.

Now, pretend that your balloon can be filled with your worries. As you release air through exhaling, imagine that you are filling your balloon with your worries. The "worries" flow in through the spout of the balloon and push against the inside walls of the balloon, making it grow bigger and lighter. Blow your breath against the balloon, and watch as it floats higher and higher. Notice that as your balloon of worries floats away, you feel lighter inside and very relaxed.

Would you like to fill another balloon with worries? If so, continue to exhale your worries into the balloon until it get lighter and floats higher. Gently blow your warm breath on it and push the balloon higher and higher. Count 1, 2, 3, 4, 5.

It is now time to begin to wake up from this daydream of blowing balloons. Notice the warm and happy feelings that surround your body. It feels good to be relaxed. Enjoy this feeling for a minute. Stretch your arms and legs to help you become totally awake once again. Smile. Your body is now awake.

Activity 29
EFT: Self-Help for Anxiety and Negative Beliefs

(Time = 15 – 30 minutes)

Objectives for Each Girl.

1. I can use self-care when I have negative beliefs about my body.
2. I can use self-care techniques for relaxation and stress management.
3. I can reframe negative beliefs that cause emotional distress.
4. I can create positive beliefs about myself and my body.

Materials Needed.

1. Handout 43, *EFT Tapping Steps.*

Explanation.

Emotional Freedom Technique (EFT) is another "emotional first aid" skill that can be used in almost any situation. EFT is an energy psychology technique that is based upon the principles of acupuncture or acupressure. As explained by Feinstein (2004), "psychological problems have a counterpart in the client's energy system and can be treated at that level" (p. 17). Instead of using needles on the acupuncture or meridian energy points, we can simply use our fingers to tap on these specific points on the body. Tapping clears the beliefs and the emotional triggers connected with a particular problem from the mind-body system. EFT can create rapid shifts in emotional states since negative emotions are released quickly, giving place for new perspectives and new positive reframes.

My favorite book for using EFT with children and adolescents is *Tap into Joy* by Susan Busen. This book has simple instructions and scripts for every problem experienced by young people. I highly recommend this book to my clients and encourage its use by parents and professionals in *Healthy Transitions for Girls* workshops. *EFT Tapping Steps* (Handout 43) uses the steps of Susan Busen's EFT approach.

Activity Steps.

1. The first step in using EFT is to ask the client to rate the level of their distress using Subjective Units of Distress (SUDs). "On a scale of 0 to 10, how distressed do you feel when you think about your distressing emotion, belief, or event? 10 means you feel completely overwhelmed, and 1 means you feel almost no distress at all." The client will choose a number subjectively, based on how they personally experience the distress. Using SUDs allows both the client and clinician to see measureable results as the client "taps" on the problem.
2. The next step in EFT is to minimize resistance to solving the problem and create "acceptance" within the client about their problem. When clients have beliefs that keep them stuck in unhealthy

behavior patterns, it is called "psychological reversal." Psychological reversal (PR) is addressed using "Even though" statements.[44] Although EFT is used for nearly any kind of problem, the examples in this chapter will focus on issues related to health and body image:

- "Even though I feel anxious whenever I sit down to eat..."
- "Even though food seems like a big battle..."
- "Even though I hate exercise..."
- "Even though I can't feel hungry..."
- "Even though I hear my mother nagging whenever I want to eat..."
- "Even though food makes me feel safe..."
- "Even though I am scared eating will make me ugly..."
- "Even though I hate the way my thighs look..."
- "Even though I am scared I am getting fat..."
- "Even though I am afraid my breasts are too small..."

To finish each of these statements, the client uses a "reframing statement" that creates acceptance, such as:

- "...I deeply and completely accept myself."
- "...I can choose to feel better."
- "...I can love myself anyway."

A complete PR statement is: "Even though I feel anxious whenever I think about food, I deeply and completely accept myself." PR statements are repeated at least three times while the client "taps" on the "karate chop point" or KC point. (See *EFT Tapping Steps*, Handout 43). PR statements can be devised based upon the client's past experiences, present moment worries, or fear of the future.

EFT can be used to tap on the sensations the client feels in the body or on a phrase that reminds the client of their distress. For example, if a girl says that she gets a "buzzing feeling" in her chest every time she thinks about her changing body, then she should tap on the "buzzing feeling." Have her describe the feeling as specifically as she can.

Using EFT with a Bodily Sensation

- "Even though I have this buzzing feeling, I deeply and completely accept myself."
- "Even though I feel stupid that I have this swirly tummy feeling, I can accept myself anyway."
- "Even though I don't know why I have this prickly hands feeling, I deeply love myself anyway."

Using EFT with a Reminder Phrase (A Short Phrase that Describes the Problem)

---

[44] I owe much of my understanding about how to use EFT with sabotage patterns from clinical psychologist and EFT Master, Dr. Carol Look. She and other EFT Master Therapists have helped literally thousands of clients all over the world with this simple tool and provided incredible insights to the field of weight wellness and health.

- "Even though <u>fear of being fat</u> makes me hate myself, I deeply accept myself anyway."
- "Even though <u>fear of growing up</u> makes me feel rage inside, I can choose to accept myself."
- "Even though <u>fear of being lonely</u> makes me cry, I love and accept myself."

3. Once the client is feels some relief and acceptance and is ready to address her problems, she can gently tap with the middle and ring fingers of one or both hands on the EFT tapping points, using her reminder phrase or bodily sensation phrase. Typically, clients start at the eyebrow point (EB) and tap on each point, working down the body; they end at the underarm point (UA). Tapping on the finger points, shown on *EFT Tapping Steps* (Handout 43) is not essential unless the client is extremely emotional; then, the finger points should be used. EFT is very forgiving in the sense that one does not need to be precise on where to tap. The main focus should be on the emotions connected with the reminder phrase. When the client "taps" their distress down to a "1" or "0," then that particular aspect of an experience or belief has been cleared.

4. Many EFT practitioners include a "forgiveness step." The "forgiveness step" of EFT helps to reduce shame-based, self-sabotage beliefs. Forgiveness phrases may include:

- "I forgive myself for hurting my body to manage my anxiety."
- "I forgive my parents for not giving me more support; they were doing the best they knew how."
- "I forgive myself for harming my body with food."
- "I forgive myself for hating my body when it is doing so much for me."

5. After clients have experienced acceptance, release of negative emotion, and self-forgiveness, they are now ready to tap in positive beliefs to replace the negative thoughts. The client may spontaneously come up with their own positive reframes as new insights pop into their minds. They can *choose* desired feelings and beliefs. "I choose to believe my body is amazing." "I choose to have a healthier relationship with food." "I choose to have better thoughts about my body." Positive affirmations can be used, such as those found on *Palace of Possibilities Affirmations* (Handout 8, in Chapter 2) or *My Body is a Miraculous Creation* (Handout 66, in Chapter 11). For affirmations to truly be effective, the "yes, but…" beliefs that challenge them must be eliminated. This is explained more fully in the *Mirror, Mirror Activity* (Activity 6, in Chapter 2).

6. Go back to the original SUDs rating which the client had prior to using EFT. Determine whether the rating has gone up or down. Decide upon a new SUDS rating.

7. If the rating is going down and the client is feeling better, you can repeat the steps until the problem can be rated at a SUDs level of 1 or 0. If the SUDS rating has gone up, that means another aspect of the problem has surfaced, since problems can have several aspects. The client may now be feeling a more specific emotion, have a more specific memory, or have a different, but related focus. Repeat Steps 1 -6, emphasizing the emotion or body sensation which is still causing distress. Continue until the client's SUDs is 1 or 0.

Using EFT with the *Mirror, Mirror Activity* (Activity 6) in Chapter 2

8. After the girls have identified negative statements on Handout 4, *Mirror, Mirror Activity Part 1* from Chapter 2, tell them to tap on the KC point of their left hand using the middle and ring finger of their right hand as they say the following:

    "Even though [fill in the blank, using the first negative statement they wrote on their handout], I deeply and completely accept myself *anyway*."

    The girls should continue to tap on the KC point, repeating this acceptance statement *three times*.

9. Next, starting at the eyebrow point (EB) and working down the face and body, ask the girls to repeat the negative statement aloud as they tap. They can pick a shortened phrase that reminds them of their negative statement. For example, if they said, "I hate my zits," then the phrase they tap on will be "my zits." They will tap approximately seven times on each tapping point using the middle and ring fingers as they repeat their negative tapping phrase. They can tap on just one side or both sides simultaneously.

10. A girl may repeat this protocol again and continue to tap until she no longer feels any emotional connection to the negative statement. She is then ready to move to the next negative statement she wrote and repeats Steps 1 and 2.

11. Once the girls tap on all of their negative statements, they are now ready for positive affirmations. Once they have written their positive affirmations on Handout 5, *Mirror, Mirror Activity Part 2*, they can tap the positive statements to help create a connection with these statements at the mind-body level. Starting at the top of the head, the girls will repeat their first positive statement while tapping about seven times on each meridian point. It is not necessary to tap on the fingers for this part of the exercise. Have them tap for each positive statement they wrote.

12. Ask them to take a moment and tune in to their bodies. Ask, "Do you feel a different feeling about your bodies after using this EFT exercise?" Ask them to share how their feelings changed.

Activity 30
What to Do When I Am Blue Card File Activity

(Time = 45 minutes)

Objectives for Each Girl.

1. I can recognize when I feel emotional, spiritual, social, or intellectual "hunger," as well as physical hunger.
2. I can choose to "feed" and care for each part of me.
3. I can choose positive activities that help me cope with life's ups and downs.

Explanation.

A vital coping skill is for girls to learn self-care when they are feeling distressed. A common practice is for girls to buy clothes or make up to relieve distress. Another common practice is for girls to eat junk food when they are distressed. Girls can also develop the habit of picking on themselves with negative self-talk when they feel distressed. These patterns lead to other problems, such as depressed mood, eating disorders, obsession with appearance, and other problems. This activity not only helps girls recognize that each part of them needs care, but it also provides ideas for self-care that can be readily used every day.

Materials Needed.

1. Index cards, 10-15 for each girl.
2. Hole punch.
3. "O" rings or colored ribbon to fasten the cards together.
4. Colored markers or stickers for decorating the cards.
5. Handout 44, *What to Do When I Am Blue Instructions.*
6. Handout 45, *What to Do When I Am Blue List.*

Activity Steps.

1. Read Handout 4, *What to Do When I Am Blue Instructions,* together. Reinforce the concepts on the handout by asking the girls if they can think of a time when they ate something because they were sad, lonely, or worried, instead of because they were hungry. Ask if there have been times when they *were* hungry but didn't eat because of those kinds of feelings. Ask if they have ever bought make-up or jewelry because they were sad, lonely, or worried. Tell them is takes practice to learn what part of us is really "hungry" and what part of us really needs attention.
2. Have the girls pick 10-15 activities from Handout 45, *What to Do When I Am Blue List,* that they would like to use when they are feeling "blue." (Explain that feeling "blue" means feeling down, sad, or lonely.) Tell them to try to choose activities from the list that would feed all parts of themselves:

social, emotional, physical, intellectual, spiritual. Tell them to write one activity from the list on each index card.

3. After the girls have written one activity on each index card, tell them they can now decorate their cards any way they wish. After they have finished, punch a hole in the left hand corner of each card. Fasten the cards together with an "O" ring or ribbon.

4. Encourage the girls to keep their card file in a place where they can see it every day, such as by the bed. Tell them that whenever they are blue, they can pull out the card file and pick an activity that will chase away the "blues."

Activity 31
My Ecomap Activity

(Time = 20 – 30 minutes)

Objectives for Each Girl.

1. I can identify people who will support me.
2. I can ask for help when I need it.

Explanation.

An Ecomap is often used by counselors to assess client resources and relationships. Since one of the common irrational belief patterns of teens is their egocentric belief that "no one can understand me" or "no one has had problems as bad as me," they can easily fall prey to the belief that their problems are beyond help. One of the warning signs of depression is when girls begin to isolate from others. Parents need to be concerned when their child seeks more and more time alone or wants to hole up in her room by herself every day. Learning to identify resources to meet needs in the many aspects of their lives and then taking steps to ask for help are two skills which will support healthier emotions and relationships.

Materials Needed.

1. Handout 46, *My Ecomap.*
2. Pens or pencils.

Activity Steps.

1. Begin with the following quote. In *Be Who You Want to Be: Dealing with Life's Ups & Downs*, author Karen Casey (2007) offers this gentle reminder that learning to ask for help is part of becoming more mature.

   Do you ask for help when you need it, or do you think you should be able to do everything all by yourself? My little sister refuses to let me help her put her shoes on. Dad says that's because of her age... It's fine to ask for help. I can ask for help with anything, in fact. If my teacher or my mom thinks I should do it alone, they say so. (p. 41)

2. As you complete this exercise with the girls, first ask how comfortable they are with asking for help. Maybe they have learned that asking for help means they are "babies." Maybe they feel that since they are growing up, it is no longer okay to ask for help.
3. Next, using the "Key" in Handout 46, help the girls identify the many areas in which they may need to ask for help. Encourage them to identify several different people who can be part of their support team. Often, teenage girls are not aware of how much the adults around them really care

about their success. Tell them that they have to be persistent and not discouraged if they ask one adult and do not get help. If they ask for help and do not receive it, then they must keep asking until they find the person who can help them. This is a skill they will use their whole lives.

4. Assign the following "Homework" activity. Ask the girls to choose a problem they have been struggling to solve. Ask them to pick someone on the Ecomap who could help them and ask for help. Have them report back in the next group meeting.

Activity 32
A 5-Step Problem-Solving Model Activity

(Time = 30 – 40 minutes)

Objectives for Each Girl.

1. I can solve my problems one step at a time.
2. I can learn from my attempts to solve problems.

Materials Needed.

1. Pencils and scratch paper.
2. Handout 46, *My Ecomap.*
3. Handout 47, *A 5-Step Problem-Solving Model.*

Special Note to Parents.

Problem-solving takes practice and encouragement. Teenagers appreciate the opportunity to make more of their own decisions even though they do not have the skills or maturity to make good decisions without practice and guidance. It is tempting to want to protect a child from poor decisions, yet sometimes reaping the consequences of a poor decision is an effective teaching opportunity. Avoid saying, "See? I told you so." Instead, say, "What did you learn from that experience?" Teens benefit greatly if parents are not critical when they make mistakes. Rather than giving your child direct advice for every problem, encourage the development of problem-solving skills by using this approach on a regular basis. Work through the steps side-by-side. Not every problem will have a simple solution, but teens can learn to take a few steps forward rather than giving up with discouragement or reacting impulsively.

Explanation.

The basic 5-step problem-solving model utilizes the following steps. By the end of the activity, the girls will hopefully be able to state the steps from memory:

1. Identify the problem.
2. Brainstorm solutions.
3. Choose the best solution.
4. Plan how to implement the solution.
5. Evaluate the results.

Activity Steps.

1. Use Handout 47. Ask the girls to pick a problem that has been bothering them. It can be a problem with a friend, a teacher, a particular academic subject, or any area of worry that they are comfortable exploring with the group.

2. Tell them that you are going to teach them to use some problem-solving steps that they can memorize and use throughout their lives. Tell them that processing their problems in writing is a good way to come up with more effective solutions. Pass out pencils and scratch paper.

3. State that step 1 is to identify the problem. Ask them to write their problem down. Ask the following questions to help them clarify the problem:

   Question 1: What would it look like if the problem was solved? Is this a realistic expectation?

   Question 2: Is this a situation you can change? (We can change our own behavior, but we can't force change in others' behavior.)

   Question 3: Can you break the problem down in smaller parts? Is there just one part of the problem you can work on at first? (For example, if the problem is a need to do better in math, they can be more specific and state that their goal is to pass the next math test.)

4. Ask the girls to clearly write a specific problem on their scratch paper.

5. For step 2, the girls need to brainstorm possible solutions. Tell them not to discount or argue with the ideas that come to their mind. Allow a free flow of ideas. They will be able to evaluate the ideas later. Ask them if they need help in the brainstorming process. This is where family and friends can help with ideas. Have them list at least three to five possible solutions.

6. In step 3, the girls should evaluate the solutions they have written. Tell them that often people struggle to solve problems because they are too quick to dismiss possible solutions with a negative attitude. Ask, "Do you believe there is a solution to your problem?" If they do not believe there is a good solution to their problem, they are likely to prove themselves right by dismissing all the possible solutions they have written down in their brainstorming. Explain that they need to identify at least one small step they can take toward a solution. Tell them that often taking one positive step can lead to more ideas and more steps.

7. Once the girls have narrowed down the list they brainstormed in step 3, ask them to write a pros and cons list for each remaining solution. This will assist them in choosing the best solution. Point out that there may not be a perfect solution but that they must simply choose what is best based upon what they understand right now. Wanting a perfect solution often keeps people stuck with no solution.

8. The next step, step 4, provides an opportunity to plan how, when, and where they can implement the solution they chose in step 3. Part of their planning will be to decide what resources they need to accomplish their task. Use Handout 46, *My Ecomap*, and have them identify what resources are available to them if they cannot readily identify available resources. Step 4 is also a good time to role-play how they would implement their solution. If time permits, allow girls to role-play their solutions. This will help them identify how to make the solutions more workable.

9. The final step, step 5, is to evaluate the results. Although the girls will not have a chance to solve their problem in this initial exercise, they can still recognize the importance of step 5. In step 5, they will be asking important questions:

- "Did the solution work?"
- "Did it almost work?"
- "Is there something I can do to improve the solution?"
- "Did I obtain more facts that would make another solution a better choice?"

10. The most important thing to emphasize here is that problem-solving requires "trial and error." Reportedly, Thomas Edison tested between 3,000 and 6,000 versions of the light bulb before he found one that would work! Emphasize that people do not "fail" until they quit trying. If they cannot solve their problem after their first few tries, it is simply time to ask for more help until they can get a solution that works.
11. Ask the girls to recite the five problem-solving steps from memory.
12. As a follow-up, tell them to implement the solution they choose and report back to the group the following week.

Activity 33
Make an Energy Circle

(Time = 15 minutes)

Objectives for Each Girl.

1. I can recognize the power of my beliefs in creating my life.
2. I can create happier emotions by choosing positive beliefs.

Explanation.

One of the most life-changing principles I have learned is that we create our realities with our beliefs. Beliefs are not merely cognitive processes that occur in our brains. Quantum science has now joined behavioral science to prove what eminent psychologist Albert Bandura (1992) explained: that beliefs "influence how people feel, think, motivate themselves, and behave" (p. 118). Beliefs "influence the types of scenarios they construct and rehearse" (Bandura, 1992, p. 118). This is a powerful discovery!

In quantum physics and energy psychology, beliefs are understood to be tangible vibrations of "energy" that surround our cells and influence our physical functioning. Emotions, or "energy in motion," create chemical reactions in our bodies; they communicate with receptors in our cells and create new neurons or pathways of thought in our brains.[45] Emotions influence our perceptions and move us to behaviors that can be negative or positive. If beliefs are powerful enough to create negative realities, then changing beliefs can empower us to change our emotions and behaviors and create positive experiences in our bodies and our environment.

Creating positive emotional "energy" is more than just thinking happy thoughts or analyzing negative thoughts. It is a creative mind-body experience. Creating "energy circles," an activity described by energy psychology practitioner, Carol Tuttle (2003), is one of my favorite activities to do with girls. Creating an energy circle as described in this activity is a simple exercise that can teach girls more about the connection between their thoughts and emotions in a few minutes than lecturing on negative cognition for hours.

Materials Needed.

1. A piece of yarn at least 36 inches long for each girl.
2. Positive affirmations, such as those written on the *Palace of Possibilities Affirmations* (see Handout 8, Chapter 2).
3. Essential oils and a misting spray bottle.

Activity Steps.

---

[45] Two well-documented books on this subject are *Molecules of Emotion* by Candace Pert, PhD., neuroscientist and pharmacologist, and *The Biology of Belief* by cellular biologist, Bruce Lipton, PhD.

1. Ask the girls to take a piece of yarn, tie the ends together, and then place it on the ground in the shape of a circle.

2. Tell them to take positive affirmations and place these "thoughts" into the circle, one by one, using their imagination. As they say the affirmations on the handout to themselves, I ask them to "feel" what it would be like to truly believe each of these affirmations. "What would it feel like if you believed your body is truly a marvelous creation? Place these positive feelings into your energy circle." I ask them to visualize in their minds some of their goals and dreams for their lives. Say, "What would it feel like if those goals came true? Place these pictures in your mind and the feelings in your heart in your energy circle."

3. To add a more tangible dimension to their "energy circle," I use a mister bottle to spray pleasant smelling essential oils around their circle.[46]

4. Once the girls have finished putting their affirmations into the circle, and I have sprayed the essential oil spray into the circle, I ask the girls to step into their energy circle and to wrap themselves up in the positive energy they have created in the circle. It is delightful to watch them experience a tangible excitement and rush of positive emotion. I invite them to remember this feeling and to recognize the positive emotions that come from positive thoughts.

---

[46] Pure, therapeutic grade essential oils stimulate positive emotional responses in the limbic system of the brain; they have profound emotional and physical benefits.

> ## Activity 34
> ### Using Assertiveness Skills to Resolve Problems

(Time = 30 – 45 minutes)

Objectives for Each Girl.

1. I can use verbal skills to solve problems.

Materials Needed.

1. Chapter 6, Handout 27, *Speaking Up: Rules that Work*.
2. Chapter 6, Handout 26, *Listening: Rules that Work*.

Explanation.

I have never had a group of girls that did not love to role-play. Fortunately, role-play is an excellent learning tool. Role-playing creates a multisensory experience that helps girls create new behaviors. Role-playing helps girls understand how to apply new concepts to their real-life experiences. Role-playing is fun; and when girls have fun, they learn more!

The communication and relationship-building skills explained in Chapter 6, listed on *Speaking Up: Rules that Work* (Handout 27) and *Listening: Rules that Work* (Handout 26), are not meant to simply be read with the girls or passed out as a handout. They are best used as guide to help girls role-play real situations in their lives. I like to ask girls to list some of their current dilemmas with their friends. An example might be, "My friend never keeps secrets. Every time I tell her something, I find out she has gossiped behind my back." Using Handout 27, I can ask her to role-play with another girl who plays the role of her friend. She practices what she could say to her friend to solve the problem. Her role-playing partner provides automatic feedback.

Since role-playing can be so unpredictable, it challenges girls to improve skills in a variety of situations. One of the favorite role-playing activities in *Healthy Transitions for Girls* workshops is role-playing how to talk to boys. In one of my groups, the girls confided that they were having a big problem with boys making lewd comments about their breasts and trying to touch them in inappropriate places. Needless to say, we spent the rest of the time role-playing how to assertively handle these situations. Role-playing is a great way to meet real-time needs.

For parents who are using this book one-on-one with their daughter, role-playing is still possible and valuable. When my daughters or granddaughters tell me about a peer problem they are having, I often pretend I am the friend and let them practice what they might say. If I think my daughter needs some awareness of how her behaviors are affecting a friend, I may ask her to pretend she is the friend, and I role-play my daughter's behavior. Then I may say, "How do you think your friend is experiencing your reaction to her?" This gives us the opportunity to role-play alternative responses that are more effective.

Activity Steps.

1. Pick a problem that can be role-played. It needs to be a problem that involves another person or group of persons. This can be a problem that is shared by everyone in the group, such as how to make friends, how to deal with a bully, how to talk to boys,[47] or how to approach a teacher about a poor grade. A girl may have a particular problem that she is willing to role-play in front of the group. Even if the other girls do not have the same problem, they can learn from the experience.

2. Use Handout 27.

3. Refer to Step 1 on the handout, "Why is this making me so upset?" Ask the girls to consider the different emotions they feel about the problem. Explain that to express themselves in a healthy way, they need to take responsibility for their own emotions about the problem, such as the following: "I am angry." "I am hurt." "I am scared." 'I am embarrassed."

4. Invite the girls to ask themselves, "What do I need this person to do for me?" as stated in Step 2 of the handout. For example, if their problem is a girl who is picking on them, they need that girl to stop. They need to express what they need instead of saying, "I hate your guts" or "You are always so mean." Identifying what they need can be a difficult step when emotions are high, but it is important for them to focus clearly on what they *do* want and not just want they don't want if they are going to solve their problems.

5. Step 3 of the handout invites the girls to construct an "I message" to state their problem. An "I message" is typically used to make a statement that describes how another's behavior affects us. "When you did this _____, I felt this _____." "I messages" invite us to take responsibility for what we feel inside and take steps to express our feelings to others in a constructive way. Giving a bully an "I message" that describes our emotions may not be effective; we may need to say "I need…" or "I will…" and state clearly what we are going to do if the bullying behavior continues. "I messages" are very effective in many other situations, however. Role-play some possible "I messages" to solve the problem being discussed in the group. Possible role-play scenarios might include:

   - How to tell a teacher that her explanations are confusing.
   - How to tell a friend that her gossip hurt you.
   - How to ask a clerk for help at the grocery store.
   - How to tell a few students in class that their whispering is disturbing you.
   - How to tell someone you don't want them cheating on your papers.

6. Step 4 of the handout invites girls to consider if there is something they have done to contribute to the problem. Explain, "This step provides a chance to apologize if you have done something that was inconsiderate. It can be difficult to know what part of a problem is our part, and what part

---

[47] Handout 28, *How to Build Friendships with Guys,* in Chapter 7, gives specific verbal skills that can be used when girls want to learn to talk to boys.

belongs to someone else. Even grownups have trouble deciding this." This is a good time for the group to offer input.

7. Finally, explain, "Step 5 reminds us that it is best to talk to someone after you and they are calmed down. Problems are never solved in the heat of the moment." They can use *My Feelings Meter* (Chapter 3, Handout 11) to help them identify the intensity of their emotions. To help with this step, role-play ways girls can tell someone that they need some time to think about a solution. Possible statements might be:

- "Can we talk about this later?" and then give a set time.
- "Can we take a timeout so I can cool down?"
- "I need time to decide how I feel. Can we get back to this later?"
- "I'm not sure I know what to do about this right now."

8. After girls have role-playing using Handout 27, tell them they are ready to have a "solo flight" on their own. Ask them to pick a problem where they could experiment with the rules. Ask them to write down the problem and to write down what happened when they use the "Speaking Up" rules to solve the problem. Tell them that it take practice to be "assertive" rather than "passive" or "aggressive" when they try to solve problems. (If girls do not know the meaning of these words, take time to explain.) Even if the girls can use just one or two of the rules, they will experience more success. Invite them to be prepared to share the experiences they recorded the following session.

Chapter 10

Gender Role: What's So Special about Being Girl?

One way to empower girls is to teach them how to develop instrumental skills such as assertiveness, independence, and goal setting... We must be particularly careful, though, not to devalue the traditionally 'feminine' characteristics of cooperation, communication, sharing, and nurturing.
~ Lecroy & Daley (2001), Empowering Adolescent Girls: Examining the Present, Building Skills for the Future with the Go Grrrls Program, p. 14, emphasis added.

A vital task for girls is to discover how they "fit" into the whole of society. What does it mean to be female in today's culture? The answer to this question is what social scientists call "gender role." In a world of "t-shirts and jeans," girls need to know there is something unique and special about being a girl. (See **Handout 49, *Don't Hide Your Femininity Behind T-Shirts and Jeans*.**)

Ask yourself: "How am I helping the girl I love to value her feminine nature?" A professional colleague who reviewed a first draft of this curriculum pleaded with me, "In your curriculum, please help girls know that it is okay to want to dress up and just be *girls*." She shared with me that her daughters and their friends loved opportunities to be "girls." They begged her to have dress-up tea parties, which grew larger as more friends wanted to share the experience. My friend's experience mirrors my own. My girls and their friends dressed up and made videos well into their high school years. **Activity 35, *Be Your Own Fashion Designer Activity*,** a favorite in my workshops, gives girls the opportunity to "dress up" and creatively explore their uniquely feminine natures.

Girls blossom with the unique gifts they bring to the world as they:

- Value their unique biology.
- Challenge cultural stereotypes.
- Internalize a working definition of *femininity*.

The Beauty and Biology of Being a Girl

Despite cultural pressures that promote androgyny, the fact remains that biological differences between girls and boys are not limited to reproductive anatomy and hormonal variations. Pert (1997) explains the neuroscience that differentiates males and females:

Women have a thicker corpus callosum—the bundle of nerves that bridges the left and right brain hemispheres—they are able to switch back and forth from the rational, or left brain, to the intuitive, or right brain, with relative ease. With fewer nerves connecting the hemispheres, men tend to be focused in one hemisphere or the other. (p. 247)

Although girls and boys share similar attributes, such as the need for emotional expression and empathy, even these attributes are expressed differently. As noted by Sapiro (1999), "women's approaches are more shaped by social connectedness and a stance of caring and relating to others" (p. 85).

A fascinating op-ed in the New York Times by psychiatrist Julie Holland (2015) challenged a cultural norm that asks women to devalue and even medicate their emotions. Dr. Holland illustrates that women's emotions are a gift they bring to their various roles in society, "When we are scared, or frustrated, when we see injustice, when we are deeply touched by the poignancy of humanity, we cry." The qualities of empathy, compassion, and vulnerability that are heightened by our unique biology aid personal growth, create balance in marriage, and lead to a more peaceful families and a more peaceful world. Dr. Holland summarizes, "We need to stop labeling our sadness and anxiety as uncomfortable symptoms and to appreciate them as a healthy, adaptive part of our biology."

What if the emotional ups and down, which are part of the menstrual cycle, were viewed a signals for self-care and reflection rather than some kind of inherent female weakness? The complex biology of a girl's reproductive system is not something to be ignored; it requires extra care. A girl who values her emotional sensitivity during the ebbs and flows of her menstrual cycle is much more likely to value her biology—and her body—as a whole.

Let's Help Girls Make Choices Based on What Really Works

Our society is full of stereotypes and myths that ignore the unique biology and capacities of females. The high rate of depression among girls and women is a signal that current stereotypes of women's roles simply aren't working. In an attempt to fix one unhealthy norm, society can swing the pendulum too far in the other extreme. For example, rejecting the Victorian stereotype of inhibition and shame about sexuality, the societal pendulum has swung radically into an exploding sexualization of girls. This shift devalues the real purpose for reproductive changes in girls' bodies and erodes boundaries essential to building healthy, long-term family relationships. (Chapter 7, **Activity 23, Heart Healthy Relationships,** addresses this issue.) This chapter challenges three common stereotypes and presents practical ideas for helping girls prepare for success in today's world.

The Traditional Woman Stereotype

The "traditional woman" stereotype says that the woman who subordinates career for home and family has "settled for less," rather than doing something "really important" with her life. She relies on her husband to be the main provider in the family while she specializes in home management and child-rearing; therefore, this stereotype insists, she lacks economic power and is doomed to male oppression. Creating a nurturing home, building healthy family relationships, or sacrificing to rear children are simply not as important as the "true" accomplishment of career success.

Rather than distinguishing between dysfunctional traditional families and traditional families as a whole, society has metaphorically "thrown the baby out with the bath water" and devalued the work and sacrifice of mothers altogether, promoting the erroneous idea that caregiving and nurturing are menial skills. In her essay, *Despising Our Mothers, Despising Ourselves*, Papazoglou (1992) stated that devaluing motherhood devalues "the primary work of most women throughout history" (p. 11). If girls can develop, without exploitation, their commitment to caregiving within their varied spheres of influence, future generations may experience, as Anne Summers (1994) described "a genuine breakthrough in our thinking about the *qualities contemporary society now has the greatest need for*" (p. 46, emphasis added).

Contrast the images of yesteryear when motherhood was valued with the images of "beauty" today. Notice that modern media images of girls and women's bodies emphasize a pre-pubescent appearance, lean, straight lines with no curves. The subtle message of these images is that rounded hips and curves, necessary for fertility and reproduction (and a by-product of reproduction in most women), are not desirable, something to be avoided. Earlier images of woman, with their rounded hips and tummies, normalized the bodily changes of puberty which meant that girls could embrace the changes of puberty as natural and could feel beautiful without obsessing about their weight.

Unfortunately, girls who are taught to devalue motherhood do not value the reproductive changes occurring in their bodies. In their minds, if reproduction is not valuable, then breasts and thighs are simply objects that attract sexual attention. They need more than the biological explanations offered in health classes. They need to acknowledge and awaken their powerful maternal natures and begin first to care for themselves.

An experience with my granddaughters, when they were ages eight and eleven, and my youngest daughter, when she was age fourteen, reinforced my belief in nurturing girls' maternal instincts. The girls pooled their money and decided they wanted to buy a toy they could enjoy during summer break. After hours of deliberation, they dragged me to the toy section of a department store to see their prize. It was a very realistic, life-size, infant doll. They were ecstatic. I admit that I was a bit surprised since I thought their doll-playing days were over; but this doll was so realistic and cuddly, they were absolutely smitten. As I picked up the doll and cuddled her to my neck, all my maternal instincts tumbled forth. I could not help but feel the same delight as my daughter and granddaughters as I hugged "Lexie Rachel" to my neck and patted her little bottom, just as I had my own babies. Even my active twelve- year-old grandson said, "I love holding this baby. She calms me down."

To increase natural empathies and respect for girls' bodies in *Healthy Transitions for Girls* workshops, we invite a mother and newborn to visit during **Activity 37, What's So Special about Being a Girl? Activity**. We ask the mother to describe how breastfeeding increases bonding. We ask her to share the nurturing emotions she feels about her baby. If the mother is comfortable with having the girls hold her baby, they are able to cuddle the baby as well.

Another impact of the "traditional woman" stereotype is that because homemaking is not valued as a career choice, girls do not prepare for it. In her essay, "Motherhood in a Corporate Culture," Ruth Moynihan, PhD, (1998) reflects:

Do your own thing. Be yourself. Follow your star. Go for the gold. All of us have heard these simple clichés of modern life again and again. But how often do people include motherhood within the list of possibilities? (p. 13)

Every girl would benefit from learning the skills necessary to manage a home and care for children since most women out of necessity must fill these roles to some degree. Creating a home is not merely the performance of menial chores, but it invites the development of a variety of creative skills, not the least of which is knowledge of nutrition and food preparation essential to the development of life-long wellness. At the end of each *Healthy Transitions for Girls* session, we make a healthy snack and give instruction on basic food preparation skills. **Handout 62, Healthy Transitions for Girls *Healthy Snacks*** (Chapter 11) offers some simple but healthy recipes that girls can share with their families.

In today's traditional family life, there are flexible options available to women who experience many "starts, stops, meander, interruptions, revisions, and detours as they accommodate the others in their lives" (McGoldrick, 2005, p. 108). In my own personal experience, I enjoyed periods of full-time homemaking and periods of part-time or full-time work out of economic necessity. When my children were grown and I decided to complete my education, I found that my experience as a mother, home manager, and community volunteer was an invaluable addition to my professional training and practice.

Suggestions for Challenging the "Traditional Woman" Stereotype

- Encourage the development of the natural maternal empathies of girls.
- Emphasize the value and nobility of motherhood roles.
- Explain that caring for their bodies now will affect the health of their children later.
- Encourage career preparation and life-long learning to prepare for economic necessities, but also value the choice of full-time homemaking as a career.
- Provide opportunities for girls to develop skills in childcare, nutrition, food preparation, financial management, and home maintenance.

Challenging the Superwoman Stereotype

The polar opposite of the passive and under-challenged "traditional woman" stereotype is the "superwoman" stereotype. She's the woman who does it all and does it all at once. She "brings home the bacon, fries it up in a pan, and never lets him forget that he's a man," as sung in an old television commercial. "Superwomen" believe they must share the provider role and participate in the workforce to make an equal contribution to society and the family. "Superwomen" believe that if they are organized enough, they can excel in demanding careers and still have ample time and energy for community activities, managing a home, nurturing and training small children, and a romantic, fulfilled marriage.

The realities of real-life "superwomen" present a different picture. Charen (2009) cited a Pew Survey which found that over 70 percent of mothers who work full-time feel their parenting is inadequate. The survey also found that 60 percent of mothers who work full-time say they would prefer part-time work; yet only 24 percent of women are able to meet financial needs by working part-time.

Our society commonly portrays women who seem to have it all, but at what cost? Celebrity marriages come and go at a dizzying rate, and stress-related diseases like Epstein Barr, migraines, fibromyalgia, and chronic fatigue syndrome are epidemic today. How many "superwomen" are using prescription drugs to cope with burnout, depression, anxiety, and insomnia? Could it be our bodies are sending us a message? Choate (2007) stated, "The message that 'you can have it all'... results in a sense of inadequacy, manifested somatically as BID [body image dissatisfaction]" (p. 321). If women are rejecting or disconnecting from their bodies in the superwoman role, perhaps it is because they are rejecting something more—their inherent needs and nature as women. Choate (2007) explained that women often feel "disconnected and isolated" in the "superwoman" role because they must sacrifice meaningful relationship connections for the hectic pace of "having it all" (p. 321).

Girls who want the experience of having children can be deceived by the Superwoman's message that you can have your career first and then wait until your 40's to have children. Hewitt (2002) documents an important biological reality, that fertility drastically decreases after 35 and that a high percentage of career women are not childless by choice. The scientific miracle of invitrofertlization (IVF) rarely compensates this fact of female biology. At age thirty-nine the chance of a live birth after an IVF attempt is 8 percent. By age forty-four, it falls to 3 percent (p. 19).

Delaying a full time career in order to have children does not impede long-term success, despite societal messages to the contrary. Moynihan (1998) notes that "women who have their children while they are young frequently experience a time of new creative energy and career potential in their 30's and 40's" (p. 13). Evidence cited by Charen (2009) shows that many women are challenging the "superwoman" myth and opting to postpone career achievement to care for their children.

The research group Catalyst, devoted to advancing women's careers in business, found that 33 percent of women with MBA degrees are not working full-time, compared to 5 percent of men. Census data from 2002 showed that 36 percent of women with college degrees who'd had a child in the previous year were staying home, up from 32 percent in 1995. (p. 321)

Additionally, the lives of real women I know challenge the "superwoman" stereotype and reinforce the flexibility that is necessary and possible in today's world.

Heather is a dentist who is married with two children. She works two days per week, sharing a dental practice with another mother who works part-time. When's Heather's husband was out of work for a period of time, she increased her working hours, but went back to working two days per week once he again became employed full-time.

Joy received her associate degree as a physical therapy assistant and then married. Her husband's income supported the family without a need for her to work outside her home; she was able to be a stay-at-home mom for 24 years while her four children were being raised. Her college training was an important resource when one of her children was born with a disability. When her youngest child was a junior in high school, she felt a desire to go back to college part-time to pursue a nursing degree.

Jennifer is an occupational therapist who nets a generous hourly income. She put her husband through college working part-time. She has a large family, but continues to supplement the family's income, working only a few hours per week.

Katie is a 20 year-old single girl who just completed 12 months training as a licensed massage therapist and certified yoga instructor. She did not enjoy high school academics and did not wish to pursue a four-year college degree. Katie's training allows her to support herself working part-time since she earns $20-$60 per hour as a massage therapist/yoga instructor. It can also provide a good supplemental income when she marries and has children. To support the possibility of running her own business, she is taking classes in business at a community college.

Andrea has a degree in health sciences but discovered an innate talent when she received on-the-job-training in business management. She makes a good hourly wage advising a non-profit organization and helping a friend manage his business. This allows her to work at home and schedule her time around her three busy teenagers, yet still contribute to the family finances during her husband's career change.

Teaching girls to consider their maternal natures as part of career planning—as illustrated by the true-life examples above—is an essential factor in supporting a healthy gender role. One area of recent debate is the fact that women are still underrepresented in science and math careers. In real-life, the best career choice is the one that allows a girl to meet financial needs, provide purpose and meaning to life, and allow flexibility to fulfill personal and family needs.

Suggestions for Challenging the "Superwoman" Stereotype

- Challenge unrealistic expectations that girls can "have it all" and "have it all at once."
- Explain that at different times in girls' lives, different roles will be more important and that they will need to prioritize and sacrifice for one role over another.
- Encourage girls to choose careers based upon talents and aptitudes, including their need for social connection and nurturing rather than trying to meet societal definitions of "success."
- Encourage girls to choose careers that allow flexible or part-time hours to give them the option of prioritizing their roles as wives and mothers during years when the demands are greatest.
- Help girls recognize that good self-care skills are vital for every woman and that the pressure to "do it all" is harmful to health.

The Sexualized Female Stereotype

The prevalence of body image dissatisfaction is evidence that modern women, despite many economic victories, have not won the battle of self-respect. As discussed in **Activity 25, *Media Detectives Activity*** (Chapter 8), girls and women trim, tuck, mold, and camouflage themselves, trying to meet an impossible and emotionally empty standard of sexual attractiveness. A study by the American Psychological Association linked the three most common mental maladies among girls--eating disorders, low self-esteem, and depression—to sexualization.

The "broad and increasing" sexualization of girls prompted the American Psychological Association to study this phenomenon and its harmful consequences. The APA defined that sexualization occurs when:

- A person's value comes only from his or her sexual appeal or behavior to the exclusion of other characteristics;
- A person is held to a standard that equates physical attractiveness (narrowly defined) with being sexy;
- The person is sexually objectified—that is, made into a thing for others' sexual use, rather than seen as a person with the capacity for independent action and decision making; and/or
- Sexuality is inappropriately imposed upon a person.[48]

Girls' minds and bodies are shamelessly exploited to sell product; even parents and mentors become numb to the harmful effects of sexualization because it is so commonplace. Girls in my workshops privately confide that entering puberty is something they fear. They feel embarrassed about the changes in their bodies, even ashamed. Some hope that if they don't think about it, it will somehow pass them by. It tugs at my heart to see them fear growing up, rather than feel joyful anticipation about the possibilities of being female.

Suggestions for Challenging the "Sexualized Female" Stereotype

Only a revolution of parents, mentors, counselors, and clergy who are willing to openly challenge these messages and set limits about girls' access to sexualized media images and clothing can change this trend.

- **Activity 35, Be Your Own Fashion Designer Activity (Activity 35)** offers a **Designer Checklist (Handout 48)** that provides guidelines for modest clothing choices. **Handout 52, Be Your Own Fashion Designer Parent Homework** invites mothers to use this list when shopping and to help their daughters avoid sexualized fashion choices.
- **Activity 36, Do You Know What You Are Attracting? Activity** informs girls about the messages they can send by their fashion choices. Modest dress is one of the premiere protections parents can offer their daughters against the sexualized messages of the media.
- Use the activities in Chapter 8, *Media Literacy and Critical Thinking: Embracing the Images of REAL Beauty* to help girls resist sexualized role-concepts.
- **Handout 20, Be a Media Conscious Parent** (Chapter 5) lists just a few of the valuable resources that can help parents protect their girls from harmful media.

---

[48] Find this article at http://www.apa.org/pi/women/programs/girls/report.aspx.

The Goal is Healthy Femininity

A working definition of femininity is the antidote for the stereotypes of modern culture. Femininity is not a "one-size-fits-all" concept. Femininity is the female expression of positive qualities such as sensitivity, creativity, charm, graciousness, character, dignity, intelligence, and strength. Femininity acknowledges the inherent beauty of the female body, which leads naturally to a desire for self-care. This occurs naturally as girls *value* their reproductive capacities, including the process of menstruation. Femininity utilizes emotional sensitivity to create positive change within self and in the lives of others. Femininity challenges the unrealistic demands of modern stereotypes. This occurs as girls evaluate their many choices based upon accurate self-understanding and accurate knowledge of female biology. Being *feminine* doesn't diminish a female's abilities—it capitalizes on them and expands them.

List of Activities, Handouts, & Figures Used in Chapter 10

Chapter 10: Gender Role: What's So Special about Being a Girl?

<u>List of Activities.</u>

<u>List of Handouts.</u>

<u>List of Figures.</u>

None.

Activity 35
Be Your Own Fashion Designer Activity

(Time = 45 – 50 minutes)

Objectives for Each Girl.

1. I can choose modest clothes that reflect my personality.
2. I can reject sexualized fashions.
3. I can choose fashions that help me to feel feminine.
4. I can challenge fashion trends that don't fit my personality or my goals.

Explanation.

If you have not tried to buy a pre-teen bra at Wal-Mart lately, you are in for an eye-opening experience. Nearly every bra is designed with underwire and one to two inches of padding. Why does a ten year-old need a padded bra? Why are little girls wearing plunging necklines, thong underwear, and little skirts that barely cover their pelvic area? These fashions influence girls' beliefs about who they are as females. The pressure to dress a certain way can be unbearable to girls who want to fit in. Yet, fashions are made with little regard for modesty or the unique figure type and preferences of individual girls.

This activity is designed to give girls the freedom to identify what they would choose to wear if they could be free of all the "fashion rules" that are reinforced in their peer groups. They are encouraged to be feminine (as opposed to sexualized or grungy) and to express their femininity in a unique way. This activity encourages girls to discover the many, many fashion choices that are possible and to expand their fashion vocabulary. I like to tell girls that their outfit is the "gift wrap" for who they are on the inside.

Importantly, the *Designer Checklist* (Handout 48) gives guidelines for both girls and their mothers on how to choose clothes that are modest and respectful of their bodies. Emphasize that this checklist is a tool they can use every time they shop. Tell them they need the encouragement of their mothers, grandmothers, and mentors in order to combat pressure from media and the fashion industry. Be sure to reinforce the bullets in the "Know the Fashion Tricks and Trends" throughout the entire activity.

Materials Needed.

1. Handout 48, *Designer Checklist.*
2. Handout 49, *Don't Hide Your Femininity Behind T-Shirts and Jeans.*
3. Handout 50, *Be Your Own Fashion Designer Instructions.*
4. Handout 51, *Be Your Own Fashion Designer Worksheet.*
5. A photocopy of Handout 52, *Be Your Own Fashion Designer Parent Homework,* for each parent, printed on cardstock if possible.
6. Colored markers and drawing paper.

Activity Steps.

1. Begin with Handout 48 and Handout 49. Review the checklist and the objectives you want to teach using Handout 48. Using Handout 49, help girls begin to develop a fresh, healthier perspective to their own "fashion."

2. Using Handout 50 and 51, tell the girls they get a chance to design a dress that might be worn on a very special occasion. Be aware that some girls may be very uncomfortable in dresses and view dresses as too "girlie." Encourage them to design a dress that reflects their interests and tastes. For example, one girl who described herself as a "cowgirl" made an outfit with a cowgirl hat, boots, and a skirt with a Western flair. Once girls are given a chance to express concerns and resistance, they relish the opportunity for creative expression.

3. After the girls have designed their outfits, allow each girl a few minutes to explain her outfit and how it expresses her tastes and personality. Try to compliment one unique aspect of each girl's design. Often girls will explain how their outfit meets standards set by their parents, such as no strapless dresses or no dresses above the knee.[49] If a design is revealing or reflects the sexualized messages of the media, simply emphasize the guidelines on the *Designer Checklist* (Handout 48) and ask what the girl might change to make her outfit comply with the guidelines. Sharing can be voluntary to honor each girl's level of trust in the group.

4. To conclude the activity, pass out the photocopy of Handout 52 as homework. Ask the girls to share this handout with their parents, then to cut along the dotted lines and make a card that can be carried with them whenever they shop for clothes to remind them of their "Designer Checklist."

5. Facilitators may wish to use Activity 36, *Do You Know What You Are Attracting? Activity* as follow-up to reinforce the need to resist sexualized fashions.

6. Another great way for mothers, mentors, and grandmothers to follow-up the learning in this activity is to actually take girls shopping. Make choosing clothes a collaborative effort where you and the girl you love are both invested in using the "Designer Checklist for Creating Your Own Style." Although finding modest styles is difficult, be aware that you can layer clothes to create more modesty. With determination, you can get what you want.

---

[49] For parents, mentors, or grandmothers who are doing this activity with the girls they love, this is a great time to establish family rules about modest dress and self-expression.

Activity 36
Do You Know What You're Attracting? Activity

(Time = 45 – 50 minutes)

Objectives for Each Girl.

1. I can recognize the messages I send with my fashion choices.
2. I can choose clothing styles that invite healthy friendships with guys.

Explanation.

This activity raises awareness of the messages girls send when they choose sexualized fashions. Sexualization of children and teens has become so commonplace that girls may think it is normal and harmless to follow fashion trends that are revealing and provocative. However, research consistently gives credence to the old-fashioned but commonsense notion that females who wear revealing clothing to gain male attention are not attracting the caring and friendship they truly desire.

Research by Peter and Valkenberg (2007) confirmed the results of other studies that "adolescents' exposure to a sexualized media environment is associated with stronger notions of women as sex objects" (p. 392). Another newly published study demonstrated that when men see women in revealing clothes, the part of their brain that is stimulated is the same part that uses a "tool," rather than the part of their brain that helps them feel empathy and real caring (Cikara, Eberhardt, & Fiske, 2010). This was particularly true when the men exhibited objectified views of women. The bottom line is that boys are socialized by the media to see the girls as objects of sexual gratification while girls are socialized to believe that they need to dress sexually to attract boys; these gratifications and attractions are not based upon an empathetic connection and thus do not encourage real caring or real friendship.

As discussed in Chapters 7 and 8, it is important for girls to challenge these sexualized messages and develop a healthy, holistic concept of gender role.

Materials Needed.

1. Several pictures of current girls' fashions from catalogs or magazines.
2. Handout 48, *Designer Checklist.*
3. Handout 53, *Do You Know What You're Attracting?*
4. Scissors and glue.
5. Pencils, pens, or markers.
6. Cardstock or construction paper.

Activity Steps.

1. Explain to the girls that they are going to make a collage of fashions that they think will help them to feel beautiful. As they prepare for this activity, ask the following questions.

    Question 1: How do you decide what fashions to buy and wear?

    Question 2: Who makes the rules about what fashions are in style?

    Question 3: Do you think the clothes you wear send messages about who you are?

    Question 4: What messages do you want to send?

2. Ask the girls if they ever buy clothes because they want boys to notice them. Explain that many girls buy clothes because they want to look attractive to boys. Fashion magazines and advertisers encourage girls to buy clothes that make them look "sexy" so they can get a boyfriend. Ask what messages they want to send to boys.

3. Explain that if they are looking for friendship and caring, girls should choose clothes that follow the fashion rules described in the *Be Your Own Fashion Designer Activity* (Activity 35). Explain that research has shown that when women wear clothes that are revealing, they do not attract the caring part of men; they attract the part that sees them as an "object" or a "tool." Women deserve to be respected for all parts of themselves, not just for the sexual parts of their bodies.

4. Use Handout 53. Tell them that this handout uses a funny and unusual analogy to describe how fashion choices affect the kind of attention they get. Share the following real-life anecdote:

    One day, a 13-year-old girl came out of her room dressed in a very short skirt. She knew her mother would not approve of the skirt, which was about 12 inches above her knee. She could not bend over without showing her underwear. Nonetheless, she thought the skirt was really "cool" and wanted to wear it. She had seen many women in magazines showing off their long legs with short skirts. She wanted to be "in style." Her mother took a look at her skirt and said, "Well, when all the flies start swarming, what are you going to do with them?" The girl was puzzled. What was her mother talking about? Why would flies swarm around her just because she was wearing a short skirt?

5. Ask the group if they can answer the girl's question. Read the handout together to discover the answer. Be sure to create a sensory experience by visualizing a table laid out with delicious food, only to have flies contaminating the food, buzzing around your face, and turning a picnic into a very annoying experience. Ugh!

6. Ask the girls if they, like the girl in the story, feel pressure to wear certain kinds of fashion. Have them share the thoughts and worries they have when they go shopping. Invite the girls to write some of their thoughts about the kinds of fashions they notice girls wearing today at the bottom of Handout 48. Then, encourage them to write down some goals about the kinds of clothes they want to wear as they grow to be young women.

7. Pass out the art supplies. Instruct the girls to cut out pictures of clothes that follow the fashion rules and that invite respect and caring from boys. Remind them that girls should feel beautiful

inside and out and not use their bodies to attract sexual feelings from boys. Have them choose clothes that they think would help them to feel beautiful and respectful.

8. After the girls have constructed their fashion collages, ask them to share their fashion choices. Help them evaluate whether these choices follow the guidelines offered in Handout 48.

9. Encourage the girls that even when they are doing their part to send the message that they want friendship and empathy, they may still receive unwanted sexual attention. If girls in the group express that this has been a problem for them, reviewing the boundary discussions from Chapter 6 may be helpful. Girls can use *Handout 27 Speaking Up: Rules That Work* (Chapter 6) to role play how to handle unwanted sexual attention.

Activity 37
What's So Special about Being a Girl? Activity

(Time = 45 – 50 minutes)

Objectives for Each Girl.

1. I can develop my natural gift for nurturing and empathy.
2. I can understand the purpose for the changes in my body.
3. I can develop respect for the changes happening to my body.
4. I can care for my body to prepare myself to be a mother someday.

Advance Preparation.

For this activity, arrange for a mother and new baby to come to the group for the last 15 minutes of the class. If you are a parent, grandparent, or mentor who is completing this activity with your daughter or loved one, arrange to visit a friend who has an infant, if possible. An alternative activity if no opportunities to interact with a real infant are possible is to spend time playing with and nurturing a lifelike doll.

Materials Needed.

1. Handout 54, *What's So Special about Being a Girl?*
2. Handout 55, *What's So Special about Being a Girl? Parent Letter.*
3. Chapter 2, Handout 1, *My Body Is Changing.*

Activity Steps.

1. Explain to the girls that in their health classes, they talk about the changes that happen to their bodies during puberty. Ask, "How many of you know what kind of changes happen to your body when you go through puberty?" Discuss changes which are listed on Handout 1. Your emphasis is not to provide a health lesson but to help girls recognize the value and potential created by these changes.
2. Ask girls how they feel about menstruation or having "periods." What kind of language do they use to describe having periods? A good indication of how they feel about their bodies and the process of reproduction is the terms they use to describe menstruation. Encourage them to use the scientific terms "menstruating," "menstruation," or a respectful term like "having my period."
3. Ask if they see having a period as a burden or something that they want to avoid. Many girls see menstruation as a meaningless hardship that girls are "stuck with." Explain that one of the gifts of being a girl or woman is the opportunity to make the sacrifice to bring a new life into the world. The physical discomfort they experience during periods helps them prepare for the physical discomfort of pregnancy and childbirth. Making a sacrifice such as this to help another human is noble and honorable. In some ways, it is like the sacrifice men and women in the military make to help others

to have freedom. The ability to give life is an important privilege and responsibility that has been given to women. They can feel proud to be girls whose bodies are preparing for this opportunity.

4. Read Handout 54 together. Use the questions on the handout to facilitate discussion. If girls in the group are too shy to answer the questions aloud, they can write their answers on Post-it Notes that you can share with the group anonymously. The important point to emphasize is that caring for their bodies now is very important. It's not just about their well-being, but also the responsibility of preparing their bodies to give life to a little baby.

5. Ask the girls if they would treat their bodies differently if they knew they had a baby inside. What would they eat or not eat? Would they rest more? Would they exercise more? Would they want to protect that baby from drugs or alcohol? Would they want to send happy thoughts to their body and their baby? Explain that even though they do not have a baby inside, and even though they will not be ready to have babies for many years, they can still develop good habits now. Most important, they can value the changes they experience as wonderful and not something "weird."

6. Invite the mother and baby to spend time with the group. For this part of the discussion, I like to have the girls and the mother and baby gather in a circle on a clean blanket on the floor. Ask the mother to share her experiences and feelings about being a mother. It is important to help the girls to awaken their own maternal instincts, since these same instincts will help them learn to value their own bodies. If the mother is comfortable with it, allow the girls to hold the baby or to play with it. Encourage the girls to ask any questions they might have about pregnancy, childbirth, or caring for an infant.

7. Use Handout 55. Tell the girls that they have an opportunity to talk with their mothers and discover how their mother felt when they were born. Girls who do not live with their mothers or who have been adopted can still benefit from this activity. Encourage them to address their letter to someone who was present when they were born. It could be an aunt, grandmother, or family friend. It could even be a father or grandfather. Tell them to ask about special memories that person remembers about them as babies. Did their little baby selves say cute things? Did people like to snuggle their little baby selves? Remind them that no matter what, every baby deserves to have a mother who will care and nurture him or her. They can each learn to be the kind of mothers who will give loving care to their bodies. They can start now by learning to care for their bodies.

Chapter 11

Physical Self-Esteem: My Body is My Best Friend for Life

Each of us is here to discover our true Self ...
that essentially, we are spiritual beings who have taken manifestation in physical form.
~ Deepak Chopra

Looking at the chapter title, "Physical Self-Esteem," one might think that physical self-esteem and positive body image are synonymous, but they are not. As shown throughout this book, positive body image is much more than having a positive attitude about one's body. Positive body image involves healthy beliefs in every area of a girl's life, the spiritual, emotional, intellectual, social, and physical aspects of self. Ideally, a girl will view her body as a "supportive partner" in every aspect of her life.

Physical self-esteem focuses on caring for the physical needs of the body *for the right reasons.* Girls typically know what behaviors contribute to good health from their health classes; but if they have disconnected emotionally from their bodies because of negative beliefs about their bodies, they will not value their bodies enough to follow through with positive health behaviors. Therefore, *a girl has physical self-esteem when she cares for her body because she has positive beliefs and positive emotional connections with her body.* Simply put, "health happens from the inside out."

Four main themes are emphasized in the activities in this chapter to promote physical self-esteem:

1. Review of basic health practices and the challenge to be health conscious, taught in *The WHOLE Me: Let's Get Physical Activity* (Activity 38) and the *Turn Over a New Leaf Activity* (Activity 41).

2. The need for positive motivation in physical exercise (exercising because you want to have good health vs. exercising because you are obsessed with being thin), taught in *The WHOLE ME: My Exercise Inventory* (Activity 39).

3. The connection between health practices and healthy emotions, taught in *The Food Mood Connection Activity* (Activity 40); *"GO GREEN" Hulk Smoothie Recipe* (Handout 59); and the *Don't Dump on Your Body Mindfulness Activity* (Activity 42).

4. An intrinsic appreciation for the body's "miraculous" functions, taught in the *I Am Thankful for All My Body Does for Me Activity* (Activity 43).

Working together, these themes help girls embrace health practices because they value their bodies as a miraculous gift. They recognize the connection between their level of care for their bodies and emotions and their overall happiness in life. When they change the way they treat their bodies, their bodies will help them experience life in a more positive way.

List of Activities, Handouts, & Figures Used in Chapter 11

Chapter 11: Physical Self-Esteem: My Body is My Best Friend for Life

<u>List of Activities.</u>

<u>List of Handouts.</u>

<u>List of Figures.</u>

None.

Activity 38
The WHOLE ME: Let's Get Physical Activity

(Time = 20 – 30 minutes)

Objectives for Each Girl.

1. I can understand basic practices that contribute to good health.
2. I can recognize holistic benefits of basic health practices.
3. I can set goals to improve my health practices.

Material Needed.

1. Handout 56, *The WHOLE ME: Let's Get Physical.*
2. Handout 57, *The WHOLE ME: Let's Get Physical—Show What You Know.*

Activity Steps.

1. Read Handout 56 together with the girls. Do not set goals yet. Just read about the 4 goal areas and how those practices contribute to good health. Explain any vocabulary words they may not understand. Tell the girls they need to really focus because you will be testing their memory.
2. After you have read about the 4 goal areas, ask the girls what areas are most difficult for them. Use the following questions to guide the discussion.

   Question 1: How many of you do all 4 of these things every day?

   Question 2: How many of you do 3 of these things every day?

   Question 3: How many of you do 2 of these things every day?

   Question 4: How many of you do 1 or none of these things every day?

   Question 5: Do you do some of these things at least some of the time?

   Question 6: What keeps you from being more consistent?

   Question 7: Which goal is the hardest for you to do?

3. Tell the girls you are going to test their memory of the 4 goal areas. Use Handout 57 to test them. They cannot look at the answers on Handout 56 but must complete Handout 57 from memory.
4. After they have written as many of the answers as they can, help them complete the rest of the handout.

5. Refer back to Handout 56. Have the girls write their goals. Have them indicate who will be their "accountability partner," someone who will follow-up with them to see how they are doing on their goals.

Activity 39
The WHOLE ME: My Exercise Inventory Activity

(Time = 20 minutes)

Objectives for Each Girl.

1. I can exercise because I love caring for my body and emotions.
2. I can recognize unhealthy exercise practices.
3. I can understand that withholding of food to support athletic performance is harmful.
4. I can set realistic and enjoyable exercise goals.

Materials Needed.

1. Handout 58, *The WHOLE ME: My Exercise Inventory*.
2. Pencil and paper.

Activity Steps.

1. Distribute pencils and paper to each girl. Tell the girls you will read several case histories. Ask the girls if they can identify any unhealthy practices or attitudes in each case history. Ask what practices or attitudes they think are positive. Ask them to record their thoughts on paper as you read each case history.
2. Read the following case histories.

> Callie is great at basketball. She plans to try out for the varsity team in high school someday. For now, she loves playing on the middle school team. It is not uncommon for Callie to work out 90 minutes at basketball practice and then run a mile after dinner. Callie is worried about staying in shape. Often she will only eat a few bites of her dinner. She has seen how tall and thin professional woman basketball players are, and she doesn't want to hurt her chances of success by gaining extra weight.

> Eva knows she needs to exercise, but she feels discouraged. No one is there to encourage her after school, and she isn't athletic enough to play on a sports team. Even though she tells herself she needs physical activity, she always ends up watching TV and eating potato chips or ice cream at night.

> Kara exercises every day. She runs at least 2-3 miles after school. The whole time she is running she tells herself, "If I don't keep exercising, my body is going to be so ugly. I hate cellulite."

> Maren plays volleyball during volleyball season, but she doesn't play any other sports during the year. She loves walking her dog before dinner every day. It feels so good to get outside. She tries to walk at least a mile or two. Some nights she gets busy and can only walk about 30

minutes. If she can't walk as much as she would like, she doesn't get down on herself. She just reminds herself how good it feels to exercise and how much she loves the outdoors when she walks.

Sarah has a fantasy exercise regimen that she has mapped out very carefully. It includes weight lifting three times per week, running five miles at least three times per week, and swimming laps at the local YMCA at least 4 nights per week. The problem is that Sarah is so busy she can't seem to work in time for exercise at all.

3. Review each case history with the girls. Ask the following questions for each case history.

   Question 1: What practices and attitudes were healthy?

   Question 2: What warning signs did you see?

   Question 3: How could these warning signs lead to health problems?

   Question 4: What advice would you give the girl in this case history?

4. Note that Maren is the only girl whose exercise practices and attitude are fully healthy. Callie and Cara are exercising for negative motivators, because they don't want their bodies to get fat. This can lead to over-exercising and obsession with thinness. Exercising because we want to feel healthy is the right reason to exercise. Eva needs ideas to help her get started with a daily exercise program. Sarah has unrealistic expectations that keep her from being successful. She needs help setting realistic goals.

5. Ask the girls to evaluate how they are doing in the area of exercise. Do any of the problems of the girls in the case history sound familiar? Brainstorm ideas on how to solve any dilemmas of girls in the group.

6. Using Handout 58, tell the girls that they will analyze their own exercise patterns. The purpose of the inventory is to help them become more aware of any unhealthy attitudes they may be developing about exercise. Have the girls select a partner. After three days of exercise, they are to report their inventory to their partner. (If you are a parent completing this activity with your child, you can both complete the three-day inventory and share with each other.)

Activity 40
The Food Mood Connection

(Time = 45 minutes)

Objectives for Each Girl.

1. I can increase mindfulness about my eating habits.
2. I can resist feeling anxious when I eat.
3. I can recognize the negative effect of certain foods on my emotions and energy level.
4. I can eat more green, nutritious foods.
5. I can choose healthy snacks, rather than "junk food."

Note.

The "Hulk Smoothie" may not be world famous—yet. But it has a pretty good following. Whenever I tell girls in my groups that we are going to make a smoothie with fresh spinach, they immediately respond with grimaces and finger-gagging gestures. After they taste a Hulk Smoothie, however, they beg for more. Whenever possible, I introduce Hulk Smoothies in my workshops. I want girls to get converted to the idea that something green, like spinach, a true "Super Food," can taste wonderful. I have adapted the recipe for girls who are lactose intolerant or who have other allergies.

Hulk Smoothies are a family tradition with my own children and grandchildren. They are skilled in making Hulk Smoothies, and every morning, a child or grandchild is given that assignment. Our amazing discovery is that when we don't have our Hulk Smoothies, our bodies feel different. A Hulk Smoothie craving is the kind of craving we want to pay attention to!

Grownups have discovered the benefit of Hulk Smoothies too. My health-minded friends like Hulk Smoothies because they help reduce cravings for the wrong kinds of food or for eating too much food. We have all discovered that when we eat the foods that are nutritious, our bodies don't feel as hungry.

Be creative with Hulk Smoothies. Make your own variations. One of my favorite mood-boosters is adding flax seed. Experiment with all kinds of fruit and greens. I wonder if the Hulk Smoothie qualifies as "green energy." It would sure be a different planet if we all had a Hulk Smoothie every day!

Materials Needed.

1. Handout 59, "Go Green" Hulk Smoothie Recipe.
2. Handout 60, Take the Food Mood Challenge.
3. Handout 61, Take the Food Mood Challenge Food Log.
4. Handout 62, Healthy Transitions for Girls Healthy Snacks.
5. Markers and paper for drawing.
6. An orange or raisin.

Activity Steps.

1. Conduct a simple "mindfulness" exercise using an orange or raisin (see **Activity 9**, Chapter 3). After the girls have practiced "mindfulness," explain that people commonly have three ways of relating to the food they eat, **mindfulness, anxiety**, and **lack of awareness**. Discuss each type of relationship.

    1) **Mindfulness** about food includes awareness of

    - what we eat;
    - how much we eat; and
    - how we are affected by what we eat.

    2) **Mindfulness** about eating is not the same as **anxiety** about eating. When someone is anxious, they are worrying about whether or not they are eating too much and whether or not they will get fat. They have images that come to their minds reminding them how much they hate their hips or thighs.

    Someone can also be anxious that they will not get enough food to eat. Maybe they have a nagging feeling that they need to fill up on food so they don't feel so empty inside.

    3) **Lack of awareness** means we just don't pay attention to the food we ingest. Eating can be such a habit that we don't even think about it. When we eat pizza, it is so yummy that we just "pig out" until our tummy hurts. Or maybe we are so busy reading good books that we go for hours without eating until our body feels kind of sick. Lack of awareness about food could also be eating so many cookies after school that we aren't hungry for dinner. Have you ever dished up your dinner, only to realize that you had piled on so many mashed potatoes you couldn't possibly eat them all? Or have you ever decided not to pack a lunch and found that you were starving at school?

2. Ask the girls if any of these scenarios sound familiar. The goal of our relationship with food is to be "mindful." That means we eat "consciously"; we are aware of what we eat and aware of body messages, such as, "I'm full" or "I need greens." Ask, "Have you ever thought to ask your body what it thinks about what you eat?"
3. Ask the girls to remember what they ate for breakfast. Ask the following questions to help girls think mindfully about their meal.

    Question 1: How did your body feel about what you ate?

    Question 2: Did you feel energized?

    Question 3: Did you get hungry an hour after breakfast?

Question 4: Did you have to starve and run on no energy until lunch?

Question 5: Did you feel "nervous" and "sickly" because all you had eaten was a sugary doughnut?

4. Ask each girl to draw a picture of her body. Then, have the girls draw what they ate for breakfast on their body pictures. Have them write down in a word balloon (like a cartoon) what their body has to say to them about what it was fed for breakfast. Instruct them, "Ask your body what it really wants for breakfast." Tell them to write down the message their body replies in a word balloon on their drawing.

5. Go around the group and allow the girls to share their body drawings and word balloons. Read the following statement:

> When our bodies feel unsatisfied or hungry, even after we have eaten, they are often telling us that even though we are feeding them, they are starving for some real nutrition. Explain that a big problem in our society is that kids are replacing nutritious food with "junk food." When their bodies give hunger signals, many girls just quiet those signals down with something unhealthy. They don't listen to their body's need for good food. For example, after a person drinks a soda, they aren't thirsty for milk. The National Center for Chronic Disease Prevention and Health Promotion (2010) reported that in the last 25 years, the consumption of milk, the largest source of calcium, has decreased 36 percent among adolescent females. As a result, eighty-five percent of adolescent females do not consume enough calcium. At the same time, soft drink consumption has doubled and even tripled, according to some studies.

6. Share the following facts on how food can affect mood.

- Caffeine drinks are known to cause anxiety and insomnia; caffeine is also highly addictive. People use caffeine to give them energy boosts instead of getting energy from good sleep and good food. Ask, "Do you think this affects mood?"
- Processed carbohydrates, such as refined sugar, can temporarily elevate mood but then cause a decrease in mood, just like a "drug" high. A rat study by Bartley Hoebel, PhD, a professor of psychology at Princeton University and reported by Tufts University (2002) found that when the rats tasted sugar, their brains released secretions that acted on the same receptors as addictive drugs (albeit with a milder effect).
- Many junk foods we commonly eat have an "addictive" quality about them. When we eat them, we feel better for a while. When we don't have them, we crave them. When we go without them, we get irritable. Some experts believe that anything that changes mood, causes cravings, and causes withdrawal fits the description of an addictive "drug."
- When adolescents don't have enough to eat, they are much more likely to experience to experience chronic depressive symptoms (dysthymia), to have thoughts about death, to want to die, and to even attempt suicide (Alaimo, Olson, & Frongillo, 2000).
- Repeatedly, diet for depression research has found that insufficient consumption of polyunsaturated fatty acids, antioxidant vitamins, folate, and vitamin B-12 (found in green leafy vegetables and whole grains) is associated with depression (Rogers, 2000).

- Some people have sensitivities to foods that cause symptoms such as anxiety, lack of concentration, aggressive feelings, or feeling down. Explain: "Being 'mindful' helps you to be aware how the food you eat contributes to feelings of sadness, irritability, or other kinds of mood issues."

6. When we decide to stop quieting our bodies and start eating healthier food, we will notice our bodies telling us they want good things to eat. When we are "mindful," our bodies will tell us, "Hey, I am starving for some veggies."

7. Refer to Handouts 60 and 61. Explain to the girls that they are going to be part of an experiment to determine how food affects their mood. Ask the girls to fill out their Food Mood Log for three days. They will practice being "mindful" by writing down everything they eat, including snacks. Encourage the girls to make a "Hulk Smoothie" every morning as part of their Food Mood Challenge. See if they feel differently. Encourage them to try healthy snacks instead of junk food.

8. They will also be "mindful" by paying attention to what they experienced in their bodies in terms of mood or energy level. They are to write down comments each day about their moods and then give their moods an overall rating at the end of each day. They will report back to the group about what they experienced. Remind them to be "mindful" of what they eat, how much they eat, and how they are affected by what they eat.

Follow-Up Activities.

During the next session or workshop, have the girls share what they noticed about the connection between food and mood during their three-day experiment. The experiment can be repeated for another three days; this time, they must follow the health regimen listed on Handout 56 and then record how their moods are affected. The results of this three-day experiment can be compared with their first three-day Food Mood Challenge. Have them commit to the following regimen:

- Go three days without soda, caffeine, or energy drinks.
- Get to bed each night by 9:30 or 10:00. Sleep at least 8 to 9 hours.
- Eat 3 smaller meals per day with 2 healthy snacks. Include at least 4-5 servings of fresh vegetables.
- Drink 6 to 8 glasses of water.
- Exercise at least 30 minutes.

In addition, the **Turn Over a New Leaf Activity (Activity 41)** can also be used as a follow-up to add new health habits to their routine. This exercise allows them to choose a goal, along with a family member, and practice the new habit for one week. There are many ideas in this activity that can be used to continually challenge the girls to have better health habits.

Activity 41
Turn Over a New Leaf Activity

(Time = 30 minutes)

Objectives for Each Girl.

1. I can start now to make changes in the way I treat my body.
2. I can choose new health habits, one by one.
3. I can give up foods and habits that do not promote a healthy mind and body.

Explanation.

This activity can be used as a stand-alone activity to initiate changes in health practices, or it can be used as a follow up to continue the benefits of *The Food Mood Connection Activity* (Activity 40). This activity also asks girls to choose an accountability partner, such as a parent, to complete the activity.

As girls accomplish one goal, they can continue the process of turning over a new leaf by choosing another goal. The *Turn Over a New Leaf Activity* can be an ongoing activity, rather than just a one week effort. Girls' willingness to take better care of their bodies is a way to access their physical self-esteem. When they value their bodies, they will increase their commitment to good health practices.

Materials Needed.

1. A watch with a second hand or a 3-minute egg timer.
2. Handout 63, *Turn Over A New Leaf*.
3. Lined sheets of paper.
4. Pens or pencils.

Activity Steps.

1. Make sure each girl has a lined sheet of paper that is folded in half lengthwise. They are going to make two columns, labeled 1) Body Builders and 2) Body Bummers.
2. Ask the girls what they know about "body builders." They make say that "body builders are guys who lift weights to build big muscles." Tell them that in this activity, a "body builder" is something that we do for our body which makes it strong and healthy, physically and emotionally. A "Body Bummer" is something we eat that does not help our body become stronger. It is something that makes our body struggle for nutrients and "fuel." If something is not helpful to our body, it is a "Body Bummer."
3. Tell the girls you are going to time them for 3 minutes. You want them to write down everything did and ate in the last seven days that helped their body to be more healthy. These belong in the "Body Builders" column. Remind them to write down how often they ate fresh, green vegetables, had a

good night's sleep, drank a glass of milk, and chose a healthy snack, as well as other healthy practices.

4. After the girls have completed the "Body Builders" list, tell them you are going to give them 3 minutes to write down all the things they did and ate in the last seven days that did not support their body's health. These belong in the "Body Bummers" column. Tell them to include things like staying up too late, skipping breakfast, and drinking soda instead of milk or water.[50]

5. When both lists are completed, ask the girls to compare which lists are longer. Ask if there are things they would like to add to their "Body Builders" list.

6. Refer to Handout 63. Ask the girls if they know what it means "to turn over a new leaf." Read the definition of this idiom at the top of the handout. Read the list of health practices listed on the handout. As the girls read this list, ask them to circle items which relate to what they have written on either their "Body Builder" list or their "Body Bummer" list. For example, if they have written that they drank soda for a snack on their "Body Bummer" list, then they would circle Item #2. Suggest they replace soda with juice or water.

7. Ask the girls to review their "Body Builder" and "Body Bummer" lists and also the circled items on the handout. Ask, "Do you see any areas where you could 'turn over a new leaf'?" Follow the instructions on the handout. Ask the girls to each commit to one goal they will work on during the week. The facilitator should also commit to a goal and ask the girls to be her accountability partners. Since everyone will be reporting back the next week, the facilitator will also report her progress, a good exercise in modeling desired behaviors. As a personal example, I had a desire to drink more water each day. A girl in the group asked to be my accountability partner and challenged me to drink more water; as her accountability partner, I challenged her to eat breakfast each day. My desire to be a good example for this girl motivated me to develop a habit of drinking more water that has continued since that workshop. In the times I have seen that girl since the workshop, I check whether she is eating breakfast, and she checks whether I am drinking water. The exercise not only influenced better health habits, but was a good rapport-building opportunity. It demonstrated that I was willing to "walk the talk" and practice what I taught.

8. If you repeat this activity over a period of time, help the girls eliminate the "Body Bummers" on their list, one by one.

---

[50] If you have not preceded this activity with *The Food Mood Connection Activity* (Activity 40), I suggest reviewing the list of health facts offered on Handout 56 prior to having the girls write their "Body Bummers" List.

Activity 42
Don't Dump on Your Body Mindfulness Activity

(Time = 30 – 40 minutes)

Objectives for Each Girl.

1. I can increase awareness of emotional body signs.
2. I can increase physical health by caring for my emotions.
3. I can increase my ability to cope with distressing emotions.
4. I can avoid eating junk food to deal with distressing emotions.

Important Note.

The purpose of this exercise is to help girls to identify how stress contributes to eating junk food and to help them use healthy self-care instead. In this activity, they will be asked to tune in to daily worries that nag at them, creating tension and stress in their bodies. They are NOT being asked to delve into big, private, emotional issues. Be sure to make this clear at the beginning of the activity. A guided imagery exercise may not be appropriate for girls with a history of trauma or mental illness and is suggested for use only by licensed professionals who have experience dealing with emotional abreaction and trauma. If a girl is going to have anxiety connected with this activity, it will typically surface at the beginning of the exercise as she is directed to focus inside her body. Anxiety will cause a girl to begin to breathe shallowly in her chest. Simply direct her to open her eyes, to focus on you, and to return her attention to the present moment. Redirect her attention back to the rise and fall of her abdomen. Explain that if an uncomfortable emotion arises, that she simply needs to observe it and allow it to pass like a "wave" or a "cloud." Remind her that as she is gently blowing warm sunshine into her abdomen, watching it rise and fall, she is surrounding her distress with warmth and love.

Additionally, a guided imagery activity should not be used if girls have not established a positive group connection. Emotional safety is always a top priority when dealing with the sensitive issues surrounding puberty. **If it is determined that a guided imagery activity is not ethically appropriate for the group, adapt this activity as an art activity. A script is provided for both a guided imagery and an art activity.**

Materials Needed.

1. Soothing music to promote relaxation.
2. A lavender essential oil mister to promote relaxation.
3. Handout 64, *Don't Dump on Your Body*.
4. Colored markers or pencils (for art activity only).
5. Several sheets of blank paper for each girl (for art activity only).

Activity Steps.

1. Prepare for the guided imagery or the art activity by playing music and using an oil mister to create a comfortable, relaxing environment.
2. Ask the girls to sit comfortably in their chairs with plenty of room between each other. You can also spread a soft quilt on the floor and allow the girls to lie comfortably on their backs on the quilt if doing the guided imagery activity.
3. Invite the girls to "turn off their left brain thinking." You want them to have a creative "right brain experience." They are going to use their imaginations.
4. With a calming voice, read either the guided imagery script or the art activity script.

Don't Dump on Your Body Guided Imagery Script

First, begin to pay attention to your breathing. Don't change it or make it faster or slower. Just notice it. Notice how it feels to breathe in through your nostrils, allowing your nose to cleanse and warm the air. Breathe out through your mouth. Feel the air pass through your lips, allowing the air to gently push against your lips, puffing them out slightly. Continue to breathe in through your nose and out through your lips. Inhale and exhale completely in this manner five times. Do not feel rushed.

Feel your shoulders droop slightly as you become more relaxed. Uncross your legs if they are crossed. Allow your arms to droop at your sides.

Now, close your eyes or focus your eyes on the end of your nose as you breathe. Allow your mind to drift. Now place your hands on your stomach. imagine as you breathe, that you have a balloon inside of your tummy. As you inhale, the balloon in your tummy grows round and full; as you exhale, the balloon in your tummy lets the air out and gets floppy. Do this five times or until you feel you have a rhythm with your breathing and you can feel your tummy going up and down as you breathe. Blow and release air in and out of your "balloon" for five breaths.

*Inside of your body, you have a place where you like to store your daily stress and worries. **You are being asked to notice just the tension or stress that comes from what you have experienced today. You are not being asked to explore big, deep, private worries**. As you breathe, notice where today's worries might be hiding. You may notice tightness in certain muscles, or butterflies in your stomach or even a slight ache somewhere in your body. Ask yourself, "If I was to draw the stress I feel in my body, what would it look like?" What colors and shapes represent the stress and worry you feel in your body today? Do you see bright squiggles? Do you see grey clouds? Do you see bold lightning bolts? [Pause for several seconds and let the girls ponder the questions.]*

Allow your creative mind to help you visualize the worries and stress that you sense in your body. This is your experience, so your stress can look like anything you desire. You don't have to carry these stress and worries in your body. You need a place to "dump" today's worries so they do not pile up, making your body feel weighed down and "stressed out."

Imagine that you have a trash can for these worries so you aren't "dumping" them in your body? Some of you may be able to visualize a trash can very clearly; for some of you, this trash may look a little fuzzy. That's okay. Everyone will have a different experience. Your trash can may look just like the one that is in your kitchen. Others of you will have a trash can that is different from anything you have ever seen. Your trash can might be very tall or very short. It may be square, or it may be round." Ask yourself, "How big does my trash need to be right now to hold all the worries or stress I have today?" The size of trash can you need to dump your worries may vary from day to day.

Now that you have created a trash can in your mind, you have a place where you can dump your daily worries.

At any time, if you start to feel nervous about your stress and worries, simply move your attention back to your breathing. Breathe slow, warm breaths into your body. Imagine that you are blowing warm rays of sunshine onto your fears and worries with each breath. Breathe 1, 2, 3, 4, 5. [Speak slowly.]

Now, imagine that you are stuffing all of today's worries into your trash can. That's right. Stuff those worries in the can! Do it with gusto! It feels good!

Imagine yourself stuffing you trash can full with today's worries. Imagine how the can expands to be as big as it needs to be to hold those worries. Then imagine yourself tying a helium balloon onto the lid of the trash can.

The helium balloon can be as big as it needs to be to carry your trash up, up, and away. Some of you will have a huge helium balloon depending on how many worries you have today; others will have a medium balloon, or even smaller.

Imagine the powerful helium balloon carrying your trash can full of worries high, higher, into the sky. Use your warm breathe and blow it higher and higher until it is so small you can scarcely see it at all. Watch until it floats out of sight and into the clouds. Now, blow out a big, deep breath. Whoosh! Slowly count your breaths as you begin to "wake up" from this "daydream," 1, 2, 3, 4, 5. [Count very slowly.] Open your eyes if they were closed.

Stretch out your arms and legs. Wiggle your fingers and toes. How does your body feel, now that you have taken out the trash? Thank your body for giving you this wonderful, creative experience. Feel a smile come from your body as it says, "You're welcome!"

Don't Dump on Your Body Art Activity Script

First, begin to pay attention to your breathing. Don't change it or make it faster or slower. Just notice it. Notice how it feels to breathe in through your nostrils, allowing your nose to cleanse and warm the air. Breathe out through your mouth. Feel the air pass through your lips, allowing the air to gently push against your lips, puffing them out slightly. Continue to breathe in through your nose and out through your lips. Inhale and exhale completely in this manner five times. Do not feel rushed.

Feel your shoulders droop slightly as you become more relaxed. Uncross your legs if they are crossed. Allow your arms to droop at your sides.

Now, close your eyes or focus your eyes on the end of your nose as you breathe. Allow your mind to drift. Now place your hands on your stomach. imagine as you breathe, that you have a balloon inside of your tummy. As you inhale, the balloon in your tummy grows round and full; as you exhale, the balloon in your tummy lets the air out and gets floppy. Do this five times or until you feel you have a rhythm with your breathing and you can feel your tummy going up and down as you breathe. Blow and release air in and out of your "balloon" for five breaths.

Inside of your body, you have a place where you like to store your daily stress and worries. **You are being asked to notice just the tension or stress that comes from what you have experienced today. You are not being asked to explore big, deep, private worries**. As you breathe, notice where today's worries might be hiding. You may notice tightness in certain muscles, or butterflies in your stomach or even a slight ache somewhere in your body. Ask yourself, "If I was to draw the stress I feel in my body, what would it look like?" What colors and shapes represent the stress and worry you feel in your body today? Do you see bright squiggles? Do you see grey clouds? Do you see bold lightning bolts? [Pause for several seconds and let the girls ponder the questions.]

Take a moment and draw the worries and stress you sense in your body in the most creative way you can. [Pause. Give the girls time to imagine and draw.] You need a place to "dump" today's worries so they do not pile up, making your body feel weighed down and "stressed out."

Imagine that you have a trash can for these worries so you aren't "dumping" them in your body? Some of you may be able to visualize a trash can very clearly; for some of you, this trash may look a little fuzzy. That's okay. Everyone will have a different experience. Your trash can may look just like the one that is in your kitchen. Others of you will have a trash can that is different from anything you have ever seen. Your trash can might be very tall or very short. It may be square, or it may be round." Ask yourself, "How big does my trash need to be right now to hold all the worries or stress I have today?" The size of trash can you need to dump your worries may vary from day to day.

Draw the trash can that your creative mind created for you. Draw it big enough to hold today's worries. [Pause while the girls draw their trash cans.]

At any time, if you start to feel nervous about your stress and worries, simply move your attention back to your breathing. Breathe slow, warm breaths into your body. Imagine that you are blowing warm rays of sunshine onto your fears and worries with each breath. Breathe 1, 2, 3, 4, 5. [Speak slowly.]

Illustrate how your trash can becomes filled up with today's worries. [Pause as the girls draw.] When your drawing shows all your worries stuffed into your trash can, draw a big helium balloon onto the lid of your can.

The helium balloon can be as big as it needs to be to carry your trash up, up, and away. Some of you will have a huge helium balloon depending on how many worries you have today; others will have a medium balloon, or even smaller.

Now draw your trash can being carried by the helium balloon into the sky. You can use several sheets of paper if you like. Draw the trash can in different stages, as it gets higher and higher, smaller and smaller. Finally, draw your trash can so small that you can scarcely see it at all. Draw a tiny speck that floats completely out of sight into the clouds. Take a moment and look at your drawings. Ponder the experience you had as you drew. Take a deep breath and blow it out, releasing any last bit of your body's tension. Whoosh!

Stretch out your arms and legs. Wiggle your fingers and toes. How does your body feel, now that you have taken out the trash? Thank your body for giving you this wonderful, creative experience. Feel a smile come from your body as it says, "You're welcome!"

5. Ask the girls to share what they felt or drew during the *Don't Dump on Your Body Activity*. Use the following questions to guide your discussion.

    Question 1: What kinds of sensations did you feel when you thought of today's worries?

    Question 2.What did your worries look like?

    Question 3: How full was your trash can when you dumped your worries?

    Question 4: How does your body feel now that you took out the trash?

    Question 5: What surprises did you have during this experience?

    Question 8: Do you have a stronger feeling that you will be okay, in spite of your problems?

6. Read Handout 64 together. Tell the girls that they can repeat this exercise on their own to help them manage stress and worries. As they become aware of the stress in their bodies, they can ask themselves the three questions from the handout:

    Question 1: **What are you aware of?** (How full is your trash can? Are you overflowing with stress and worries?)

    Question 2: **What do you want?** (Instead of junk food, what are you really longing for? What do you need right now, in the moment?)

    Question 3: **What can you do to care for yourself in a healthy way?**

    Brainstorm with the girls to help them answer Question 3. Handout 64 suggests *several Healthy Transitions for Girls* handouts for self-care. (This is not a comprehensive list.) *You may follow up this activity by teaching or reviewing one or two of the following:*

    - Be Your Own "Cheerleader" (Handout 7, Chapter 2).
    - *Palace of Possibilities Affirmations* (Handout 8, Chapter 2).
    - "The Butterfly Hug Self Soothing Technique" (Handout 42, Chapter 9).
    - EFT Tapping Steps (Handout 43, Chapter 9).
    - "Blowing Balloons" Relaxation Activity (Activity 28, Chapter 9).
    - *What to Do When I'm Blue Card File* (Handouts 44 and 45, Chapter 9).
    - *Healthy Transitions for Girls Healthy Snacks* (Handout 62, Chapter 11).

Activity 43
I Am Thankful for All My Body Does for Me Activity

(Time = 45 minutes)

Objectives for Each Girl.

1. I can recognize the amazing things my body does each day.
2. I can develop gratitude for my body's physical capacities.

Materials Needed.

1. Handout 65, *I Am Thankful for All My Body Does for Me.*
2. Handout 66, *My Body is a Miraculous Creation.*
3. National Geographic *Incredible Human Machine* DVD.[51]
4. A small snack, such as a graham cracker or carrot sticks.
5. A heavy object that the girls can pick up with a moderate effort, such as a pile of books, a cement brick, or a gallon of milk.
6. Pencils and paper.

Activity Steps.

1. Ask each girl to name everything her body has done for her since she woke up this morning. After all the girls have finished their lists, tell them you are going to show them a movie that documents the things their bodies do for them first thing in the morning.
2. Play the introduction to the National Geographic *Incredible Human Machine* DVD, the **first 2:42 minutes.**[52] The introduction to the video does an excellent job portraying the miracle of the human body and its function. The photography is mesmerizing.
3. After showing the introduction, ask the girls if they can once again comprehend what their bodies did for them since they woke up this morning.
4. Next, give the girls a snack. As they eat, ask them to list all the things their bodies do to help them enjoy the snack and bring nutrition to their bodies.
5. Show Scene #10 of the DVD, "Feed the Machine." After they have watched this scene, ask them if they are amazed at everything their bodies do to eat and digest food. Ask them if they think what they eat makes a difference in how the body does its job.
6. Put the heavy objects(s) on the floor. Give each girl a chance to pick up the object.

---

[51] Selected scenes are suggested since this video is almost an hour long; also, some scenes present partial nudity that may be embarrassing and inappropriate for younger girls.

[52] The menu of the DVD allows for scene selection and also has a photo gallery. Scenes I typically show are #10 "Feeding the Machine," and Scene #11 "Pushing Limits." The photo gallery has informative and inspirational captions that showcase interesting facts and features of the human body.

7. Show Scene #11 of the DVD, "Pushing Limits." (You may want to stop the DVD before the segment that shows a man receiving surgery to repair the nerves in his arm. It is instructive, but may be a little graphic for some girls since it does show blood. I would let the girls at least have a chance to turn away if watching blood disturbs them. It is hard to inspire them if they are feeling anxious.)

8. Ask the girls if they can now understand more of what the body has to do just to pick up a simple object. Ask them to consider what their bodies must do to help them participate in sports. Using Handout 65, have each girl fill out the list of things her body has done for her today, reviewing some of the things she saw on the DVD.

9. Ask, "Do you have a greater appreciation for all that your body does for you? Do you think it is time to say 'thank you' to your body?"

10. Lead the girls in the "Body Appreciation Exercise."

Body Appreciation Exercise

1) Have each girl find a partner. If you are a parent doing this activity with your child, you can be each other's partner. Each girl needs to be in a chair facing her partner. Explain that each girl will have an opportunity to talk to her body. The partner is going to play the role of "My Body."

2) Tell the girls this may feel funny at first, but to be the best "actresses" they can. Tell them you expect them not to be silly, but to take the exercise seriously and really focus. If they do this, they will be surprised how much they will learn.

3) Tell them to look at their partner sitting in the chair across from them and pretend that they are looking at their own body. Tell them to think about the **muscles, nerves, brain signals,** and **cells** that are constantly at work. Tell them to think of the miraculous things they saw in the movie. Remind them to think of activities they love to do with the help of their bodies. As they think of these things, they are to verbally express their appreciation to "My Body" (the partner seated across from them.) Take a few minutes and give each girl a chance to talk to "My Body."

4) Next, ask the girls how they have been treating their bodies lately. Have they been giving them enough sleep? Have they been giving them the right kind of fuel (food)? Have they been complaining about them or criticizing them? Tell them it is time to apologize to their bodies for not being better caretakers. Tell them as part of this apology, they need to tell their bodies what they will do differently to be better caretakers. Encourage them to be very specific.

11. After the girls have completed the "Body Appreciation Exercise," read Handout 66 together. Tell each girl these are ways to show her body that she is grateful for the big job it does for her. Invite the girls to sign the pledge at the bottom of the handout. Tell them that whenever they start to be critical of their bodies, they can look at this pledge and remember that their bodies are miraculous!

Chapter 12

Curriculum and Workshop Planning

Planning a series of workshops can be daunting, but the helps in this chapter make it easy to feel like a pro. This chapter provides detailed workshop plans using the activities in Chapters 1-11 for a 12-week workshop series comprised of weekly, 60-minute sessions; and a 3-week summer or after-school workshop series comprised of bi-weekly, two hour sessions. It also offers essential tips in maximizing the success of your *Healthy Transitions for Girls* groups.

Utilize These Strategies to Create Emotionally Safe and Dynamic Groups

At an age when girls are pressured to compete with each other, *Healthy Transitions for Girls* groups offer a supportive way to resolve growing-up worries. Girls have wonderful bonding experiences in *Healthy Transitions for Girls* groups and are often sad for them to end. In my experience, it is best to limit groups to 6 to 8 girls who are near the same age and at the same maturity level. When possible, I prefer heterogeneous groups that mix girls who are at risk with girls who appear to be more adjusted, rather than a group of all at-risk girls. Encourage mentoring and modeling in your groups to break down some of the barriers that exist between peer groups or cliques. At the same time, protect girls who are inexperienced and innocent from girls who have been participated in risky behaviors, such as sexual experimentation and alcohol and drug use.

Because the maturity and experience level of girls varies, even within same age groups, you will need to choose and adapt the activities to best fit the experience of the girls you are working with. For example, most eight-year-olds have not started to think about being romantically affectionate with boys, so **Activity 23, Heart Healthy Relationships Activity (Chapter 7)** would not be appropriate; however, since helping eight-year-old girls develop communication skills and appropriate boundaries is very appropriate, you may choose **Activity 20, "Conversation and Diplomacy Rules" Role Play Activity (Chapter 7)**. On the other hand, in some groups, girls may already be experimenting with sexual behaviors as young as ten; therefore, **Activity 23** would be an essential activity to present. Look for the suggestions on choosing age-appropriate activities in the workshop plans provided in this chapter.

As explained in **Figure 3, Healthy Transitions for Girls Consent Form,** *Healthy Transitions for Girls* is a skills group, not a therapy group. A group experience may not be advisable for vulnerable girls who have a history of mental illness or trauma. The **Parent Consent Form (Figure 3)** asks parents to disclose to the facilitator if there are mental health concerns or self-harm behaviors affecting their daughters. Although *Healthy Transitions for Girls* can be an excellent adjunct to therapy, it is not a replacement for therapy. The **Parent Consent Form** advises that girls who have a therapist need to consult with their therapist before participating. Finally, girls who have severe acting out behaviors or constant attention-seeking behaviors may not be a fit for a group experience.

Although the completed **Parent Consent Form** and a discussion with the parents can assist in assigning girls to a particular group, prescreening of girls *for Healthy Transitions for Girls* groups is recommended. Preferably, prescreening includes a brief interview process. Interview questions that can be included are:

- Why do you want to be in the group?
- What do you want to experience in the group?
- Do you have any questions about what it is like to be in the group?
- Is there anyone who causes you to feel unsafe that might be in the group?
- Have you been in girls' groups before? What kinds of behaviors made those groups work or not work?
- Are you committed to come to every group and to do the assigned homework? (Explain that is fun and engaging homework, not like academic homework.)

It is <u>essential</u> that each prescreening interview include a discussion on appropriate disclosure. If you do not conduct prescreening interviews, make sure this is addressed as part of creating group rules in **Activity 46, Format for a First Workshop Session**. Girls are not to discuss sexual experiences or sexually explicit media, use profanity, or boast about anti-social behaviors, such as bullying, vandalism, cheating, truancy, etc. If an inappropriate disclosure or discussion does occur between girls in the group, you must inform parents immediately. This is essential to protect you and the girls from harm and to preserve the trust of the parents.

Every member of the group has to be committed to a positive experience for the group to be safe and beneficial, so enlisting a commitment from each participant as part of prescreening is encouraged. *Healthy Transitions for Girls* groups are <u>closed groups</u>, meaning that once the group starts, new participants are not allowed. This helps to create the bond that is necessary for girls to feel safe and to grow through shared activity. If girls commit to participate but have sporadic attendance or leave in the middle of the workshop series, this changes the dynamics of the group and can create a sense of loss for the girls who remain. The idea is not to force girls to attend but to help build a sense of loyalty to the others in the group who will potentially become close friends.

Healthy Transitions for Girls Workshops can serve as a screening tool to help you identify girls who need professional help but are not currently receiving help. For example, in one of my groups, a girl made subtle statements that indicated an unusually high level of sexual knowledge for a 5th grade girl. I worked to build rapport with her during group activities, and then I arranged for some one-on-one time with her. During our one-on-one discussions, she made statements that caused me to suspect she had been sexually abused by a family member. I was able to refer her case to the appropriate authorities and work to get needed intervention. Anytime you suspect that a girl might be a danger to herself or others, bring your concerns to the parents. Be very careful not to take on situations that are beyond your training and competency.

Leadership Skills That Will Make Your Job Easier

Successfully facilitating a group of adolescent girls requires special skills, which are outlined by Jacobs, Masson, and Harvill (2006): (1) take charge, (2) use structure, and (3) make it interesting (p. 401). I have made every attempt in these workshop plans to help you accomplish these goals. Know that if you are ill-prepared or do not show assertiveness as a leader, the girls will likely steer the group from its intended focus. So, make sure you are well-prepared and know the concepts you are sharing. Be ready to deal with the girl who tries to dominate the group with her sharing and the girl who barely says a word. Be enthusiastic in your approach; your enthusiasm is contagious!

Most important, build rapport and trust with the girls. This requires you to be genuine in your approach and to respect the confidences they share. They don't need you to try to be one of their peers, nor do they need you to take a "I know it all and you don't know anything" stance. Girls will respond as you reflect accurate understanding of their dilemmas while at the same time providing genuine leadership. Pay attention to whether or not you are connecting with them. Be flexible. If something isn't working, try another approach. If you discover that a certain problem is at the forefront of the girls' minds, and there is an opportunity for a "teaching moment," then pick one of the exercises in Chapter 9, Coping Skills and Problem-Solving Skills, and help the girls work through some problem-solving steps.

One final suggestion involves financial payment. In groups where parents are paying for their daughters to participate, arrange for money to be collected at parent meetings or any time other than class time and on teaching days. Accepting a payment in an envelope is okay, but generally, you will be much too busy with the girls to be worrying about financial matters. A payment plan that works well is to require that 50 percent of the cost is paid before the classes start, and the remainder is paid by the half-way point of the workshop series. As explained in **Figure 3, *Healthy Transitions for Girls Consent Form,*** refunds will not be given after the third session. This helps sustain commitment from parents and girls and saves you from getting entangled in refunds and disputes for girls who miss sessions.

How Chapter 12 Activities Set You Up for Success

Activity 44, *Initial Planning Format* explains the basics of planning successful workshops. **Activity 48, *Basic Workshop Format,*** provides a generic outline that can be used to construct additional workshop sessions using the activities in Chapters 1-11. The workshop plans provided typically include more material than you can actually cover. Using the basic workshop format provided, you can add a second workshop series as a follow-up to your initial group to complete activities not covered in the first workshop series. There are more than enough activities in Chapters 1-11 for an additional series of workshops.

I always initiate a *Healthy Transitions for Girls* Workshop Series with **Activity 45, *Parent Workshop Activity*.** This 90-minute introductory workshop orients parents and invites their support and participation, a vital factor in developing positive body image. A sample promotional flyer is provided as **Figure 1** to assist schools and agencies in advertising this introductory workshop. In the ***Parent Workshop Activity,*** parents have an opportunity to increase understanding of adolescent development, enhance communication skills, view the curriculum, and give consent for girls to participate. Since parents, not girls, must consent for participation, making sure the parents understand what is being taught is an important ethical safeguard.

Additional parent workshops can be used to elicit parent support throughout the workshop series. I suggest that you meet with parents after the first six sessions to discuss their feelings about their daughters' progress, hear concerns, and reinforce the principles being discussed. An excellent activity to do with the mothers/mentors during a mid-series parent workshop would be **Handout 3, *Who's Been Writing on My Walls?* (Chapter 2).** This activity will help mothers/mentors connect to their own formative experiences and examine the beliefs and self-talk that may be negatively influencing the girls they love.

Specific plans are provided in **Activity 46, *Format for a First Workshop,*** which includes **Activity 47, *One Body Activity*.** This activity helps the girls to express their individuality and to form unity as a group. I love how the synergy of the girls in the group makes each group unique. Since every *Healthy Transitions* group is unique, you will find continual satisfaction and discovery as you help girls to build strengths through the transition of puberty.

List of Activities, Handouts, & Figures Used in Chapter 12

Chapter 12: Curriculum and Workshop Planning

List of Activities.

The workshop plans in this chapter use all activities in Chapter 1-11 and the following activities from Chapter 12.

List of Handouts.

The workshop plans in this chapter use all handouts from Chapters 1-11.

List of Figures.

Activity 44
Initial Planning Steps
Organizing a *Healthy Transitions for Girls* Workshop

Planning.

1. **Meeting Times.** If you decide not to use the 12-week or 3-week curriculum plans offered in this chapter, decide how many workshop sessions you want to have and how long each session will be, such as "10 weeks for 90 minutes each week" or "7 weeks, bi-weekly, for 2 hours," or "15 weeks for 60 minutes each week." Even if you decide to use the 12-week or 3-week curriculum plans provided in this chapter, you can easily add additional sessions to these plans. You can also organize a school-based program, such as a series of lunchtime workshops or after-school workshops.

2. **Planning for Essential Concepts.** Be sure that you plan for enough workshops to thoroughly cover the essential factors needed to promote positive body image that are discussed in Chapter 1. An effective body image program must build strengths in each of these essential areas:

   - Reframes negative belief systems and creates positive belief systems.
   - Supports the mind body connection and a holistic view of wellness.
   - Supports strong parent and peer relationships.
   - Teaches media literacy and critical thinking.
   - Encourages healthy concepts of femininity and challenges stereotypes (gender role).
   - Teaches coping skills.
   - Supports global and physical self-esteem.

Preparation.

1. **Materials Needed.** Once you decide which activities you want to include in your workshops, make a list of materials needed. **Figure 5, Comprehensive Materials List,** suggests materials you need for the entire workshop series. Give yourself plenty of time to order necessary DVDs and books. I highly recommend that you obtain a model castle and a Palace of Possibilities Display Board.[53] You need to have tangible learning materials when working with younger girls. Additionally, a materials list is provided at the beginning of each activity.

2. ***Healthy Transitions for Girls* Handouts.** Once you know how many girls will attend the workshop, make sure that you obtain a copy of the ***Healthy Transitions for Girls Handout Pages Workbook*** for each girl. These can be ordered from www.amazon.com.

3. **Other Resources.** In addition to the materials provided in the *Healthy Transitions for Girls* curriculum, you can also supplement your curriculum with activities from other resources, such as *104 Activities That Build: Self-Esteem, Teamwork, Communication, Anger Management, Self-Discovery, Coping Skills* by Alanna Jones. *Healthy Transitions for Girls* integrates well with other prevention programs, such as bullying prevention and substance abuse prevention.

---

[53] I provide instructions for obtaining these resources in Chapter 2, Figure 1, and Figure 5.

Setting.

1. **Privacy.** You need to have a room people cannot walk through and disturb the meetings or sit and stare at the girls. Due to the personal nature of the concepts taught, the quality of your meetings will be hindered if you do not have a private setting.

2. **Space.** It is best if you have enough space where the girls can sit on the floor in a circle as well as work at tables. One success secret is that girls' attention spans are typically limited to about 20 - 30 minutes. I keep their interest piqued by moving back and forth between a sitting on a quilt on the floor and working at the table. Attention-grabbing shifts like these are critical when you are conducting two-hour workshops.

3. **Food Prep Area.** Make sure you have a space where the girls have a table for cutting fruit for snacks and a place to plug in a blender to make "Hulk Smoothies."

Promotional Materials and Letters of Consent.

1. **Involve Parents.** Every workshop series should begin with **Activity 45, Parent Workshop Activity**. While much of the material in this curriculum is directed at girls and women, fathers can have an incredible impact on their daughters' body image. Consider the impact of a father who assures his daughter that she is beautiful without trying to wear sexualized clothing, who helps her select modest clothing, and who helps her to establish healthy dating boundaries. In your planning, decide whether you want to promote your parent workshop as a mother-daughter activity or whether fathers should be included too. **Chapter 5** lists specific activities and handouts that require parent collaboration. **Figure 2, Promotional Parent Flyer,** can be filled in and photo copied to advertise your parent workshop. Then at the parent workshop, you can have the parents review curriculum materials and sign a consent form. A sample consent form is provided as **Figure 3**; however, please make sure that you have covered necessary legalities required by your institution. This form is only a sample template.

2. **Summarize Learning.** Additionally, a sample workshop evaluation is included in **Figure 4**. Using this evaluation is a great way to help girls summarize what they have learned at the end of the workshop and can help you know which areas still need more attention. You can support the ongoing evaluation and development of this curriculum by submitting your evaluation results and suggestions to peggy@healthytransitionsforgirls.com.

Activity 45
Parent Workshop Activity

(Time = 90 minutes)

Objectives for Each Girl.

1. I can increase positive communication with my parents and mentors.
2. My parents and I can recognize the harmful effects of media.
3. My mother and I can improve negative self-talk about our bodies.
4. I can recognize beliefs that support a healthy view of my body.

Materials Needed.

1. Name tags for each parents and girl.
2. A 36-inch piece of yarn for each girl.
3. A yard stick or broom handle.
4. A copy of Handout 16, *What's Happening to My Little Girl?* (Chapter 5) for each parent or mentor.
5. A copy of Handout 18, *Open the Door to Better Talk* (Chapter 5) for each parent or mentor.
6. A copy of Handout 20, *Be a Media Conscious Parent* (Chapter 5) for each parent or mentor.
7. *Killing Us Softly 3* Handouts.[54]
8. A copy of Handout 33, *Media Words You Should Know* (Chapter 8) for each parent or mentor.
9. Palace of Possibilities Display Board. (See directions for making this on Figure 1.
10. A copy of Chapter 2, Handout 8, *Palace of Possibilities Affirmations* for each parent or mentor.
11. Chapter 9, Activity 33, *Make an Energy Circle Activity* (optional).
12. Figure 3. *Parent Consent Form.*
13. Essential oil mister spray (optional).
14. Pens or pencils for each girl.
15. Make posters that display healthy behaviors and display them in the room. (Optional).

Activity Steps.

Part I: Introduction to the Problem of Body Image (15- 20 min.)

1. Ask the following questions. List the answers on a chalkboard or poster board. As parents respond, put tally marks next to answers that are given by multiple parents, such as: dieting III low self-esteem II moodiness III

---

[54] These can be obtained free on the Internet from the Media Education Foundation (MEF). To download this free resource, go to www.mediaed.org. Click on "Materials & Resources." Then, click "Handouts & Articles." Scroll down the page. Under "Handouts," you will see the "Killing Us Softly 3 Study Guide Handouts." Click on the link to download the .pdf file. Print off the pictures provided in this packet to use with this activity. The web address for the handouts at the time of this printing: http://www.mediaed.org/assets/products/206/studyguidehandout_206.pdf

- *What brought you here?*
- *What concerns do you have?*
- *What experiences have you had that have made you feel concern for the pressures girls are facing today?*

2. Use Handout 16. Use this handout to confirm parent's concerns and to explain the normal challenges their girls face. Explain that this workshop will provide information that will confirm their concerns, enhance their understanding of the problems they see, and offer suggestions they can use at home and in the community to support the girls they love.

3. Do the "Double Bind Object Lesson." Give each girl a piece of yarn and tie it in a big circle. They are to put the circle on the floor and then stand in the circle. The leader displays the yardstick or broomstick and tells the girls that if they stay in the circle, she is going to hit them with a stick. The leader then tells them that if they get out of the circle, she is going to hit them with a stick. Of course, the girls soon realize that no matter what they choose, they are going to get hit with a stick. Explain that the media and cultural messages of today put girls in a double bind. Even though it is normal for them to put on between 30-50 pounds during puberty, they are made to feel that if they gain any weight they are "fat." The next part of the presentation will deal directly with specific media messages.

Part II: Media and Cultural Messages (20-25 min.)

1. Define MEDIA: MEDIA IS COMMUNICATING. Media includes movies, TV, social media images, all forms of advertising, music, music videos, billboards, and magazines.

2. Tell parents and mentors, "We want to help you to fully understand how the media is putting images in your daughter's brain. The most powerful form of media is music videos that engage emotions through music and plant images and beliefs into the mind. It is a form of brainwashing. Research has shown that the more a girl or woman views popular media, the more she is at risk for eating disorders, risky sexual behaviors, and other behaviors that lead to unhappiness."

3. Using Handout 33, write the following words on the chalkboard or on a poster board: *objectification, dismemberment, thinness, isolation, sexualization, victimization, unrealistic perfection.* Follow the directions for Step 4 in Chapter 8, **Activity 25, *Media Detectives Activity,*** using the advertising photos from *the Killing Me Softly* Study Guide. As you present the definitions for the words on Handout 33, have the girls write the definitions on their copy of Handout 33.

4. Summarize the activity with this important statement: "Advertisers and media gurus knowingly encourage harmful behaviors to sell products. Corporate marketing giants seek out the 'edgiest' kids they can find and flash these images again and again to create new definitions of what is 'cool.' They don't look for trendsetters who are positive role models but look instead for charismatic deviants who erode moral and social norms. The astounding intent of pop culture media is to fuel impulsive behaviors and create emotional distress in teens. They want to exploit and create greater levels of *need*, especially in the areas of base, innate human desires, such as sexual gratification. A distressed teen without moral and social restraints will buy, buy, and buy to satisfy her unmet needs.

5. Use Handout 20. Read the quote by Mary Pipher, PhD at the top of the page. Invite the parents and mentors to protect their daughter from the harmful messages of the media culture after reading the *WHAT YOU CAN DO* section together as a group.

Part III. Building Strengths (30 min.)

1. Tell parents and mentors, "If we can help a girl to develop positive body image, we can help her resist eating disorders, depression, substance abuse, risky sexual behaviors, girl bullying, and unhealthy dating relationships." Explain that there are several important strengths shown by research to help a girl to create a positive body image. Say, "When some of these strengths are not developed, girls have a more difficult time resisting the negative messages of the media and developing a positive attitude about herself and her body. In some studies, as many as 80 percent of 4th grade girls were dissatisfied with their bodies. Addressing body image is critical in today's culture!"
2. Explain that research has shown that one of the most important factors is for girls to have supportive parent/grandparent/mentor relationships.
3. State, "We want you to know that you are important in your child's life. Even though this is a time when she is learning to be more independent, she craves your support and encouragement. The generation gap is a creation of the media. One research project that surveyed girls living in Denver, CO showed that the top wish of girls is for their parents to communicate better with them" (Dove, 2008).
4. Explain the life stage task of adolescence. Tell parents and mentors, "Since the psychological task of adolescent girls is become more independent and prepare for adulthood, it may seem that they don't value our opinions anymore. It is important for them to begin to feel that we value their opinions; at the same time, we must set important limits that they may not understand. The media tries to erode girls' self control; parent structure is needed to combat this. Girls with structure at home have better self-esteem, even if they resist that structure. Building communication can help girls and their parents and mentors improve relationships during this challenging phase."
5. Use Handout 18. Say, "This handout teaches active listening, a tool that supports girls by building trust, helping them feel you understand them. Sometimes, they just want to be understood and figure out the problem on their own. Sometimes, by active listening, you can open the door so girls will tell you things that are important for you to know."
6. Perform an "active listening" role-play. Have girls first pretend that they are the parent. The parent (or mentor or grandparent) will play the role of the daughter. The "daughter" is to think of a scenario or problem that she can bring to her "parent." The "parent" is to use the "door openers" listed on the handout to respond to what the "daughter" says. Reverse the roles. Continue to use the "door openers" listed on the handout. After both adults and girls have had a chance to role-play, open up the discussion. Ask if using "door openers" made a difference in the dialogue. Ask, "What did you experience in this role-play?" "Is there a particular door slammer that you want to change?"
7. Another important strength girls learn in *Healthy Transitions for Girls* is to develop positive beliefs about their body. Ask, "Girls, what kind of things do you say to yourself in front of the mirror?" Let the girls share these self-statements.

8. Using the Palace of Possibilities Display Board you made from the directions in Figure 1, first read aloud the beliefs on the board that create negative body image. These are the kinds of beliefs girls say in front of the mirror. Explain that negative self-talk is emotionally harmful. Contrast these negative statements with the positive statements that are written on the *Palace of Possibilities* display board.

9. Emphasize to the mothers, grandmothers, and mentors who are assisting the girls that their own self-talk is critical to their own daughter's body image. Invite them to team with the girls they love and establish a new family rule to eliminate negative body talk from their dialogue.

10. (Optional). Do **Activity 33, *Make an Energy Circle,*** from Chapter 9. You can use the yarn used in the "Double Bind Activity" for this activity. Check to make sure parents are okay with the use of essential oils in this activity.

Part IV. Conclusion: What Can Parents Do? (10-15 min.)

1. Recap the concerns parents listed at the beginning of the class. Summarize how these questions were addressed during the presentation. Explain that girls will have homework to share with their parents as part of their *Healthy Transitions for Girls Workshops*. This homework will give the parents opportunities to build strengths with their daughters and address areas of concern.

2. Ask the parents to commit to being a partner with the girl they love as she participates in the *Healthy Transitions for Girls Workshops*. Invite them to review the curriculum and sign Figure 3, *Parent Consent Form*, if a workshop series for girls is being offered.

Activity 46
Format for a First Workshop Session

(Time = 55 – 60 minutes)

Explanation.

The first meeting is an important time to begin building rapport between the facilitator and the girls. As a facilitator, your goal is to create a "safe space" where the girls can come and share their experiences and concerns. With the right kind of meeting structure, the girls have the opportunity to develop support and trust, even if they do not "hang out" with each other outside the group.

Materials Needed.

1. A large poster board for writing group rules.
2. A long piece of butcher paper or newsprint (approximately 5 ft long), for the icebreaker activity described in Activity 47.
3. Colored markers or crayons.
4. Tape.
5. Chapter 2, Handout 1, *My Body is Changing*.

First Meeting Steps.

1. **Establish group rules.** (10 min.) Ask, "What rules do we need to help you feel safe and valued in this group?" Write down the rules the girls agree upon—usually four or five rules. Make sure one of the rules involves appropriate/inappropriate sharing. Girls are not to use profanity, discuss sexual experimentation or sexually explicit movies, reveal self-harm behaviors, or brag about anti-social behaviors, such as, bullying, vandalism, cheating, truancy, etc. Have the girls each sign their name at the bottom of the rule page. Keep the rules posted in a visible place at every workshop. Refer to these rules any time the girls need a reminder during upcoming sessions. At this juncture, I also explain that while the rules of the group are not negotiable, the activities in the group are voluntary. That means if there is an activity that makes a girl feel uncomfortable, she can politely indicate that she prefers not to participate. It puts girls at ease knowing they have the freedom to opt out of an activity if is too challenging or embarrassing for them.
2. **Use an ice breaker activity.** (25-30 min.) See Chapter 12, Activity 47, *One Body Activity*.
3. **Follow the directions for Chapter 2, Activity1, *My Changing Body Activity*.** (15-20 minutes). If you are short on time, omit Steps 4 and 5.
4. **Check out.** (5 min.) As a final reinforcement of the things discussed in the group, give each girl an opportunity to summarize her experience. Ask girls to share if they had worries coming in to the group and if they feel differently after the first group meeting. Remember, first impressions are important. Even though I may not be able to remember each girl's name until after the second workshop, I still try to make a connection with each girl by sharing something we have in common or by praising a unique trait that she has as the meeting concludes.

Activity 47
One Body Activity[55]

(Time = 25-30 Minutes)

Objectives for Each Girl.

1. I can recognize my contribution and importance to the group.
2. I can recognize common traits I share with other girls.

Materials Needed.

1. A long piece of butcher paper or newsprint (approximately 5 ft long).
2. Colored markers or crayons.
3. Tape.

Activity Steps.

1. Tell the girls they are going to draw one big person to represent the mascot of their group. Each girl will be asked to draw a part of the mascot's body, such as arms, legs, face, clothing, and accessories. Girls take turns adding parts to the drawing until it is completely finished. The only rule I give them is that each item they add to the poster must represent something about their own personality or preferences. I advise them that when the poster is done, they will be asked to describe what they drew.
2. Allow 15-20 minutes for the girls to create the poster. When the girls are done with the poster, process the drawing. Each girl shares about what she drew. Then, hang up the poster and evaluate the overall look of the mascot (which is usually quite absurd, but fun). Since the mascot needs a name, take the first letter of each girl's name and organize those letters to create a name for the mascot. For example, if you have Sue, Jen, Pam, Michelle, Ann, and Rachel in the group, you might name your mascot, J-P-A-R-M-S ("J'Parms"). Of course, the mascot's name is nonsensical, but that is part of the fun. I emphasize to the girls that coming together as a group is always the beginning of an original creation; every group is unique.
3. To emphasize the value of each group member and the need for safety in the group, I ask what would happen if we, for example, "lopped off the arm that Pam drew." The girls answer that the body would be missing an important part. I use this object lesson to illustrate that each member is needed, and that when one girl feels she can't be herself in the group because she feels worried about the ridicule of others, then the whole group is missing an important part.

---

[55] This activity is adapted from the activity, "One Body," from 104 Activities That Build : Self-Esteem, Teamwork, Communication, Anger Management, Self-Discovery, Coping Skills by Alanna Jones. This excellent book is available at www.amazon.com.

Activity 48
Basic Workshop Format

This is the basic format for creating a successful 60 to 90 minute workshop session. This format can be used to assist in creating additional workshops using the Activities in Chapters 2 through 11.

Basic Workshop Steps.

1. **Check-in.** (5-10 min.) Check-in is a time to re-connect with each girl and build rapport. Ask the girls if any issues have arisen that need to be addressed, such as confidentiality, "girl drama" issues that might impact the group, or "burning" issues that need to be discussed before girls can move on to other activities. The check in is also the time where you have girls report on homework assigned at the previous session. A final suggestion for check-in time is to spend a few minutes doing a "mindfulness" exercise each week. This can be as simple as asking girls to tune in to their breathing and send their breath more deeply into their abdomen, or doing a "Butterfly Hug" (Chapter 9, Handout 42), or *A Simple Mindfulness and Acceptance Activity* (Chapter 3, Activity 9).

2. **Use *Healthy Transitions for Girls* concepts and activities.** (35-45 minutes for a 60-minute workshop; 60-75 minutes for a 90-minute workshop.) As you discuss what is on girls' minds during check-in, direct their thoughts to the concepts you will cover in the activities that has been chosen for this week's session.

3. **Check-out and assign homework.** (5-10 min.) Before girls leave, make sure they have 1) a homework assignment that will be reported at the next workshop; and 2) an opportunity to share their "take-away," or what they learned, from that day's workshop session. Some examples of "take-away" questions appear below.

   - In what way do you feel stronger after today's activities?
   - What will you do differently after today's workshop?
   - What do you want to practice after today's workshop?

Activity 49
12-Week Workshop Plan with 60-Minute Weekly Sessions

Week 1: Use Activity 46, *Format for a First Workshop Session*[56]

Week 2: I Am a Palace of Possibilities: Building Positive Belief Systems

Materials Needed.

1. Palace of Possibilities Display Board (Chapter 2, Figure 1).
2. Palace model (as described in Chapter 2).
3. Scrapbook paper (optional).
4. Post-It notes and pencils.
5. Paper and drawing materials for each girl (if using Activity 2 as an art activity).
6. Make a photocopy of Chapter 2, Handout 8, *Palace of Possibilities Affirmations for each girl.*

Preparation.

Prepare to present Activity 1, *My Body is Changing*, Activity 2, *Palace of Possibilities Guided Imagery (or Art) Activity*, and Activity 3, *My Changing Beliefs Activity* (Chapter 2).

Activity Steps.

1. **Check in.** (15 min.) Review the group rules and *One Body* poster that were made in the first workshop. Focus the girls on their changing bodies with the "My Body is Changing Pretest" (Step 1, Activity 1, *My Body is Changing,* Activity) if you did not have time for this activity in the first workshop session. Review the girls' answers and present information to challenge existing myths (Steps 2 and 3). If you were able to complete these steps in the first workshop session, complete Step 5, from Activity 1, *My Body is Changing* Activity.

2. **Teach concepts and activities.** (30 -35 min.) Present Chapter 2, Activity 2, *Palace of Possibilities Guided Imagery (or Art) Activity.* Follow-up with Chapter 2, Activity 3, *My Changing Beliefs Activity.*

3. **Check out.** (5-10 min.) Pass out a photocopy of Handout 8, *Palace of Possibilities Affirmations.* Follow the directions for Steps 1 and 2 on the handout. Ask the girls to hang these affirmations near their mirror and repeat Steps 1 and 2 as they stand in front of the mirror each morning. Ask them to promise to avoid critical self-talk in front of the mirror and to invite their mothers or grandmothers to take this challenge with them. They will report on their experience next week.

Optional or Additional Activities.

An optional follow-up activity to Activity 2, *Palace of Possibilities Guided Imagery (or Art) Activity* is Activity 4, *My Palace of Possibilities Body Drawing Activity* (Chapter 2).

---

[56] Start Week 1 after you have done Activity 44, *Parent Workshop Activity.*

Week 3: More Help with Positive Self-Talk

Materials Needed.

1. A full length mirror (at least one, but two is preferable).
2. A black hat and cape.
3. A tiara and wand.
4. Chapter 2, Handout 4, *Mirror, Mirror Activity Part 1*.
5. Chapter 2, Handout 5, *Mirror, Mirror Activity Part 2*.
6. Pencils or pens.
7. Chapter 9, Handout 42, *The Butterfly Hug Self-Soothing Technique*.
8. Chapter 2, Handout 3, *Who's Been Writing on My Walls?*
9. A photocopy of Chapter 2, Handout 8, *Palace of Possibilities Affirmations* for each girl.

Preparation.

Prepare to present Activity 6, *Mirror, Mirror Activity*.

Activity Steps.

1. **Check in.** (10 min.) Briefly review the homework from the previous session, Handout 8, *Palace of Possibilities Affirmations*. (You will have more time to review this individually later.) Ask the girls if they noticed any changes in their mood as they used positive affirmations in the mirror. Explain to the girls that the discoveries they made about their self-talk will help them in this week's activity.
2. **Teach concepts and activities.** (45 min.) Teach the steps from Handout 42, *The Butterfly Hug Self-Soothing Technique. When the girls are proficient with this technique,* follow the directions for Activity 6, *Mirror, Mirror Activity*. While girls are waiting for their turn at the mirror, take time to discuss the Handout 8 homework experience in more depth with each girl. Help them to add some new affirmations to Handout 8, *Palace of Possibilities Affirmations* in the lines provided.
3. **Check out.** (5-7 min.) Remind the girls to use the "Butterfly Hug" anytime they have negative thoughts in front of the mirror. For homework, use Handout 3, *Who's Been Writing on My Walls?* Ask them to complete this handout with their mothers. Tell them the group will discuss their experience with this assignment during the next workshop session.

Optional or Additional Activities.

If you have a group of older girls who are not comfortable dressing up as suggested in *Activity 6, Mirror, Mirror Activity,* you may omit Activity 6 and use Activity 7, *Watch Out for the "Imaginary Other,"* and Activity 8, *Be Your Own Cheerleader Activity* (see Chapter 2). Both of these activities reinforce positive self-talk in the real-life situations that girls face.

Week 4: The Mind Body Connection

Materials Needed.

1. A simple object, such as an orange or raisin for each girl.
2. A photocopy of Chapter 2, Handout 2, Healthy Transitions for Girls *Body Drawing* for each girl.
3. Chapter 3, Handout 9, *My Body Talks*.
4. Chapter 3, Handout 10, *Emotional Body Talk*.
5. Chapter 3, Handout 11, *My Feelings Meter* (optional).
6. Ruler for each girl (optional).
7. Pens or pencils.

Preparation.

Prepare to present Activity 9, *A Simple Mindfulness and Acceptance Activity*, Activity 10, *Body Talk Activity*, and if time, Activity 11, *My Feelings Meter* (Chapter 3.)

Activity Steps.

1. **Check in.** (5-10 min.) Allow the girls to share what they learned as they completed Handout3, *Who's Been Writing on My Walls?* with their mothers. Share that no matter what has been written on their walls, they have the power to "erase" old beliefs and "write" new positive beliefs.
2. **Teach concepts and activities.** (35 - 40 min.) Begin with Activity 9, *A Simple Mindfulness and Acceptance Activity*. Explain the principle of "mindfulness" and how learning to connect the messages that come from their bodies is an important part of learning to be healthy and happy. Complete Activity 10, *Body Talk Activity*. If there is sufficient time, complete Activity 11, *My Feelings Meter*.
3. **Check out.** (5-7 min.) Mindfulness is a skill that can be used every day to support emotional regulation. For homework, pass out a photocopy of Handout 2, Healthy Transitions for Girls *Body Drawing*, and ask the girls to make notes of emotional body signs they notice during the week. Ask them to write where they felt this "body talk" on the handout and return it next week.

Optional or Additional Activities.

Activity 42, *Don't Dump on Your Body*, is an excellent follow-up mindfulness activity from Chapter 11. Chapter 9, Activity 28, *"Blowing Balloons" Relaxation Activity* can be taught and used to help girls increase mindfulness and body awareness and reduce distress.

Week 5: Holistic Wellness

Materials Needed.

1. Chapter 4, Handout 12, *The WHOLE ME: Discovering My WHOLE Self*.
2. Chapter 4, Handout 13, *The WHOLE ME: Blossom into the WHOLE You* (optional).

3. Index cards, 10-15 for each girl.
4. Hole punch.
5. "O" rings or colored ribbon to fasten the cards together.
6. Colored markers or stickers for decorating the cards.
7. Chapter 9, Handout 44, *What to Do When I Am Blue Instructions.*
8. Chapter 9, Handout 45, *What to Do When I Am Blue List.*
9. Pens or pencils.

Preparation.

Prepare to present Activity 30, *What to Do When I'm Blue Card File Activity* (Chapter 9).

Activity Steps.

1. **Check in.** (5-10 min.) Allow the girls to share the "body talk" they wrote on Handout 2, Healthy Transitions for Girls *Body Drawing*, during the week. Tell them that this week, they are going to learn more about themselves and discover that they have many different parts that make up the whole of who they are.
2. **Teach concepts and activities.** (45 min.) Using Handout 12, *The WHOLE ME: Discovering My WHOLE Self,* introduce the concept that while the media emphasizes only physical appearance, the girls have many parts of them that need care. Follow the instructions for Activity 29, *What to Do When I'm Blue Card File Activity.*
3. **Check out.** (5-7 min.) For homework, they can share how they used their card file during the week, or they can complete Handout 13, *The WHOLE ME: Blossom into the WHOLE You,* and share how they are developing goals in all areas of their lives.

Optional or Additional Activities.

You can omit Activity 29, *What to Do When I'm Blue Card File Activity and use it in another workshop session. Fully* complete Activity 12, *The WHOLE Me Activity* (Chapter 4), in class to facilitate a more thorough discussion of holistic wellness.

Week 6: Developing the Spiritual, Intuitive Aspects of Self

Materials Needed.

Chapter 4, Handout 15, *The Wise Place Inside of Me.*

Preparation.

Prepare to present Activity 14, *The Wise Place Inside of Me Activity* (Chapter 4).

Activity Steps.

1. **Check in.** (5-10 min.) Ask the girls to share successes in using the "What to Do When I Am Blue Card File" during the week. If the girls completed Handout 13, *The WHOLE ME: Blossom into the WHOLE You* for homework, ask them to share some of the goals they set.
2. **Teach concepts and activities.** (45 min.) Tell the girls that this week you are going to focus on how caring for their spiritual self is an important part of learning to protect themselves from harmful situations. Follow the instructions for Activity 14, *The Wise Place Inside of Me Activity*.
3. **Check out.** (5 min.) For homework, ask the girls to share what they learned with a parent or mentor. Tell them to ask a parent or mentor about a time when intuition or "gut feelings" helped them know how to make an important decision or avoid an unsafe situation. They will report their discussions the following week.

Optional or Additional Activities.

Activity 31, *My Ecomap Activity*, teaches girls how to discover who they can turn to for help in crisis situations. A follow-up activity to Activity 14, *The Wise Place Inside of Me Activity*, is to invite a law enforcement officer to come to class and teach girls about personal safety skills or provide information about cyberbullying and Internet safety.

Week 7: Building Supportive Girl Connections

Materials Needed.

1. Chapter 6, Handout 21, *Friend or Competition?*
2. Chapter 6, Handout 22, *Don't Be an Identity Thief.*
3. Chapter 6, Handout 23, *My Space, Your Space.*
4. A long piece of yarn, at least 36 inches, for each girl.
5. Pens or pencils.
6. Index cards (8-10 cards for each girl in the group).
7. Envelopes (one for each girl).
8. Paper clips or clothespins.
9. A section of clothesline, thin rope, or heavy string.

Preparation.

Prepare to present Activity 15, *Measure Your Friendship IQ Activity*, Activity 16, *Identity Theft Activity—Taking Steps to End "Girl Drama,"* and Activity 17, *My Space, Your Space Part 1.* (See Chapter 6.)

Activity Steps.

1. **Check in.** (15 min.) Ask girls to share any opportunities they had to use their intuitive "gut feelings" as discussed the previous week. Urge them to continue to honor their intuitive gifts. Introduce this week's concepts by following the instructions for Activity 15, *Measure Your Friendship IQ Activity*.

2. **Teach concepts and activities**. (30 -35 min.) Follow the instructions for Activity 16, *Identity Theft Activity—Taking Steps to End "Girl Drama."* Follow the instructions for Steps 1-4, and 6 in Activity 17, *My Space, Your Space Part 1*.

3. **Check out**. (5-10 min.) Introduce the "Love Lines" Activity found in *104 Activities That Build: Self-Esteem, Teamwork, Communication, Anger Management, Self-Discovery, Coping Skills* by Alanna Jones. The "Love Lines" Activity asks girls to observe positive qualities of the other girls in the group. A "Love Line" (clothesline or heavy yarn) will be hung during the remaining groups. Each girl will have an envelope with her name on it hanging from the line. In the next few weeks, girls will place an index card with a positive compliment written on it into the envelope of each of the other girls in the group. This activity will be a termination activity in Week 12. For homework, tell the girls that you want them to report next week on how resisting gossip reduced "girl drama" with their friends.

Optional or Additional Activities.

An additional session to help girls understand the concept of personal boundaries would be extremely valuable. For an additional session, follow the role-play instructions given in Activity 17, *My Space Your Space*, Steps 3 through 5, from Chapter 6. Then follow the instructions for Activity 18, *My Space, Your Space Part 2*. A follow-up art activity is included in Activity 19, *My Space, Your Space Part 3*.

Week 8: Building Healthy Girl-Boy Friendships

Important Note.

The activities you choose for this session will depend specifically upon the age and maturity of the girls in the group.

Materials Needed.

1. *Cinder Edna*, written by by Ellen Jackson and Kevin O'Malley (for younger girls).
2. *A lunch tray with various sections for food (for younger girls)*.
3. *Lima beans or some other sortable object (for younger girls)*.
4. *Princess Academy, written* by Shannon Hale.
5. *Chapter 7, Handout 28, How to Build Friendships with Guys*.
6. Chapter 7, Handout 30, *Heart Healthy Relationships* (for older girls).
7. Chapter 7, Handout 31 *My Timeline* (for older girls).
8. Chapter 7, Handout 32, *My Timeline Events* (for older girls).
9. Paper and pencils.
10. Scissors and glue sticks (for older girls).

Preparation.

For younger girls, prepare to present Activity 22, Cinder Edna Bibliotherapy Activity. Follow up with Activity 20, *"Conversation and Diplomacy" Rules Role Play Activity*. **For older girls**, prepare to present

Activity 23, *Heart Healthy Relationships Activity* or Activity 24, *Relationship Timeline Activity.* If time, follow up with Activity 20, *"Conversation and Diplomacy" Rules Role Play Activity.*

Activity Steps.

1. **Check in**. (5- 10 min.) Ask the girls if they practiced the skills they learned the previous session in their relationships with other girls. Did they notice a change in "girl drama"? Do they still need help in this area? Tell them that this week, they are going to work on developing healthy friendships with guys. Explain that since much girl drama is related to jealousy over boys, much girl drama could be eliminated if they were willing to challenge the peer pressure for romance and steady dating.
2. **Teach concepts and activities.** (45- 50 min.) Follow the directions for the activities you have chosen based upon age and maturity level. If you feel you will not have enough time to present all the activities suggested, you may choose only to use certain steps from each activity.
3. **Check out.** (5 min.) Encourage the girls to share what they learned with their parents and ask for help in building healthy friendships and resisting romantic relationships. This stage in the workshop series is a good time to have follow-up communication with parents to discuss the concepts being taught and to get feedback. The girls will not be able to set boundaries to resist sexualized romantic relationships without guidelines from parents. Handout 30 can be an excellent resource for parents to guide their daughters.

Optional or Additional Activities.

Girls never seem to get enough of Activity 20, *"Conversation & Diplomacy Rules" Role Play Activity.* You could spend a whole session role-playing the situations they face every day. Handout 26, *Listening: Rules That Work*, and Handout 27, *Speaking Up: Rules that Work* from Chapter 6, can also be used to role play effective communication in difficult situations. Activity 21, *Codependency Versus Healthy Relationships Activity* (Chapter 7), can be used as a follow-up to help older girls recognize the traits of healthy relationships since codependency is consistently modeled in media portrayals of romance.

Week 9: Media Literacy and Critical Thinking

Materials Needed.

1. *Killing Us Softly 3* Handouts.[57]
2. Chapter 8, Handout 33, *Media Words You Should Know*
3. Chapter 8, Handout 34, *Media Mind Games.*
4. Chapter 8, Handout 35, *Be a Media Detective.*
5. Chapter 8, Handout 36, *Media Detective: Case Solving Score Sheet.*
6. Chapter 8, Handout 38, *The Truth about Barbie (optional).*

---

[57] These can be obtained free on the Internet from the Media Education Foundation (MEF). To download this free resource, go to www.mediaed.org. Click on "Materials & Resources." Then, click "Handouts & Articles." Scroll down the page. Under "Handouts," you will see the "Killing Us Softly 3 Study Guide Handouts." Click on the link to download the .pdf file. Print off the pictures provided in this packet to use with this activity. The web address for the handouts at the time of this printing: http://www.mediaed.org/assets/products/206/studyguidehandout_206.pdf

7. Chapter 8, Handout 40, *Let's Celebrate REAL Beauty.*
8. Chapter 8, Handout 41, *REAL Beauty Is … .*
9. Optional Handouts: Handout 37, *Media Detectives: Sleuthing for More Hidden Messages* (Chapter 8), and Handout 46, *My Ecomap* (Chapter 9).
10. Choose at least 10–12 advertisements clipped from magazines that target teen girls and women.
11. Poster paper and markers (for optional workshop follow-up activities).
12. Optional: A good resource to demonstrate how makeup and photo tricks are used to create unrealistic perfection is the Dove Real Beauty Project.[58] The STAR Magazine's "Stars without Makeup" issues also show how stars look in real life when their looks have not been enhanced with makeup and photo tricks. Not only do these pictures show what famous stars really look like without their makeup, but the text also criticizes stars' physical features and why they lost their last boyfriend based upon their physical "flaws." This demonstrates how the media encourages competition between girls that causes isolation.
13. Use a palace model or Palace of Possibilities Display Board as described in Chapter 2. These are tangible tools to show girls how media influences impact their belief systems.

Preparation.

Prepare to present Activity 25, *Media Detectives Activity* (Chapter 8).

Activity Steps.

1. **Check in.** (5-10 min.) Ask the girls whether or not they talked to their parents about family values regarding steady dating and physical affection. If a girl states that she has difficulty talking about these things with her parents, use Handout 46, *My Ecomap*, to identify an adult who can help her to establish goals and boundaries and help her resist romantic relationships. Also, remind the girls to write their "Love Lines" cards about each person before the last workshop session.
2. **Teach concepts and activities.** (40-45 min.) Follow the directions for Activity 25, *Media Detectives Activity.* Part of this activity will be valuable review from the *Parent Workshop.*
3. **Check out.** (10 min.) Use Handout 40, *Let's Celebrate REAL Beauty*, and Handout 41, *REAL Beauty Is …* Ask the girls to complete the "Real Beauty Challenge" this week. They will describe the results of their challenge next week. For another homework option, Use Handout 38, *The Truth about Barbie.* Ask the girls what kind of message this image sends about "real beauty" as they grow up.

Optional or Additional Activities.

Enough ideas are provided in Chapter 7 for several one hour workshops. Additional art and role-play activities are provided at the end of Activity 25. Handout 37, *Media Detective: Sleuthing for More Hidden Messages,* is an excellent follow up to help girls challenge harmful media messages. Activity 26, *My Image Activity* (Chapter 8), is an additional workshop activity that addresses the effect of media icons and peer pressure on self image. Activity 27, *What Is Real Beauty? Activity* (Chapter 8) can be used as a workshop activity instead of homework.

---

[58] See http://www.campaignforrealbeauty.com.au.

Week 10: Gender Role

Materials Needed.

1. Chapter 10, Handout 48, *Designer Checklist.*
2. Chapter 10, Handout 49, *Don't Hide Your Femininity behind T-Shirts and Jeans.*
3. Chapter 10, Handout 50, *Be Your Own Fashion Designer Instructions.*
4. Chapter 10, Handout 51, *Be Your Own Fashion Designer Worksheet.*
5. A photocopy of Chapter 10, Handout 52, *Be Your Own Fashion Designer Parent Homework* for each parent, printed on cardstock if possible.
6. Colored markers and paper.

Special Note.

For Week 11, you will need to invite a mother who has a new infant to come for Chapter 10, Activity 37, *What's So Special about Being a Girl? Activity,* Step 6. She will just need to come for 15-20 minutes. You can also invite the mothers to participate in this activity and to discuss Handout 55, *What's So Special about Being a Girl? Parent Letter,* with their daughters as part of the workshop.

Preparation.

Prepare to present Activity 35, *Be Your Own Fashion Designer Activity* (Chapter 10).

Activity Steps.

1. **Check in.** (5-10 min.) Ask the girls to share their experience with the "Real Beauty Challenge" during the previous week.
2. **Teach concepts and activities.** (35-45 min.) Complete the steps for Activity 35, *Be Your Own Fashion Designer Activity.*
3. **Check out.** (5-7 min.) For homework, pass out a photocopy Handout 52, *Be Your Own Fashion Designer Parent Homework* to each girl. Ask the girls to share this handout with their parents, then to cut along the dotted lines and make a card that can be carried with them whenever they shop for clothes in the future to remind them of their "Designer Checklist."

Optional or Additional Activities.

For older girls, Activity 36, *Do You Know What You Are Attracting? Activity* (Chapter 10), can be used as a follow-up to help girls resist sexualized fashions and sexualized stereotypes of girl. Handout 38, The Truth about Barbie (Chapter 8), can also be used to discuss the unrealistic, objectified images that impact girls' understanding of femininity.

Week 11: Gender Role and Physical Self-Esteem

Materials Needed.

1. Chapter 10, Handout 54, *What's So Special about Being a Girl?*
2. Chapter 10, Handout 55, *What's So Special about Being a Girl? Parent Letter.*
3. Chapter 11, Handout 63, *Turn Over a New Leaf (optional).*

Preparation.

Prepare to present Activity 37, *What's So Special about Being a Girl? Activity* (See Chapter 10).

Activity Steps.

1. **Check in.** (5-10 min.) Tell the girls that in today's activity, they are going to learn more about why caring for their bodies is so important, not only for them, but for people who will depend upon them in the future.
2. **Teach concepts and activities.** (35-40 min.) Follow the directions for Activity 37, *What's So Special About Being a Girl? Activity.*
3. **Check out.** (5-7 min.) Remind the girls that they need to have all their "Love Lines" cards completed for next's week final session. They can complete these cards as homework if they are not complete. For homework, ask the girls to share Handout 55, *What's So Special about Being a Girl? Parent Letter* with their mothers or grandmothers if they were not present at the workshop. They can share next week what they learned about their own birth experience. Additional homework: Ask the girls to pick a goal from Handout 63, *Turn Over a New Leaf*, as their homework activity. They should ask their mothers to partner with them on this activity.

Optional or Additional Activities.

You may begin working on Chapter 11 activities as a follow up to the need for girls to care for their bodies in preparation for their future roles as mothers. You may make any of the healthy snacks on Handout 62, encouraging girls that proper nutrition skills are important for families. Few girls realize the effect that food has upon their emotional health and mood; therefore, Activity 40, *The Food Mood Connection Activity*, is valuable if you want to encourage girls to avoid depressed mood.

Week 12: Physical Self-Esteem and Termination

Materials Needed.

1. Chapter 11, Handout 59, *"Go Green" Hulk Smoothie Recipe (optional).*
2. Chapter 11, Handout 65, *I Am Thankful for All My Body Does for Me.*
3. Chapter 11, Handout 66, *My Body is a Miraculous Creation.*
4. National Geographic *Incredible Human Machine* DVD.
5. Smoothie ingredients listed in Handout 59, The "Go Green" Hulk Smoothie (optional).
6. Blender (optional).
7. Paper cups & napkins (optional).
8. "Love Line" materials listed in Week 7.
9. A photocopy of Figure 4, *Workshop Evaluation Form* for each girl.

Preparation.

Prepare to present Activity 43, *I Am Thankful for All My Body Does for Me Activity* (Chapter 11).

Activity Steps.

1. **Check in.** (5-10 min.) Give girls an opportunity to place their "Love Lines" index cards in the envelopes hanging on the "Love Line" if they have not already done so. Tell them that since this is the last week of the group, you hope they will leave with new skills and an appreciation of the relationships they made in the group. Ask the girls to share what they learned as they discussed Handout 55, *What's So Special about Being a Girl? Parent Letter*, with their mothers or grandmothers. Optional homework: Ask the girls to share what they have noticed since setting some new goals from Handout 63, *Turn Over a New Leaf.*
2. **Teach concepts and activities.** (30 min.) Follow steps 1-3 and 8 in Activity 43, *I Am Thankful for All My Body Does for Me Activity.* Have the girls sign the pledge in Handout 66.
3. **Final check out and termination activities.** (10 - 15 min.) Have the girls complete the workshop evaluation form (Figure 4). When they are finished, have them pull the envelope with their name on it off the "Love Line." As they read the positive things others have said about them, encourage them to continue to create a "Palace of Possibilities" with more positive thoughts about themselves and their bodies.

Optional or Additional Activities.

There are other steps that can be completed in Activity 43 if there is additional time. Chapter 11 has several additional activities which can be presented, such as making the Hulk Smoothie, following the directions on Handout 59. An art activity can also be used as a termination activity; have the girls make a poster to share what they've learned with others. Use these posters to help advertise future *Healthy Transitions for Girls* Workshops.

Activity 50
Workshop Plan for 3 Weeks, 2 Hour Bi-Weekly Sessions

Week 1, Day 1, 10:00 a.m. to 12:00 p.m.

Materials Needed.

1. Quilt, blanket, or individual carpet squares.
2. Large poster board.
3. A long piece of butcher paper or newsprint (approximately 5 ft long).
4. Colored markers or crayons.
5. Tape.
6. Snack ingredients. See Chapter 11, Handout 62, *Healthy Transitions for Girls Healthy Snacks*.
7. Palace model and/or Palace of Possibilities Display Board (Chapter 2).
8. Post-it Notes or squares of scrap book paper.
9. Chapter 9, Handout 42, *The Butterfly Hug Self-Soothing Technique*.
10. Chapter 2, Handout 3, *Who's Been Writing on My Walls? (Activity 5)*.

Preparation.

Prepare to present Activity 46, *Format for a First Workshop Session*, Step 1.
Prepare to present Activity 47, *One Body Activity* (Chapter 12).
Prepare to present Activity 1, *My Body is Changing* (Chapter 2).

10:00 -10:15
Invite all the girls to sit in a circle on a quilt that is placed on the floor. Using one of the pieces of poster paper and a marker, help the girls to create class rules as instructed in Activity 46, *Format for a First Workshop Session*, Step 1.

10:15 – 10:45

While the girls work at a long table, complete the directions for Activity 47, *One Body Activity*. Be sure to hang up the poster at each session to represent the girls' group mascot.

10:50 – 11:00

Give the girls a break to use the restroom, stretch, and get a drink.

11:00 – 11:15

Make a healthy snack using one of the recipes given on Handout 62.

11:15 – 11:45

As the girls sit at a table, follow directions for Activity 1, *My Body Is Changing* (see Chapter 2). Have the girls share how their beliefs have changed on a Post-It Note and place it on the walls of the palace model or the Palace of Possibilities Display Board (See Chapter 2, Figure 1).

11:45 – 12:00

Ask the girls to sit in a circle on the blanket. Teach the Butterfly Hug Self-Soothing Technique (see Chapter 9, Handout 42.) Encourage them to use this simple technique whenever they feel worried about their changing bodies or with other stressors. Assign Handout 3, *Who's Been Writing on My Walls? (Chapter 2, Activity 5),* as homework to be completed with their mothers. Depending upon their ages, girls may only be able to fill out one or two of the sections of this handout.

Week 1, Day 2, 10:00 a.m. to 12:00 p.m.

Materials Needed.

1. Quilt, blanket, or individual carpet squares.
2. Snack ingredients. See Handout 62, Healthy Transitions for Girls *Healthy Snacks.*
3. Palace model and/or Palace of Possibilities Display Board (see Chapter 2).
4. A full length mirror (at least one, although two is preferable).
5. A black hat and cape.
6. A tiara and wand.
7. Drawing materials and several sheets of blank paper for each girl (if using Activity 2, *Palace of Possibilities Guided Imagery (or Art) Activity* as an art activity).
8. Post-it Notes or squares of scrapbook paper.
9. Chapter 2, Handout 4, *Mirror, Mirror Activity Part 1.*[59]
10. Chapter 2, Handout 5, *Mirror, Mirror Activity Part 2.*
11. A photocopy of Chapter 2, Handout 8, *Palace of Possibilities Affirmations* for each girl.
12. Chapter 8, Handout 33, *Media Words You Should Know.*
13. Chapter 8, Handout 34, *Media Mind Games.*
14. Chapter 8, Handout 35, *Be a Media Detective.*
15. Chapter 8, Handout 36, *Media Detective: Case Solving Score Sheet.*
16. Chapter 9, Handout 42, *The Butterfly Hug Self-Soothing Technique.*

Preparation.

Prepare to present Activity 2, *Palace of Possibilities Guided Imagery (or Art) Activity* and Activity 6, *Mirror, Mirror Activity* (Chapter 2). Prepare a follow-up activity for Activity 2, such as Activity 3, *My Changing Beliefs Activity,* or Activity 4, *Palace of Possibilities Body Drawing Activity* (Chapter 2).

---

[59] Most girls love to dress up, but in the event you have older girls who may not want to dress up as part of the *Mirror, Mirror Activity,* you may choose Activity 7, *Watch Out for the "Imaginary Other" Activity* or *Activity 8, Be Your Own Cheerleader Activity,* as a substitute.

Prepare to present Activity 25, *Media Detectives Activity* (Chapter 8).

10:00 – 10:30
Begin this session seated in a circle on the quilt. Discuss the homework from the previous session, Handout 3, *Who's Been Writing on My Walls? Tell the girls they will learn more about the "writing on their walls" in this workshop session.* Ask the girls to find a comfortable position sitting on the quilt on the floor. Follow the directions for Activity 2, *Palace of Possibilities Guided Imagery (or Art) Activity.* If conducting Activity 2 as an art activity instead of a guided imagery, ask the girls to be seated at the table.

10:30 – 10:50

Explain that the next activity will help them to recognize and challenge the negative beliefs that are "written on the walls of their palace." Follow the directions for Activity 6, *Mirror, Mirror Activity.* While the girls are waiting to go the mirror, work with each girl to complete the steps to Activity 3, *My Changing Beliefs Activity* or Activity 4, *My Palace of Possibilities Drawing Activity.* The girls will be seated at a table while they are not at the mirror.

10:50 – 11:00

Give the girls a break to use the restroom, stretch, and get a drink.

11:00 – 11:15

Make a healthy snack using one of the recipes given on Handout 62.

11:15 – 11:45

Follow the directions for Activity 25, *Media Detectives Activity.* Part of this activity will be a review from the *Parents Workshop.*

11:45-12:00

Ask the girls to sit in a circle on the blanket. Using Handout 8, *Palace of Possibilities Affirmations,* follow the steps and demonstrate that positive beliefs create feelings of emotional safety and acceptance about the body. Ask the girls to take this handout home and to hang it by their mirror and to do this exercise every morning. They should also ask their mothers to support them by doing the affirmation steps with their daughters. Ask the girls to notice if they start to have more automatic positive thoughts in front of the mirror and report back at the next session.

Week 2, Day 3, 10:00 a.m. to 12:00 p.m.

Materials Needed.

1. Quilt, blanket, or individual carpet squares.

2. Snack ingredients. See Handout 62, Healthy Transitions for Girls *Healthy Snacks.*
3. Pencils and scratch paper.
4. Index cards, 10-15 for each girl.
5. Hole punch.
6. A ruler.
7. "O" rings or colored ribbon to fasten the cards together.
8. Colored markers or stickers for decorating the index cards.
9. Chapter 3, *Handout 9, My Body Talks.*
10. Chapter 4, Handout 12, *The WHOLE ME: Discovering My WHOLE Self.*
11. Chapter 4, Handout 13, *The WHOLE ME: Blossom into the WHOLE You (Optional).*
12. Chapter 9, Handout 44, *What to Do When I Am Blue Instructions.*
13. Chapter 9, Handout 45, *What to Do When I Am Blue List.*
14. Chapter 9, Handout 46, *My Ecomap.*

Preparation.

Prepare to present Activity 10, *My Body Talks Activity* (see Chapter 3).
Prepare to present Activity 12, *The WHOLE Me Activity* (see Chapter 4).
Prepare to present Activity 28, *"Blowing Balloons" Relaxation Activity* (optional).
Prepare to present Activity 30, *What To Do When I'm Blue Card File Activity* (see Chapter 9).

10:00 – 10:10

Ask the girls to share their experience using Handout 8, Palace of Possibilities Affirmation while they were in front of the mirror. If time, invite them to participate in Activity 28, *"Blowing Balloons" Relaxation Activity*, or Handout 42, *The Butterfly Hug Self-Soothing Technique* (both from Chapter 9).

10:15 – 10:50

Follow the directions for Steps 1-4 in Activity 12, *The WHOLE Me Activity*. If time complete Step 5 and Handout 13.

10:50 – 11:00

Give the girls a break to use the restroom, stretch, and get a drink.

11:00 – 11:15

Make a healthy snack using one of the recipes given on Handout 62.

11:15-11:45

Follow the directions for Activity 30, *What To Do When I'm Blue Card File Activity* (Chapter 9). The girls will work at a table as they complete this art activity.

11:45-12:00

As the girls sit in a circle on a blanket, use Handout 10, *My Body Talks*. Follow Step 4 through 6 in Activity 10, *Body Talks Activity* (Chapter 3). Before the girls leave, encourage them to use the skills they have learned to deal with their emotions and to learn to care for each part of themselves.

Week 2, Day 4, 10:00 a.m. to 12:00 p.m.

Important Note.

For Week 3, Day 6, the final workshop, you will need to invite a mother who has a new infant to come for Chapter 10, Activity 37, *What's So Special about Being a Girl? Activity*, Step 6. She will just need to come for 15-20 minutes. You can also invite the mothers to participate in this activity and to discuss Handout 55, *What's So Special about Being a Girl? Parent Letter* with their daughters as part of the workshop.

Materials Needed.

1. Quilt, blanket, or individual carpet squares.
2. Snack ingredients. See Handout 62, Healthy Transitions for Girls *Healthy Snacks*.
3. A raisin or orange for each girl.
4. A long piece of yarn, at least 36 inches, for each girl.
5. An envelope and several index cards for each girl.
6. A rural-type mailbox with a lid/door that opens and closes (optional).
7. Chapter 4, Handout 15, *The Wise Place Inside of Me*.
8. Chapter 6, Handout 23, *My Space, Your Space*.
9. Chapter 6, Handout 27, *Speaking Up: Rules that Work*.

Preparation.

Prepare to present Activity 9, *A Simple Mindfulness and Acceptance Activity* (see Chapter 3).
Prepare to present Activity 14, *The Wise Place Inside of Me Activity* (see Chapter 4).
Prepare to present Activity 17, *My Space, Your Space Part 1* (see Chapter 6).

10:00 – 10:15

Have the girls sit in a circle on a blanket as in previous sessions. Using a raisin or an orange, follow Activity 9, Step 1, *A Simple Mindfulness and Acceptance Activity*. Have the girls use the steps of mindfulness for at least 1 minute. Tell them that it is important to use mindfulness to listen to the "messages" their bodies give them.

10:15 – 10:50

Follow the directions for Activity 14, *The Wise Place Inside of Me Activity*. Optional: For the last 10 minutes of the activity, you can have a law enforcement officer come to the group and explain how intuition or gut feelings to help girls know how to set appropriate boundaries. The speaker could also address the need for setting personal boundaries in internet use and texting.

10:50 – 11:00

Give the girls a break to use the restroom, stretch, and get a drink.

11:00 – 11:15

Make a healthy snack using one of the recipes given on Handout 62.

11:15-11:45

Have the girls put their chairs in a circle for this activity. Follow the directions for Activity 17, *My Space, Your Space Part 1*. Be sure to give the girls an opportunity to role-play, not only to have a more effective learning experience, but also to help with their wiggles in this second hour.

11:45-12:00

As the girls sit in a circle on the floor, introduce the "Love Lines" Activity found in *104 Activities That Build: Self-Esteem, Teamwork, Communication, Anger Management, Self-Discovery, Coping Skills* by Alanna Jones. The "Love Line" Activity asks girls to be observant and write down something positive about every other girl in the group on an index card. A "love line" (clothesline or heavy yarn) will be hung during the remaining groups. Envelopes with each girl's name will hang from the line. Girls will each place an index card in each envelope whenever they have time during the remaining sessions until Week 12 when every girl will have an envelope with positive comments from her peers hanging on the "Love Line." This activity will be a termination activity in Week 12. Ask them to be watching for positive traits in each other that they can write on the "Love Line." Give the girls an opportunity to share what they learned.

Week 3, Day 5, 10:00 a.m. to 12:00 p.m.

Materials Needed.

1. Quilt, blanket, or individual carpet squares.
2. Snack ingredients. See Handout 62, Healthy Transitions for Girls *Healthy Snacks.*
3. A lunch tray with various sections for food (for younger girls).
4. Lima beans, or some other sortable object (for younger girls).
5. Post-It Notes and a pen.
6. Colored markers or crayons and drawing paper.
7. Glue sticks.
8. Scissors.

9. *Cinder Edna*, written by by Ellen Jackson and Kevin O'Malley (for younger girls).
10. *Princess Academy*, written by Shannon Hale.
11. Chapter 7, Handout 28, *How to Build Friendships with Guys*.
12. Chapter 7, Handout 30, *Heart Healthy Relationships* (for older girls).
13. Chapter 7, Handout 31 My Timeline (for older girls).
14. Chapter 7, Handout 32, *My Timeline Events* (for older girls).
15. Chapter 10, Handout 48, *Designer Checklist*.
16. Chapter 10, Handout 49, *Don't Hide Your Femininity Behind T-Shirts and Jeans*.
17. Chapter 10, Handout 50, *Be Your Own Fashion Designer Instructions*.
18. Chapter 10, Handout 51, *Be Your Own Fashion Designer Worksheet*.
19. A photocopy of Chapter 10, Handout 52, *Be Your Own Fashion Designer Parent Homework* for each parent, printed on cardstock if possible.

Preparation.

Prepare to use Chapter 9, Activity 28 *"Blowing Balloons" Relaxation Activity* or Activity 29, *EFT: Self-Help for Anxiety and Negative Beliefs*.
Prepare to present Chapter 7, Activity 20, *"Conversation and Diplomacy" Rules Role Play Activity*.
Prepare to present Activity 22, *Cinder Edna Bibliotherapy Activity (for younger girls)* or Activity 23, *Heart Healthy Relationships Activity* and Activity 24, *Relationship Timeline Activity*, (for older girls) depending upon which activity you feel is most appropriate for the girls in the group.
Prepare to present Activity 35, *Be Your Own Fashion Designer Activity* (Chapter 10).

10:00 – 10:15

Ask the girls to sit comfortably on the blanket. Ask them to take a few moments and use "mindfulness" skills to tune in to their breathing and the sensations they feel in their bodies. Use Activity 28 *"Blowing Balloons" Relaxation Activity* or Activity 29, *EFT: Self-Help for Anxiety and Negative Beliefs* to help them release any stress they may feel.

10:15 – 10:55

For younger girls, present Activity 22, Cinder Edna Bibliotherapy Activity. Follow up with Activity 20, *"Conversation and Diplomacy" Rules Role Play Activity*. They can listen to the story seated on the quilt and then put their chairs in a circle to act out the role play activity.

For older girls, present Activity 23, *Heart Healthy Relationships Activity* or Activity 24, *Relationship Timeline Activity*. They need to work at the table for these activities. Follow up with Activity 20, *"Conversation and Diplomacy" Rules Role Play Activity*. They can act out the role play activity with their chairs in a circle.

10:55 – 11:05

Give the girls a break to use the restroom, stretch, and get a drink. Remind the girls to be working on their "Love Lines" cards.

11:05 – 11:15

Make a healthy snack using one of the recipes given on Handout 62.

11:15-11:45

Follow the directions for Activity 35, *Be Your Own Fashion Designer Activity.* The girls will need to work at the table for this art activity.

11:45-12:00

Have the girls move from the table to a blanket on the floor. Give them a chance to share their fashion creation with each other. Encourage them to share what they learned about their unique fashion style. For homework, have the girls share Handout 52, *Be Your Own Fashion Designer Parent Homework* with their mothers.

Week 3, Day 6, 10:00 a.m. to 12:00 p.m.

Materials Needed.

1. Quilt, blanket, or individual carpet squares.
2. Smoothie ingredients and blender.
3. "Love Line" materials.
4. Chapter 10, Handout 54, *What's So Special about Being a Girl?*
5. Chapter 10, Handout 55, *What's So Special about Being a Girl? Parent Letter.*
6. Chapter 11, Handout 59, *"Go Green" Hulk Smoothie Recipe.*
7. Chapter 11, Handout 66, *My Body is a Miraculous Creation.*
8. Figure 4, *Workshop Evaluation Form* (a copy for each girl).

Preparation.

Prepare to present Activity 37, *What's So Special about Being a Girl? Activity* (see Chapter 10).
Prepare to present Activity 43, *I Am Thankful for All My Body Does for Me Activity* (see Chapter 11), Steps 9 through 11.
Prepare to make a "Hulk Smoothie," from Chapter 11, Handout 59.

10:00 – 10:15

Give the girls a few minutes to complete their "Love Line" index cards. Each girl should have written a note on an index card for every other girl in the group and placed the notes in the envelopes on the "Love Line."

10:15-10:50

Follow the directions for Activity 37, *What's So Special about Being a Girl? Activity.* If you have mothers or grandmothers attending this activity, give them time to discuss Handout 55, *What's So Special about Being a Girl? Parent Letter,* with their daughter.

10:50-11:00

Give the girls a break to use the restroom, stretch, and get a drink. Remind the girls to finish their "Love Lines" cards.

11:00 – 11:30

Demonstrate how to make "Hulk Smoothies." As the girls drink their smoothies, have them do Activity 43, *I Am Thankful for All My Body Does for Me Activity,* Steps 9 through 11.

11:30-11:45

Give the girls time to complete their workshop evaluations, Figure 4.

11:45-12:00

Have the girls take the envelope with their name off the "Love Line" and read the positive comments written by the other girls. As they read the positive things others have said about them, encourage them to continue to create a "Palace of Possibilities" with more positive thoughts about themselves and their bodies. Invite them to verbally share how they felt about being in the group.

Part II
Handouts, Figures, References & Index

Chapter 1: This Book Is Written for the Girls You Love

None.

Chapter 2: Building Positive Self-Talk: "I Am a Palace of Possibilities"

Chapter 3: The Mind-Body Connection: Building a Partnership with My Body

Chapter 4: Holistic Wellness: Reclaiming the WHOLE ME

Chapter 5: Building Parent Connections: Less Conflict, More Collaboration

Chapter 6: Building Supportive Connections with Other Girls

Chapter 7: Building Healthy Boy-Girl Friendships

Chapter 8: Media Literacy and Critical Thinking: Embracing the Images of REAL Beauty

Chapter 9: Coping Skills and Problem-Solving Skills

Chapter 10: Gender Role: What's So Special about Being a Girl?

Chapter 11: Physical Self-Esteem: My Body is My Best Friend for Life

Chapter 12: Curriculum and Workshop Planning

MYBODY IS CHANGING

Hey! What's happening to my body?

It's changing!

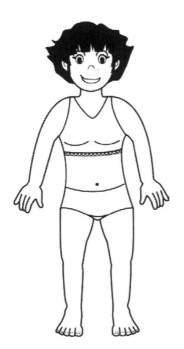

- ✓ Acne appears.
- ✓ Breasts develop and enlarge.
- ✓ Hips widen.
- ✓ Fat pads appear.
- ✓ Waistline narrows.
- ✓ Hair grows in pubic area, under arms, and on legs.
- ✓ Sweat glands develop.
- ✓ Uterus and ovaries enlarge.

Did you know that the average girl gains 30 to 50 pounds during puberty? Most of that weight develops on the hips and thighs. This normal weight gain is a healthy part of growing up. It doesn't mean you are "getting fat."

You might wonder, "If gaining weight during puberty is normal, why do all the girls in the movies and magazines look so skinny?" That is a GREAT question!

Be aware that only 5 percent of women can be as thin as they portray in the media without unhealthy dieting. Also, be aware that the media has many tricks to make people look thinner than they really are. Being ultra-thin is not REAL beauty; it's just a fad. Standards of beauty change from decade to decade, but the need to eat healthy and care for your body never changes!

**My body is changing in wonderful ways.
I can resist fears about being "fat" as my body develops.**

Handout 2
Healthy Transitions for Girls Body Drawing

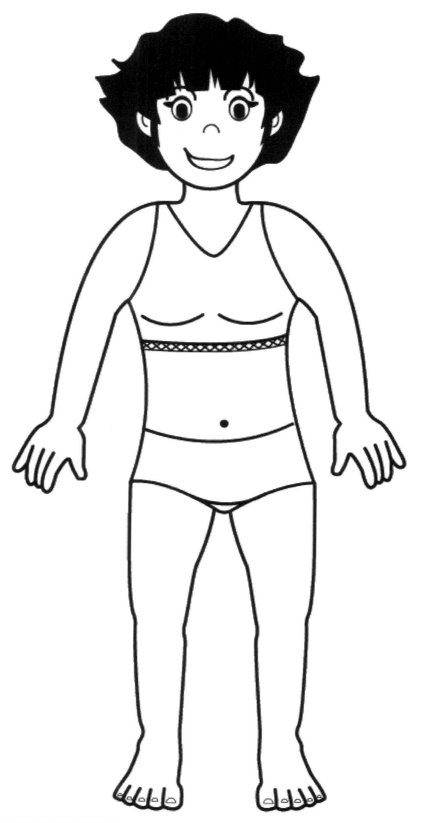

www.healthytransitionsforgirls.com

Handout 3
Who's Been Writing on My Walls?

Revisit each stage of your life so far. First ask: *How do did I feel about my body at this stage?* Then answer: *What are the messages that affect how I feel about my body (the "writing" on my walls)? Who or what do I think I should look like?* Consider things you learned from family, friends, television, movies, and magazines. Ask, *Do I want to change those messages?*

Early Childhood (up to age seven):
How Do I Feel About My Body?

What Messages Are Written on My Walls?

Later Childhood (age 7 to 10):
How Do I Feel About My Body?

What Messages Are Written on My Walls?

Early Adolescence (age 10 to 12):
How Do I Feel About My Body?

What Messages Are Written On My Walls?

Adolescence (age 13-14):
How Do I Feel About My Body:

What Messages Are Written On My Walls?

Handout 4

Mirror, Mirror Activity Part 1

Mirror, Mirror Activity—Part I

There's a "villainess" looking at you in the mirror. Say the positive body affirmation out loud to yourself as you look in the mirror. It is written in bold. Then, notice the negative thoughts that come to your mind to challenge or argue with the positive affirmation. Write down these negative thoughts.

Beauty comes in ALL shapes, sizes, and colors.

Negative things I'm saying in the mirror:

I am changing in wonderful ways.

Negative things I'm saying in the mirror:

My body is a miraculous creation.

Negative things I'm saying in the mirror:

I can recognize negative self-talk when I look into the mirror.

Handout 5

Mirror, Mirror Activity Part 2

Mirror, Mirror Activity—Part II

You are the princess of your own palace, and you have control over the beliefs that are written on your walls. You can use "mindfulness" and "acceptance" skills to challenge negative self-talk about your body. Learn to observe your body *without criticism*. Pay attention to simple facts about your body, but don't judge what you see. Practice these skills every time you look in the mirror! Read each positive affirmation statement. Then, write down the positive things you think in response.

Beauty comes in ALL shapes, sizes, and colors.

Positive things I observe in the mirror:

I am changing in wonderful ways.

Positive things I observe in the mirror:

My body is a miraculous creation.

Positive things I observe in the mirror:

I can choose positive self-talk when I look in the mirror.

www.healthytransitionsforgirls.com

Handout 6
Watch Out for the "Imaginary Other"

Watch Out for the Imaginary Other!

Have you ever noticed a little voice in your head that likes to stir up worries? It's like an "Imaginary Other" is peeking from behind a secret hiding place, watching everything you do. She makes mischief in your mind by exaggerating and making you feel self-conscious and left out.

If you hear these words, WATCH OUT! The "Imaginary Other" is at work: **NEVER, ALWAYS, NOBODY, EVERYBODY, ALL, NOTHING, EVERYTHING.**

- **Everybody** is going to notice my new zit.

- I **never** do anything right.

- **Nothing** ever goes the way I want it to.

- My parents **never** understand me.

- People are **always** talking behind my back.

- **Everything** I do is second rate.

- **Nobody** ever compliments the good things I do.

- **Nobody** but me has that problem.

- **All** the girls are going to have a boyfriend except me.

Write some statements the "Imaginary Other" says to you.

_____
_____
_____
_____
_____
_____
_____

I can challenge exaggerations that cause discouragement.

Handout 7

Be Your Own Cheerleader

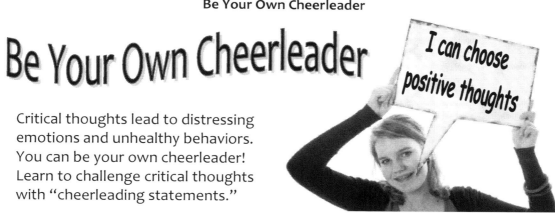

Critical thoughts lead to distressing emotions and unhealthy behaviors. You can be your own cheerleader! Learn to challenge critical thoughts with "cheerleading statements."

Write a "cheerleading statement" on the line under each distress-causing belief.

Hint: Start with phrases like "It's okay if…." Replace "I can't" with "I can." Change words like "everyone," "never," "always," to "someone," "sometimes." Ask yourself: Is *that statement an exaggeration? How can I make it more accurate?*

If my best friend is mad at me, everyone must hate me.

_____

If someone belittles me, I have to believe it.

_____

I'm the only one who has this problem.

_____

When I am unhappy, I just can't control it.

_____

I know everyone thinks _____ about me.

_____

I can't face this situation.

_____

There is a perfect solution to every problem.

_____

I feel sad today so life is awful.

_____

It is my fault if my parents _____ (fight, drink, are getting divorced).

_____

Because I have problems, I feel awful.

_____

I will never feel good about myself.

_____

I can encourage myself with more positive thoughts.

Handout 8

Palace of Possibilities Affirmations

My Palace of Possibilities

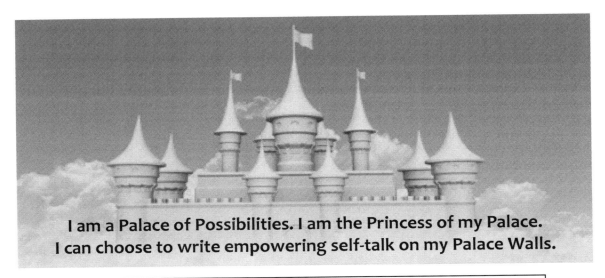

**I am a Palace of Possibilities. I am the Princess of my Palace.
I can choose to write empowering self-talk on my Palace Walls.**

1. Hang this list by your mirror where you can see it every day.
2. Write these messages in your heart: Make a fist and move it in a clockwise circle over your heart as you say each affirmation.

3. Add some of your own affirmations to write on your palace walls.

- ❖ Beauty comes in all shapes and sizes.
- ❖ I am a wonderful mixture of talents and challenges.
- ❖ I am learning to respect myself and others.
- ❖ I am responsible for the life I create.
- ❖ My body is a miraculous creation.
- ❖ I am changing in wonderful ways.
- ❖ I can resist media messages that tell me I can't measure up.
- ❖ I am gentle when I notice my shortcomings.
- ❖ I thank my body for all it does for me.
- ❖ _____
- ❖ _____
- ❖ _____
- ❖ _____

I can choose beliefs and self-talk that create a happier life.

Handout 9
My Body Talks

MYBODY TALKS

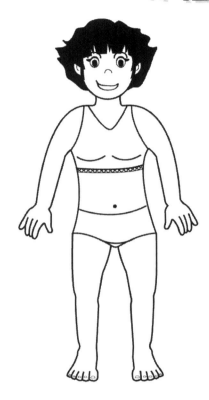

Listening to your body is important. It has a big job to do for you.

When you are hungry, your body says, "I need food." What kind of food is your body telling you it needs? Are you listening?

When you have pain in a certain area, your body is saying, "I need care."

When your body is tired, it is saying "I need rest." How can you give your body what it needs?

Where does your body tell you there is danger? Where does your body tell you it feels stressed? Where does it tell you it feels anger?

I can listen to my body talk.

Handout 10

Emotional Body Talk

EMOTIONAL BODY TALK

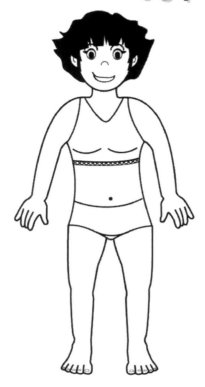

Recognizing your emotional body talk is an important part of being "alive." On the body drawing, write down where you feel the following emotions:

- Embarrassment
- Fear
- Lack of Self-Confidence
- Worry
- Homework Pressure
- Happiness
- Love

By learning to recognize your emotional body signs, you can learn to understand yourself. You can learn self-soothing skills, like the "Butterfly Hug," (Handout 42) so you will not feel so overwhelmed.

I can listen to my body's emotional messages.

Handout 11
My Feelings Meter

    I have a feelings meter inside my body. It helps me recognize what I'm feeling and how intense my feelings are. By paying attention to my body signs, I can understand my feelings. Understanding my feelings is a first step in knowing how to handle them.

    Negative feelings can lead to unhealthy behaviors. I can learn how to handle my feelings in healthy ways.

10. Very Upset, Worried, or Scared

8. Upset, Worried, or Scared

6. Bothered or Nervous

4. Okay

2. Happy

1. Very Happy

0. Not Sure

Three Important Questions
What are my body signs?
What do I feel?
How intense are my feelings?

I can recognize that not all feelings are an emergency.

www.healthytransitionsforgirls.com

Handout 12
The WHOLE Me: Discovering the WHOLE Self[1]

Discovering My Whole Self

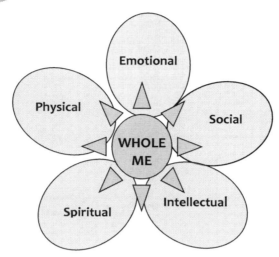

You have many parts of yourself that all work together. Getting to know yourself better means you take time to recognize all parts of yourself. Write a few words in each category to describe something about you. For example, under "Intellectual," you might write, "a fast reader" or "I like learning." Under "Spiritual," you could write, "I feel peaceful in nature" or "I pray often." Share your thoughts with a parent or friend. How are you alike or different from others? Which part of you needs more attention right now?

SPIRITUAL_____

_____

SOCIAL_____

_____

EMOTIONAL_____

_____

INTELLECTUAL_____

_____

PHYSICAL _____

_____

I can learn about the many parts of myself.

_____

[1] From *Thinking, Feeling, Behaving: An Emotional Curriculum for Adolescents, Grades 7-12,* (pp. 11-12) by Ann Vernon, 2006, Champaign, IL: Research Press. Adapted with permission.

www.healthytransitionsforgirls.com

Handout 13
The WHOLE Me: Blossom into the WHOLE You

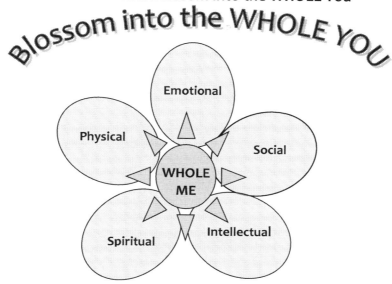

Blossom into the WHOLE YOU

The media wants you to think that all that matters is how you look on the outside, but there is so much more to you. All parts of you need care and attention. You can blossom into the WHOLE ME when you spend time on all aspects of yourself and not just your appearance.

List one or two goals you have for each area of your life.

SPIRITUAL_____

_____

SOCIAL_____

_____

EMOTIONAL _____

_____

INTELLECTUAL _____

_____

PHYSICAL _____

_____

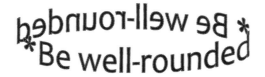

* Be well-rounded

I can make choices that support every part of my life.

Handout 14
The Spiritual Part of ME: Discovering My Authentic Self

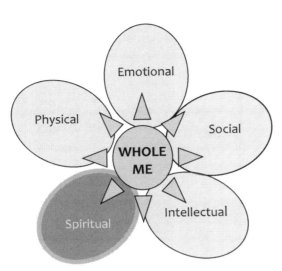

The Spiritual Part of ME
Discovering My "Authentic" Self

My Spiritual Self reminds me to follow personal rules and values like honesty and kindness, even when the crowd is doing something different. **My Spiritual Self** guides me to be true to myself. It leads me to find a positive purpose for my life. It guides me to know how to avoid harmful situations.

I cannot see **My Spiritual Self**, but it plays a big role in who I am. Sometimes, I cover up or change who I am—"wear a mask"—to fit in with my friends and lose touch with my authentic self.

Happiness Happens from the Inside Out.
Spend Time Inside Your Heart.

My Spiritual Journey

1. When you say the word "spirituality," what other words come to your mind?

2. Do you feel a loving connection to God or a Higher Power?

3. What can you do to strengthen your spiritual self?

4. What are some of your values?

5. Whose values do you admire?

6. Where do you go if you have questions about your life's purpose?

7. How can your spirituality help you when problems arise?

8. What would you like to be proud of when you are very old?

I can nurture the spiritual part of me.

Handout 15

The Wise Place Inside of Me

The Wise Place Inside of Me

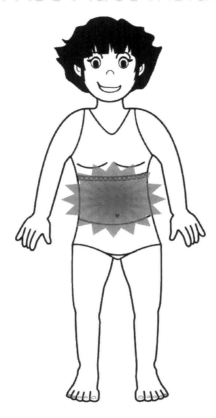

You can learn to be still in your mind so you can tune in to the wise place inside. Learning to listen to sensations you feel inside helps you tune in to messages called "intuition" or "spiritual guidance." These feelings whisper inside your heart and your body. They help you to know what is right and wrong. They help you to know whether a situation is safe or unsafe. They help you to know whether a situation is going to lift you up emotionally or drain you emotionally.

When a situation or person may be harmful, you will get an "ick" feeling or a "stay away" feeling. Learn to trust those feelings, even when others around you don't understand why you feel that way.

When a friendship is harmful, you may feel "down" or "confused" whenever you are with that person. That means you need to set stronger boundaries or find ways to be around that person less.

Your wise place feels "sparkly" or "warm" when something is healthy for you.

I can tune into feelings that guide and protect me.

What's Happening to My Little Girl?

All of a Sudden, She...

- Worries more about what her friends think.
- Puts herself down.
- Wants to wear revealing or tight clothing.
- Complains of being left out of the group.
- Obsesses about her appearance.
- Acts "boy crazy."
- Argues with family rules.
- Spends more time alone in her room.
- Tries out weird fads.

Adolescence: What's Normal?

- A roller coaster of emotional ups and downs.
- Irrational beliefs seen as absolutely true.
- A need for independence from parents.
- Worries and conflicts about peer relationships.
- Preparing for a future occupation.
- Preoccupation with self.
- Preoccupation with abstract and often unrealistic philosophies.
- A need to conform with peers and fads.
- A desire for self-expression (sometimes through acting out).

> ## Teens Need More Independence.
> ## At the Same Time, They Need Structure
> ## and Affection from Their Parents.

- ✓ DO set rules and boundaries.
- ✓ DO say "Yes" whenever you can, but set limits.
- ✓ DO explain the reasons when you say "no."
- ✓ DO invite your teen's input on family rules.
- ✓ DO give lots of hugs and encouragement.
- ✓ DO take time out when you are frustrated or angry.
- ✓ DO model the kind of respect you want from your teen.
- ✓ DO get help when you feel overwhelmed.

I can adapt my parenting skills to fit my child's new life stage.

Handout 17
The Emotional Roller Coaster Starts with These Beliefs

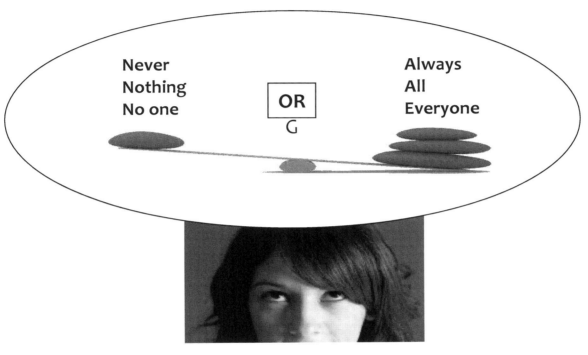

The Emotional Roller Coaster Starts with These Beliefs

Never
Nothing
No one

OR

Always
All
Everyone

Common Irrational Beliefs of Teens

- I must be liked by everyone, and if I am not, I can't handle it.
- If someone belittles me, I have to believe it.
- I'm the only one who _____ (ever has this problem, ever does any work, ever gets in trouble).
- When I am unhappy, I just can't control it.
- I know everyone thinks _____ about me.
- I can't face this situation; therefore, I have to avoid it.
- There is a perfect solution to every problem, and I have to figure out the perfect solution. Otherwise, there is no solution.
- I can achieve success even if I don't have any goals.
- I can't stand discomfort because it is awful.
- It is my fault if my parents _____ (fight, drink, are getting divorced).
- Because I have problems, my life is awful.
- Because I experienced some form of abuse in my past, I don't deserve to be happy.

I can recognize and patiently challenge my child's unhealthy thinking.

www.healthytransitionsforgirls.com

Handout 18

Open the Door to Better Talk[2]

Open the Door to Better Talk

Four Steps to Show You'll Listen:

1. Stop what you are doing.
2. Look at your child.
3. Listen quietly to what is said.
4. Clarify what you think you heard ("Do you mean…?").

Examples of Door Openers:

- What do you think?
- Would you like to share more about this?
- I don't know, but I'll find out.
- I'm interested in what you are saying.
- Do you know what that means?
- That sounds important to you.
- Do you want to talk about it?

> "Many kids don't need a person with a PhD as much as they need someone who knows them, is a good listener, and is a good problem solver."
> ~ Mary Pipher, PhD

Examples of Door Slammers:

- You are too young to understand.
- If you say that again, I'll….
- That's none of your business.
- I don't care what your friends are doing!
- We'll talk about that when you need to know.
- That's just for boys/girls.
- Why are you asking me that?
- You don't need to know about that.
- Don't come to me if you mess up.

I can listen in a way that helps me understand what's going on inside my child.

---

[2] "Door Openers" is a concept explained by Thomas Gordon (2000/1975). *Parent Effectiveness Training.* New York, NY: Three Rivers Press. This book is an excellent resource for parents and professionals.

Handout 19
Create a Safe Space for Problem Solving[3]

Create a "Safe Place" for Problem Solving

> 1. Take **Time Out** when emotions are high.
> Nothing is ever solved in the heat of the moment.
> 2. **Emphasize** what you **DO want,** not what you don't like.
> 3. Use the **"Sandwich Approach."**
> (Compliment-Constructive Feedback-Compliment)
> 4. Use **Active Listening Skills.**
> (See Handout 18, *Open the Door to Better Talk.*)
> 5. Work together using the **"Four Square" Problem Solving Model.**

Let's Play "Four-Square"

Map out the rewards and consequences of obeying a parent request or a family rule. It is best to complete the square on your own and then with your child. For example, if you ask your daughter to give up going to a dance because she is too young, your four square table will look like this:

	What I am GIVING UP	What I RECEIVE
If I COMPLY...	• Can't be with friends. • My friends might think I'm a baby. • Won't get to have fun at the dance.	• Less pressure to have a boyfriend. • More time to develop friendships. • Parent will be happier. • More privileges later.
If I Don't COMPLY...	• Parent will be mad. • Dances will be old news by the time I'm older. • I will be pressured to focus on dating when I am not ready.	• I will still feel like part of the crowd. • I will have fun. • I can do something on my own.

Benefits of Playing "Four Square"
- Supports communication & cooperation.
- Supports problem-solving skills & autonomy for child.
- Challenges irrational beliefs of teens.

I can use a teamwork approach when solving problems with my child.

---

[3] Adapted from Tracy Todd (2000). Solution focused strategic parenting for challenging teens: A class for parents. *Family Relations,* 49(2). 165-168.

www.healthytransitionsforgirls.com

Handout 20
Be a Media Conscious Parent

Be a "Conscious Parent." Don't Just Let Culture Happen

*"You need to **protect** your kids from what's ugly and obnoxious, and **connect** with what's good and beautiful."* ~Mary Pipher, PhD

ASK YOURSELF:

✓ What are your values?
✓ What do you want your child to understand about her changing body and sexuality?
✓ Do the movies, television programs, magazines, Internet sites, and music in your daughter's life reflect your values?

DID YOU KNOW?

The 2002 PBS film *The Merchants of Cool* documents that media moguls and advertisers **encourage unrestrained, risky and irresponsible behaviors** because **distressed kids buy products** to feel better. In a 2010 study of the **25 most popular teen TV shows**, girls were depicted **in sexual situations nearly twice as often** as adult women. **Ninety-three percent** of these sexual incidents are qualified as **"unhealthy"** by the American Psychological Association. (See www.4everygirl.com or www.parentstv.org)

WHAT YOU CAN DO

✓ Use an Internet contract to establish family Internet rules. (See http://www.protectkids.com/parentsafety/pledge.htm.)
✓ Get the facts about social networking at www.connectsafely.org.
✓ Preview movie, TV, and music choices at www.pluggedin.com.
✓ Do not buy magazines that emphasize unhealthy thinness, unreal depictions of beauty, or sex and dating.

We can ALL be MEDIA DETECTIVES!

I can **protect** my home from unhealthy media influences.
I can **connect** my child to *positive* activities, music, movies, and books.

Handout 21
Friend or Competition?

FRIEND OR COMPETITION?

A lot of "girl drama" centers on the belief that girls have to compete with their friends to get guys' attention. They think they have to compete for popularity. When friendships are competitive, girls think they have to be "better" than others to measure up or fit in.

Take this quiz and discover how competition is affecting your friendships.

Rate your answers on a scale of 1 to 5. Write the number after each statement.

1	2	3	4	5
Never true	Rarely true	Sometimes true	Often true	Always true

1. I have to be prettier than other girls in order to be popular.

2. I hope boys will notice me more than my friends.

3. It's not possible for more than just a few girls to be popular.

4. I would rather not have my friends around when I am with boys I like.

5. I think I would be more popular if my friends were not prettier than me.

6. When I am just with my girlfriends, I don't care what I look like.

7. I lose friends because they are jealous of me.

8. I have lost a friend because we fought over a boy.

What would you like to change in your relationships with other girls?

_____
_____
_____
_____
_____

I can take steps to be a true friend and avoid "girl drama."

Don't be an Identity Thief

SIGN THE "NO GOSSIP" PLEDGE

Gossip can steal the reputation and "identity" of you and girls you know. Rumors fuel "girl drama" and ruin friendships. **BE the kind of friend who doesn't listen to gossip and doesn't pass it on.**

Name a time when a friend gossiped about you and caused people to believe things that weren't true. How did you feel about that "theft" of your reputation and identity?

_____

_____

_____

Write 3 things you can say the next time someone wants to gossip to you about someone you know or about a close friend:

1._____

2._____

3._____

I WILL NOT LISTEN TO GOSSIP AND I WILL NOT PASS IT ON.

Signed: _____

Handout 23
My Space, Your Space

My Space, Your Space

As you look at this picture, would you guess these girls are close friends or just acquaintances? What non-verbal clues help you decide?

Everyone has something called "personal space." This is how close people can get to you physically before you get uncomfortable. Your personal space is different with a person you trust—you will let her or him get closer, right next to your face. You may want people you don't trust to stay far away from you—a couple feet or more. Your sense of personal space may be different from others. Respect and protect your personal space.

My Personal Space

You have a right to set boundaries around your personal space. You can move away when people are getting "too close for comfort." Your personal space also includes how private you are about your feelings. You can determine how much your want to share with others.

Many girls think they need to share *all* their feelings with *everyone.* Other girls keep everything to themselves. **The best approach is to find a balance.** Private things should be shared only with people you trust. People should prove to you that they are trustworthy over a period of time. It is not wise to share private information with people you have just met. Private feelings should definitely NOT be shared on Facebook or Social Media.

Setting boundaries around your personal space helps define and protect who you are as a person. Pay attention to boundaries that help you feel your best.

I can choose to say "yes" or "no" about what I will share with others.

My Space, Your Space: Find the Balance

BOUNDARIES ARE TOO LOOSE
- You can't say no because you are afraid of being criticized.
- You often change yourself to be what others think you should be.
- You feel constant guilt about others' problems.
- You share personal information before you have built a trust relationship.
- You let others treat you disrespectfully.
- You worry about helping others, but you don't ask to them to help you.
- You have difficulty identifying what you want, need, or feel.
- You don't have a sense of moral values and limits.

BOUNDARIES ARE TOO RIGID
- You say no to any request that takes you out of your "comfort zone."
- You rarely share your feelings with anyone.
- You are scared that if people really knew you, they would reject you.
- You have difficulty identifying what others want, need, or feel.
- You rarely ask for help.
- You hate to admit you are wrong.
- You usually blame others when problems arise.

HEALTHY BOUNDARIES
- You enjoy helping others, but you can say no to others' requests if you need to.
- Your relationships are a mutual give and take.
- You respect and act on your values, even when others disagree.
- You know when the problem is yours and when it belongs to someone else.
- You share personal information gradually as you develop trust.
- You don't hang around with people who put you down or hurt you physically.
- You communicate your needs and feelings clearly in your relationships.
- You are responsible for your own happiness and fulfillment. You allow others to be responsible for their own happiness and fulfillment.
- You value your opinions and feelings as much as those of others.
- You are able to ask for help when you need it.

I can have healthy "giving" and "receiving" in my relationships.

---

[1] *Used with permission from Loretta Sparks, LMFT, D.CEP, EFT Master at www.selfcarepower.com.*

Handout 25

My Space, Your Space: Good Boundaries Make Good Friendships Better[1]

My Space, Your Space

Good Boundaries Make Good Friendships Better

Knowing how to set boundaries makes friendships better. Have you ever tried to please a friend by doing something you did not want to, only to feel resentful later? Do you hesitate to say "yes" because you worry friends will take advantage of you? You can learn to say YES or NO for the right reasons.

My Personal Space

How To Strengthen Boundaries that Are Too Loose:

If you have difficulty saying "No," <u>no matter what</u> do not say "Yes." Instead, say, "Let me get back to you," or "I need some time to think it over." Say "Yes" only if you can answer each of these questions affirmatively. Do not say "Yes" if it will make you feel resentful.

> 1. *Do I want to do what I have been asked?*
> 2. *Do I have the time to do it?*
> 3. *Do I have the physical and emotional capacity to do it?*

How To Be More Flexible When Boundaries Are Too Rigid:

If you have difficulty saying, "Yes," look for opportunities to say "yes" more often. Volunteer to help whenever possible. If someone makes a request of you, say "Yes" if you can answer "Yes" to these questions.

> 1. *Will doing it improve my relationship or improve someone's life?*
> 2. *Can I make time to do it?*
> 3. *Do I have the physical and emotional capacity to do it?*
> 4. *Will doing it increase my self-respect?*

---

[1]*Used with permission from Loretta Sparks, LMFT, D.CEP, EFT Master at www.selfcarepower.com.*

Listening: Rules That Work

Listening is not as easy as we think. We often hear what a person says without really "hearing" or understanding the message they are trying to send.

1. Check the message by saying, "Did you mean.....?"

Misunderstandings occur easily when we respond without understanding what a person really meant. It's easy to ask questions, so we understand their meaning. Don't rush to respond before you know the message that was sent.

2. Validate.

Most of the time people don't want advice; they just want to know someone understands them. Don't you love it when someone says, **"It sounds like you are feeling…."** Validation feels so good; great listeners are good at validating.

3. Pay attention to what you see and feel.

If someone says, "I'm fine," but they look sad, there is more going on. Pay attention to their body clues. Sometimes someone will tell you something and it just doesn't feel right. Pay attention to how a person's words make you feel.

I can build friendships by being a good listener.

Speaking Up: Rules That Work

Things I say when I am upset or hurt can make a big difference in whether the problem gets better or worse. Here are some RULES for expressing myself that can make the problem better.

1. Take a slow, deep breath. Ask: Why is this making me so upset?
Anger is usually covering up other feelings and needs that we haven't thought about.

2. Express what you DO need or want, rather than what you don't want.
We waste a lot of time criticizing and complaining without explaining what we REALLY need the person to do for us. We have to take responsibility for our needs and wants.

3. Use an "I" message, rather than blaming.
For example: "When you did that, I FELT….."
Watch for exaggerations like, "ALWAYS" or "NEVER."

4. Take responsibility for my part of the problem.
Maybe you're having a bad day and just feeling grumpy; or maybe you're worried about a test or some other unrelated problem.

5. Know when it's the right time to talk.
Solutions never happen in the heat of the moment. Cool off and take a break, then try talking when you're calm.

I can build friendships by expressing my needs and boundaries.

How to Build Friendships with Guys
(Even when you are nervous)

Remember when talking to boys used to be easy? Puberty seems to make relationships with guys more complicated. In the popular book, *Princess Academy*[1], the heroine, Miri, discovers that growing up has made it very awkward to talk to her life-long friend, Peder. But Miri attends a Princess Academy and learns a whole range of grown-up skills, including rules for "Conversation and Diplomacy."

Every "princess" needs a little help now and then. When you find yourself "tongue tied" and don't know what to say. These rules from *Princess Academy* can help.

Princess Rules for Conversation & Diplomacy

1. <u>Say his name</u>. Look him in the eyes. Smile and call him by name instead of "Hey you," or "Hey Dude." Everyone loves to hear their name spoken in a friendly way.

2. <u>Make observations, not judgments</u>. Resist criticism and sarcasm as a way to start a conversation. State something you observe, such as, "Hi John, I noticed that you were concentrating during the science test," rather than, "Looked like you really bombed the test."

3. <u>Return the conversation back to him by asking questions</u>. Conversation is like tossing a ball back and forth. You can keep the "ball" going by sharing information about yourself and by asking him questions.

4. <u>Recognize strengths, give compliments</u>. Resist putting guys down to make yourself feel confident. Show respect by recognizing unique strengths and giving compliments.

5. <u>Build upon common ground</u>. Share your interests and ask questions to discover his interests. Your goal is to discover shared interests and build upon them.

I can build healthy friendships with guys based upon mutual interests and sharing.

---

[1] Hale, Shannon (2007). Princess Academy. Bloomsbury USA Childrens.

Handout 29

I Can't Live Without Him ... and Other Lies You Hear in Country Songs

"I can't live without him"...
(and other lies you hear in country songs)

Are you someone who has to have a boyfriend to feel good about yourself?

Much of what the media portrays about "love" is really unhealthy **codependency**.

Know the signs. Avoid the drama.

Healthy Friendship	vs.	**Codependency**

Healthy Friendship	Codependency
• I stay in touch with my feelings.	• I try to figure out what he thinks, but I'm unsure of my own feelings.
• I set clear boundaries about physical affection, and they are respected.	• I give physical affection to make him like me.
• We can talk comfortably; I am not afraid to say what I really feel.	• We are physically attracted, but we don't talk much; I hold in my real thoughts.
• I hold him responsible for his choices and behaviors.	• I make excuses when he hurts me; I lie about things he does so others will like him.
• I feel accepted just as I am; I don't have to change my looks to please him.	• I change my preferences and my appearance to please him.
• We enjoy spending time together, but I have many other interests and friends.	• I give up my friends and interests to be with him.

I can choose to have healthy friendships.

www.healthytransitionsforgirls.com

Handout 30

Heart Healthy Relationships[1]

HEART HEALTHY RELATIONSHIPS

Heart Healthy Relationships stay "HORIZONTAL."

Heart Healthy

Relationship Stage	Physical Affection
Acquaintance	Handshake
Friendship	High-five, Brief Hug
Casual Dating	Hand holding
Serious Dating	Kiss on the lips
Engagement	Lingering kiss
Marriage	Sexual relations

Not Heart Healthy

Relationship Stage	Physical Affection
Acquaintance	Handshake
Friendship	High-five, Brief Hug
Casual Dating	Hand Holding
Serious Dating	Kiss on the lips
Engagement	Lingering kiss
Marriage	Sexual relations

Physical Affection must correspond to the appropriate Relationship Stage in order to develop into a permanent, secure relationship. Use this chart to help you CHOOSE the boundaries you need to have healthy relationships later in your life.

---

[1] Adapted from Jeanette Smith (2008). Unsteady: What Every Parents Absolutely Must Know About Teenage Romance, American Fork, UT: Covenant Communications. Used with permission.

Handout 31
My Timeline

MY TIMELINE

Now	High School/College	Building a Family, Marriage, Children

I have so much to accomplish before I worry about serious boy/girl relationships. **NOW is the TIME** to learn to build friendships, learn about myself, develop my talents, pursue my education, and other priorities that will prepare me for a happier future.

I can stay focused on today's important priorities.

Ideas I Have About My Future.

Write or draw about what you want your life to look like in 20 years.

MY TIMELINE EVENTS

Cut along the dotted lines. You will have 28 different milestones that will be accomplished in the next five to ten years. Place these 28 milestones in the appropriate column on the timeline. For example: "Steady date" should occur as a preparation for marriage, so it will be placed in the "Building a Family" column.

Get my diploma	Steady date	Earn a scholarship	Learn Communication Skills
Learn problem solving skills	Traveling abroad	Plan my wardrobe	Learn to manage money
Gain sexual experience	Learn parenting skills	Establish my spiritual values	Practice daily exercise
Learn to cook	Discover my likes and dislikes	Take a trip with my friends	Buy a house
Live in my own apartment	Learn to make friendships with boys	Participate in extra-curricular activities	Improve my GPA
Date many different guys	Develop my talents	Become a mother	Get my driver's license
Learn to be patient	Eat healthy	Do good deeds for others	Get my first kiss

To everything there is a season, a time for every purpose under the sun.
~ Ecclesiastes 3:1

230

Media Words You Should Know

To be a MEDIA SLEUTH, you have to know the language. Add these words to your SECRET CODE BOOK. TOP NOTCH MEDIA SLEUTHS can DECODE these tricks and messages on TV, magazines, billboards, and on the Internet.

OBJECTIFICATION

DISMEMBERMENT

THINNESS

ISOLATION

SEXUALIZATION

VICTIMIZATION

UNREALISTIC PERFECTION

I can learn to recognize hidden messages in media.

Handout 34
Media Mind Games

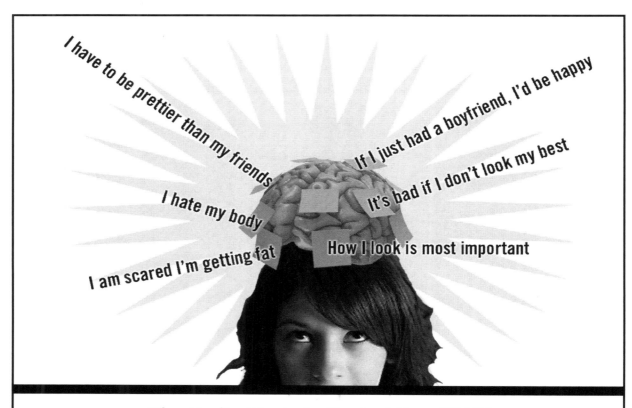

The Media Wants to Control Your BRAIN
TAKE BACK YOUR TERRITORY!

**Don't think the advertisers really care about how you look and feel.
They need you to feel DISTRESSED so you will buy products.
You are being "brainwashed" with media messages
that encourage "RISKY" behavior and NEGATIVE self-talk.
Watch out for these lies.**

- Photography tricks that portray unrealistic expectations of beauty.
- Overemphasis on appearance as a key to happiness.
- "No consequences" lies about sexual behaviors.
- Pressure to steady date rather than build friendships.
- Sexualized images of girls and women.
- "Girl drama" rather than supportive friendships.

I can challenge the distressing messages that come from media images.

Handout 35
Be a Media Detective

Be a Media Detective

Advertisers pretend to care about what you want and need, but the media really just wants to get your money. The media sells a point of view and a product—at the expense of your self-esteem! Don't BUY the lies! You can be a MEDIA SLEUTH as you learn to DECODE media messages.

Follow these important CLUES:

1. Is the ad using a woman's body to sell a product?

2. Has computer-enhanced photography been used? Do the people or objects in the ad look like people or things I see everyday?

3. Are only certain body parts emphasized? (For instance, thighs, legs, lips, hair, breasts, or midriff.)

4. What does the ad promise that the product can do for me based on the picture, the words, and the feeling I get? (Hint: What EMOTION words are used?)

5. Does the ad use sexuality to sell the product?

6. How do I feel as I compare myself to people in the ad? Do I suddenly feel like something is wrong with me? (This is a very important clue!)

7. Is the ad honest? Is it stirring up emotions to sell the product, or is it just stating facts?

8. Is the ad using a movie star to sell the product? Do I think, "Wow, I better use that product so I can be cool like _____."?

9. Does the ad promote supportive friendships, or does it promote popularity as a means to being happy?

10. Is the ad realistic? Can it really do what it says?

I can decode harmful media messages every day!

Media Detective: Case Solving Score Sheet

Description of Ad Evaluated _____

_____

Clue 1 Yes _____ No _____
Notes _____

_____

Clue 2 Yes _____ No _____
Notes: _____

_____

Clue 3 Yes _____ No _____
Notes: _____

_____

Clue 4 Yes _____ No _____
Notes: _____

_____

Clue 5 Yes _____ No _____
Notes: _____

_____

Clue 6 Yes _____ No _____
Notes: _____

_____

Clue 7 Yes _____ No _____
Notes: _____

_____

Clue 8 Yes _____ No _____
Notes: _____

_____

Clue 9 Yes _____ No _____
Notes: _____

_____

Clue 10 Yes _____ No _____
Notes: _____

_____

Handout 37

Media Detective: Sleuthing for More Hidden Messages

Be a Media Detective
Sleuthing for More Hidden Messages

Advertisers tell you lies to sell products, even if those lies are harmful. Every time you hear or see an ad, you can say, *"Is that really true?"* Practice being a media sleuth. For each one of these media messages, write your own argument to challenge the untrue message. (The first one is done for you.)

- ❖ "If I look different, I will be happier."
- ❖ There's a lot more to being happy than how I look.

- ❖ "Experimenting with sex has no consequences and doesn't hurt anybody."
- ❖ _____

- ❖ "Drinking soda, junk food, and high-caffeine Monster drinks doesn't hurt my body that much."
- ❖ _____

- ❖ "Part of growing up is fighting with my parents. They have no idea how I feel. They are just old-fashioned and clueless."
- ❖ _____

- ❖ "Looking sexy and wearing revealing clothes makes my body look good."
- ❖ _____

- ❖ "I have to compete with other girls to get guys' attention."
- ❖ _____

- ❖ "I *have* to have a boyfriend to be important and okay."
- ❖ _____

Homework: Pick a television commercial or a magazine ad. What does the advertiser want you to buy? Using the message list above, write down two hidden (false) messages the ad is selling you. How did the ad make you *feel?*

**I can choose to resist negative media messages and
remember messages that really support me.**

Handout 38
The Truth about Barbie

Healthy Transitions for Girls
SPECIAL REPORT: *THE TRUTH ABOUT BARBIE*
By P. McFarland, Body Image Editor

"I'm not blaming Barbie...She's one small factor, an environmental factor. I'm blond and blue-eyed, and I figured that was what I was supposed to look like. She was my idol. It impacted the way I looked at myself."

Galia Slayen speaks out against eating disorders. She built a life-size Barbie to demonstrate that many images of "ideal beauty" are unrealistic. Girls who diet to look like Barbie or models they see on TV and magazines put themselves at risk for eating disorders and other problems.

Galia isn't the only who believes Barbie has had a negative influence on girl's culture. Many researchers agree. A 1999 study by Kuther (2004) supported Galia's claim.

Galia's freakish re-creation, with its 30 inch bust, 18 inch waist, 33 inch hips, and 6-foot height, is a reminder that all girls are tempted to be "Barbies" in today's culture. They are tempted to be a de-humanized collection of body parts with emphasis on big breasts, abnormal thinness, and a painted-on face. Galia's "Barbie" model serves to remind girls that the beauty and body image ideals of the media are unrealistic.

Be smart, girls! Resist the temptation to be a "Barbie doll," a collection of body parts and a painted-on face. Be real. Be YOU.

Used with permission from Galia Slayen, 2011.

Handout 39

My Image

My Image

What is my IMAGE? Is my IMAGE real?
Who created my IMAGE?

Your "image" is the way you present yourself to other people. It is who you want other people to think you are. You have images in your mind about how you should look and act. Many of these images came from celebrities you see on television. Some of these images come from others around you that you think are "cool."

Celebrities create a glamorous image that is quite different from their real personalities to help them to get parts in movies or record deals. When you look in a magazine or at a friend you think is pretty and try to imitate how that person looks or acts, you are trying to create an image that is just an imitation of someone else, but not the REAL YOU.

You may present one image of yourself to one group of friends and another image of yourself to another group of friends. You may present a different image of yourself to your parents and teachers than with your friends. Everyone's behavior changes in different situations and different mood states, but trying to have a different image with different groups of people means you aren't really being your "authentic" or "real" self. It is like wearing a mask. Being authentic means you are guided by values that don't change, no matter who you are with. It means you try to be honest at all times. It means you act on what you know is right and not on what or who your friends think you should be.

Use the following questions to help you understand more about your IMAGE.

1. What image do you try to portray to your friends?
2. Do you portray a different image to adults?
3. Do you get a sad feeling when you compromise what you believe?
4. Do you act like a clown or hide your skills or talents so other people will like you?
5. Do you hide your emotions to appear "cool" with your friends?
6. Do you feel people don't know the real you?
7. Are there people who know the real you?
8. Does your confidence increase when you stick up for your beliefs with your friends?

Happiness Happens from the Inside Out.
Spend Time Inside Your Heart.

Let's Celebrate REAL Beauty

Where do you find REAL beauty, the kind that warms you heart and makes you smile? What about the women you see walking into Wal-Mart? What about the women who help you at school? What about the women in your own family?

TAKE THE REAL BEAUTY CHALLENGE:

1. Read the definition of real beauty listed on the handout *REAL BEAUTY IS...*

2. Add your ideas about real beauty to the list.

3. Think of someone you know who fits the definition of real beauty. On the handout REAL BEAUTY IS..., write your thoughts about why this person is beautiful to you.

4. Now let's pass some real beauty around! Take your completed REAL BEAUTY IS... handout and share it with the person you wrote about. Let them know what they mean to you.

Real Beauty is something that warms your heart.

REAL BEAUTY is...

- *Respect for my body, mind, and spirit self.*
- *Caring for others.*
- *Wearing makeup that enhances my natural qualities.*
- *Taking responsibility for my choices.*
- *Discovering and using my unique talents.*
- *Being honest with myself and others.*
- _____
- _____

What makes someone beautiful to me?
Write a few thoughts about someone special.

_____
_____
_____
_____
_____

Handout 42

The Butterfly Hug Self-Soothing Technique[1]

The Butterfly Hug

By Lucina Artigas

Follow These Steps:

1. Close your eyes or keep your eyes half open looking towards the tip of your nose. Begin to focus on your breathing. Slowly inhale and exhale through your nose. Move the air deeply into the bottom of your stomach. Place your hands on your stomach and feel it move in and out, like a balloon. Take about 5-6 deep slow breaths.

2. Next, place your hands over your chest, with your fingers spread, so that with the fingertips of each hand you can touch the area that is located under the connection between the clavicle (collar bone) and the shoulder. You may interlace your thumbs simulating the body of the butterfly.

3. Next, alternate the movement of your hands, simulating the movement of the flapping wings of a butterfly.

4. As you flap your butterfly wings, observe what goes through your mind and body without changing it, judging it, or suppressing it. By doing this, you are helping your brain to comfort the rest of your body.

5. Continue to breathe gently and stop when you feel in your body that it has been enough.

6. Use the "Butterfly Hug" any time you notice thoughts or sensations in your body that are unpleasant or uncomfortable. Watch for the pleasant thoughts, emotions, and sensations in your body that you have as you do the Butterfly Hug.

---

[1] The Butterfly Hug is a self bilateral stimulation method that was developed by Lucina (Lucy) Artigas during her work performed with the survivors of Hurricane Pauline in Acapulco Mexico (1997). It is now used all over the world to help people reprocess traumatic memories. Used with permission.

Handout 43
EFT Tapping Steps

EFT TAPPING STEPS

Adapted from *Tap into Joy* by Susan Jeffrey Busen

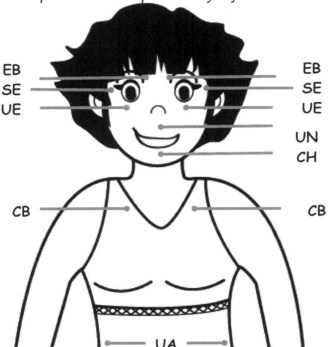

EB = eyebrow
SE = side eye
UE = under eye
UN = under nose
CH = above chin
CB = under collar bone
UA = under arm (under breast)
KC = karate chop

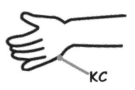

STEP 1: Rate the intensity on a scale of 0 to 10. (10 is highly distressed.)

STEP 2: Tap the KC and say your set-up phrases at least 3 times.
"Even though I [state problem or emotion], I love and accept myself."

STEP 3: Tap each point about 7 times as you say the negative phrase or body sensation that describes your negative emotion. Use the index and middle finger of each hand to tap the points in this order: EB, UE, SE, UN, CH, CB, UA. After you are done tapping, take a big breath and slowly blow out the air.

STEP 4: Hold one hand in a fist over your heart; rotate your fist in circles over your heart and say your forgiveness phrases. After you finish, take another big breath and slowly blow out the air.

STEP 5: Tap each point about 7 times as you say your POSITIVE phrases.

STEP 6: Rate the intensity.

STEP 7: Repeat the whole process (Steps 1-6) until the intensity is down to 0 or 1.
Used with permission.

Handout 44
What to Do When I Am Blue Instructions

What to Do When I Am Blue

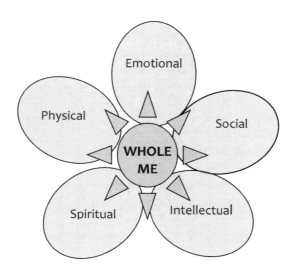

Every part of you needs care and nourishment. Every part of you can generate feelings of emptiness or "hunger." Often, when you are feeling blue, you try to "feed" only your Physical Self by worrying about your appearance, eating junk food, or buying clothes or jewelry, etc. What may really be "hungry" is your Spiritual Self or your Social Self. All parts of you must be nourished to keep you balanced.

Make a *What to Do When I'm Blue Card File* of activities you can do to nurture the different parts of yourself when you are feeling blue.

How to Make *a What to Do When I'm Blue Card File*:

1. Get 10-15 index cards. On each card, write one action item from the *What to Do When I'm Blue Activity List*.
2. Decorate each card with markers, stickers, etc. Have fun!
3. Punch a hole in the corner of each card. Fasten cards together with a ribbon.
4. Keep this card file by your bed or other place where you can use it often.
5. When you are blue, pick a card and do the activity to lift your mood.

What to Do When I Am Blue List

- Buy one beautiful flower.
- Make one space in a room pretty.
- Light a candle and watch the flame.
- Set a pretty place at the table, using your best things, for a meal.
- Look at nature around you.
- Go out in the middle of the night and watch the stars.
- Look at beautiful pictures in a book.
- Listen to beautiful or soothing music or to invigorating and exciting music.
- Pay attention to the sounds of nature (waves, birds, rainfall, leaves rustling).
- Sing your favorite songs or hum a soothing tune.
- Light a scented candle.
- Bake cookies, cake, or bread and share them with someone.
- Smell the roses, daisies, or any other flowers.
- Chew your favorite gum.
- Really taste the food you eat; eat one thing mindfully.
- Take a bubble bath.
- Put clean sheets on the bed.
- Pet your dog or cat.
- Have a massage.
- Soak your feet.
- Put creamy lotion on your whole body.
- Brush your hair for a long time.
- Hug someone.
- Read a book with characters you admire.
- Write a secret note to tell someone how much you appreciate them.

- Write your feelings in a journal.
- Say or write a heartfelt prayer.
- Look up a topic you enjoy on the internet, such as: whales, birds, bread making, travel, etc.
- Share your thoughts with a friend or listen to a friend's thoughts.
- Make a list of all the things you are thankful for.
- Go for a vigorous walk or run.
- Ask someone you trust for help.
- Punch a pillow.
- Vigorously scrub the bathtub.
- Draw a picture that expresses your feelings or dreams.
- Eat a crunchy apple.
- Hug a baby.
- Look up clean jokes on the internet and have a hearty laugh.
- Try out a new recipe.
- Make a list of things you love to do.
- Say a prayer for someone else.
- Offer to cook dinner.
- Give yourself a "Butterfly Hug." (Handout 42).
- Write a make-believe story.
- Have a good cry.
- Give someone a sincere compliment.
- Dance when no one is looking.
- Apologize for something you did or said that was careless.
- Play a musical instrument.
- Clean out a drawer or closet.
- Do 10 "jumping jacks."

Handout 46

My Ecomap

My Ecomap

An ecomap can help me solve problems. It helps me figure out who can help me with the many different kinds of problems that challenge me.

1. Write your name in the middle.
2. Write names of people who help you in the ovals. (you can draw more ovals if you need to.)
3. Use the Ecomap Key to identify the ways each person can help you.
4. In each oval, write the symbol from the Ecomap Key that matches how that person can help you. For example, if you have written "mom," now write all the symbols that describe how mom can support you.

Ecomap Key

H = Homework help.

$ = Help with clothes, food.

♥ = Feeling sad.

W = Feeling worried or scared.

^ = Getting picked on.

** = Really confidential stuff.

? = Questions about God, death, and the purpose of life.

+ = Help with aches and pains.

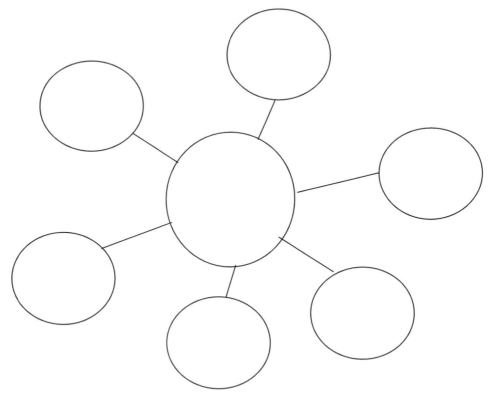

I can ask for support when I need help.

www.healthytransitionsforgirls.com

5-Step Problem-Solving Model

1. Identify the problem.
What would it look like if the problem was solved? Are your expectations realistic? Can you change the situation or the person involved? Can you break the problem down into parts and address one part of the problem?

2. Brainstorm solutions.
Don't worry about whether the solution is workable in this step. Just let your ideas flow.

3. Choose the best solution.
Don't worry about a perfect solution. Use a pros and cons list to help you choose the best solution. Go with your best choice at the time, knowing that if you learn more, you can decide that another choice is better.

4. Plan how to implement the solution.
Decide how, when, and where you will take action. What resources do you need? Who can help you? What "first step" can you take?

5. Evaluate the results.
Did the solution work? Did it almost work? Is there something you can do to improve the solution? Did you learn more facts that would make another solution a better choice?

Remember: You haven't failed until you have quit trying!
It took Thomas Edison over 6,000 tries to invent the light bulb.

I can solve problems one step at a time.

Handout 48
Designer Checklist

Designer Checklist for Creating Your Own Style.

Use this list when shopping to choose a style that is right for you.

- ✓ Can you bend over and not worry that you are revealing anything in the front or back?
- ✓ Does your outfit give you room to move freely?
- ✓ Does it fit in a way that does not call attention to your breasts, thighs, navel area (midriff), or buttocks (rear end)?
- ✓ Do the colors and style help you express YOUR personality, rather than trying to imitate what the media says you should look like?
- ✓ Does the outfit have colors that help you feel cheerful and energetic?

Outsmart the Fashion Tricks and Trends!

- ➤ YOU can OUTSMART fashion trends that may not showcase who YOU are inside. Remember, the fashion industry is trying to SELL A MESSAGE about what makes girls "pretty" and "popular."

- ➤ YOU can reject media messages that portray femininity as sexy, grungy, passive, "in-your-face," and materialistic.

- ➤ YOU can adapt the latest fashions to fit your own personality and reject styles that are too revealing or tight. Your UNIQUENESS is what COUNTS!

- ➤ YOU can OUTSMART media and advertisers who want to HOOK YOU in to wanting to be sexy and pretty, so you will BUY MORE AND MORE products.

- ➤ YOU can look "inside" for answers rather than letting the media "write on YOUR walls" and define who YOU are.

- ➤ YOU can change your style as you grow. As YOU come to know yourself better, YOU will have more ideas about what YOU want to wear.

- ➤ Choosing YOUR own style is a way of choosing the messages YOU believe about YOURSELF. Choosing YOUR own style is a way of choosing the messages YOU want OTHERS to believe about you, too.

I can resist social pressure and choose styles that represent who I am inside.

Handout 49
Don't Hide Your Femininity behind T-Shirts and Jeans

Don't Hide Your Femininity behind T-Shirts and Jeans

Girls can get stuck in the "t-shirt and jean rut." Dressing casual is great, but it's important to let the feminine part of being a girl shine through.

Dressing feminine means you resist sexualized styles and choose styles that bring out the real girl INSIDE of YOU. Truly feminine fashions increase your self-respect. What does "femininity" mean to you?

> **FEMININITY IS** *more than makeup, hair styles, and trendy clothes.* **FEMININITY IS** *the female expression of positive qualities, such as sensitivity, creativity, charm, graciousness, character, dignity, intelligence, and strength.* **FEMININITY IS** *expressed in* **unique and meaningful ways for each girl.**

BEWARE! Don't let the media put you in a BOX that portrays femininity as "sexy," "risky," "passive," or "revealing."

Advertisers know that if you are constantly trying to be "sexy," "risky," or "trendy," you will buy more products.

Your clothes reflect who you are on the inside—they are the "gift wrap" for the unique girl inside of YOU.

Sexy
Risky
Passive
Revealing

> ### FEMININITY...
> It comes in all shapes, and sizes. It is expressed in different ways and different styles in different settings. It's not "one-size fits all."

I can choose fashions that help me to feel feminine.

BE YOUR OWN FASHION DESIGNER INSTRUCTIONS

Instructions: Create a favorite outfit that you might wear for a special occasion, such as church, a party, a dance, a play, a concert, or a visit with the President of the United States. This outfit should reflect your personality rather than current fads. The guidelines in the Designer Checklist will help you design an outfit that avoids the pitfalls of immodest or revealing sexualized fashions that detract from you true feminine beauty.

Designer Checklist for Creating Your Own Style:

✓ **Can you bend over and not worry that you are revealing anything in the front or back?**
✓ **Does your outfit give you room to move freely?**
✓ **Does it fit in a way that does not call attention to your breasts, thighs, navel area, or buttocks (rear end)?**
✓ **Do the colors and style help you express YOUR personality rather than trying to imitate what the media says you should look like?**
✓ **Does the outfit have colors that help you feel cheerful and energetic?**

As you begin planning your outfit, remember the definition of FEMININITY.

FEMININITY IS *more than makeup, hair styles, and trendy clothes.* **FEMININITY IS** *the female expression of positive qualities, such as sensitivity, creativity, charm, graciousness, character, dignity, intelligence, and strength.* **FEMININITY IS** *expressed in* **unique and meaningful ways for each girl.**

Ask yourself: what styles help me to feel FEMININE?

Now that you know the guidelines for choosing styles that reflect your *true* personality, use the fashion words on the next page to give you ideas on how to make your design truly unique.

I can choose modest clothes that reflect my personality.

BE YOUR OWN FASHION DESIGNER

Circle all the adjectives that describe your fashion style.

Polka dots	Jacket	Kelley Green	Sparkles
Floral	Short-sleeve	Baby Pink	Satin
Striped	Long-sleeve	Fluorescent	Ball gown
Solid color	Lacey	Yellow	Sweetheart
Bright	Balloon sleeve	Ruffled	Tropical
Pastel	Bell sleeve	Baby Blue	Pencil skirt
Shiny	Bias cut	Beaded	Pin striped
Soft	Monochrome	Faded	Cotton
Geometric	Western	Flared	Polyester
Multi-colored	Gold	Fitted	Silky
Mid-length	Navy Blue	Rhinestones	¾ Sleeves
Knee Length	Hot Pink	Scarf	Boots
Gathered	Purple	Shawl	Slip-ons
Square neck	Spring Green	Buttoned	Tassels
Round neck	Hunter Green	Zippered	Collar
V-Neck	Royal Blue	Hat	Sweater
Ankle-length	Orange	Heels	Cap sleeve
Cropped	Scarlet Red	Tights	Pockets
Shrug	Coral	Gloves	Classy

Now you are ready to design your own fashion creation.

What does your outfit say about who YOU are INSIDE?

_____

_____

_____

_____

I can be creative in my fashion choices rather than following the latest fad.

Handout 52
Be Your Own Fashion Designer Parent Homework

Dear _____:
(Mom, Grandmother, Mentor)

Today in our *Healthy Transitions for Girls* Workshop, we learned about choosing clothes that reflect our own personality and style. The media promotes fashions that are over-sexualized, rather than supporting a true definition of femininity. The media also promotes wearing too many black and drab colors that drag down my mood. I really want to wear clothes that represent my true self, rather than wearing clothes that make me feel like I have to try to be "sexy" or "revealing" in order to get boyfriends and popularity.

In our discussion today, we were given a checklist to help us make smart fashion choices. Will you please remind me about this list when we shop for clothes? Modest dress is a vital way to protect me against the over-sexualized media culture.

Thanks for all you do to guide me to make healthier choices!

Love,

_____

🔖 Save for Future Reference

Designer Checklist for Creating Your Own Style:

✓ **Can you bend over and not worry that you are revealing anything in the front or back?**

✓ **Does your outfit give you room to move freely?**

✓ **Does it fit in a way that does not call attention to your breasts, thighs, navel area, or buttocks (rear end)?**

✓ **Do the colors and style help you express YOUR personality rather than trying to imitate what the media says you should look like?**

✓ **Does the outfit have colors that help you feel cheerful and energetic?**

Handout 53
Do You Know What You Are Attracting?

Do You Know What You Are Attracting?

Have you ever been on a picnic and noticed how the flies swarm around the food? Gross! People have to "cover up" the delicious food to keep the flies away. Making fashion choices is like going to a "picnic." What you wear attracts attention, but is it the kind of attention you *really* want?

What do you really want to attract from boys when you choose your clothes? Do you want guys to see you as a sexual "object" or "tool," or do you want them to care about you for who you are inside? Wearing revealing clothing is like attracting "flies" that spoil the "picnic." "Cover up" and get the "picnic" you deserve!

Make conscious fashion choices. You can create the relationships you really want. Share your thoughts and concerns. Write down your goals about fashion choices.

_____
_____
_____
_____
_____
_____
_____
_____
_____

I can be powerful by choosing clothes that attract real friendships.

www.healthytransitionsforgirls.com

Handout 54
What's So Special about Being a Girl?

What's So Special about Being a Girl?

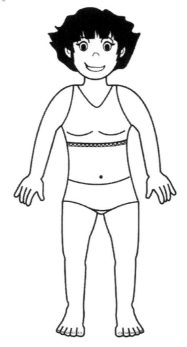

There are a lot of changes going on in my body. Some I can see. Some I can't. These changes feel embarrassing sometimes, but they have a wonderful purpose. My uterus or womb is changing to become a place where someday, a new little person can grow inside of me. That little person needs a healthy place to develop and feel safe so he or she can get off to a good start in life.

My breasts are changing inside and out. Inside, glands are developing that can one day help me feed my baby with nutritious milk. Babies need good nutrition and nurturing to be healthy and happy. Someday, I will be able to snuggle and feed my baby right next to my *heart*. I have a responsibility to respect and care for my body. Someone special is depending upon ME!

Write some of the feelings you have about the changes in your body?
- How do you feel about being a mother someday?
- Do you like to snuggle babies?
- What are you learning to help you be a loving mom?
- Do you think taking care of your body NOW is an important gift you can give your baby someday?

I am changing in wonderful ways.
I can prepare today to care for a new life.

www.healthytransitionsforgirls.com

Handout 55

What's So Special about Being a Girl? Parent Letter

What's So Special about Being a Girl?

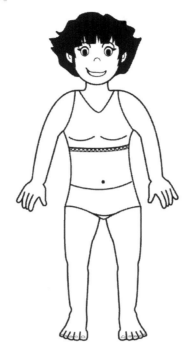

Dear _____:

Today in *Healthy Transitions* we talked about the big responsibility we have to care for our bodies NOW so that we are prepared someday be mothers.

Can you tell me how you feel about being a mom? Do you have some memories you can share with me about what I was like as a baby? I love learning about ME!

I am really trying not to be so embarrassed about my body and all the things that are changing. The media and other kids are sending a lot of weird messages that make me feel even more embarrassed.

I really need your help to feel good about the normal and natural things that are happening to me.

Love,

254

The WHOLE ME: Let's Get PHYSICAL

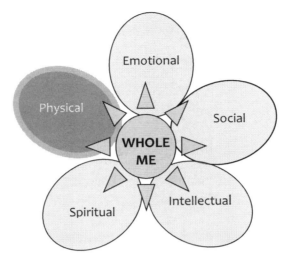

Goals to Support the **Physical** Part of Me:

Goal	How It Helps Me
1. Get a good night's sleep (8-9 hours).*	Restores body's normal chemistry; gives me a daily stress tune up.
2. Participate in 30 minutes aerobic exercise daily.	Releases negative emotional energy; suppresses cravings for unhealthy food; stimulates endorphins (the "feel good" hormones).
3. Eat 3 healthy smaller meals throughout the day, plus 2 healthy snacks between meals.	Keeps metabolism up; staves off excessive hunger and binge eating; levels out blood sugars to keep you energized.
4. Drink 6-8 glasses of water daily.	Helps flush out toxins; keeps your cells hydrated so they work better *Do NOT use caffeine as a substitute for rest.

Write at least 3 things you can do now to care for your PHYSICAL Self:

1._____

2._____

3._____

Who can be your accountability partner to help remind you?

_____

I can know and practice basic rules for health.

Handout 57
The WHOLE Me: Let's Get Physical—Show What You Know

The WHOLE ME: Let's Get Physical
SHOW WHAT YOU KNOW

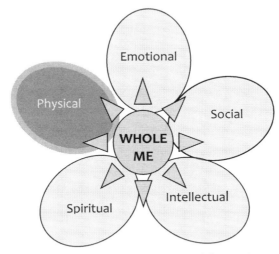

What 4 health practices will keep you physically healthy? Hints are given to help you remember what you have learned. The hints look like a weird math formula, but it a formula for GOOD HEALTH. How do these health practices help your body and your emotions? Fill in the blanks. The first letter of the answer is given for you. Show what you know. Set 3 goals to help you have better health.

1. (Hint: S8-10)_____

    Helps restore body's normal **c** _____.

    Gives the **b**_____ a **s** _____ tune up.

2. (Hint: M3+S2)_____

    Levels out blood **s**_____ to keep you **e**_____.

    Staves off excessive **h**_____ and **b**_____ eating.

3. (Hint: D6-8)_____

    Flushes out **t**_____.

    Keeps your **c**_____ **h**_____.

4. (Hint: 30m)_____

    Releases **n**_____ **e**_____ energy.

    Supresses cravings for **u**_____ **f**_____.

    Stimulates the **f**_____ **g**_____ hormones.

I can know and practice basic rules for health.

Handout 58
The WHOLE Me: My Exercise Inventory

The WHOLE ME: My Exercise Inventory

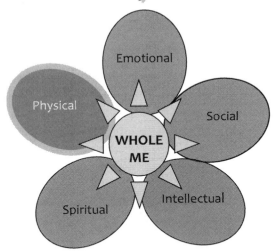

Your body needs exercise to be healthy emotionally and physically, at least 30 minutes of aerobic exercise daily. However, even a good thing like exercise can get out of balance. Girls who want to be thin can become obsessed with exercise; they exercise to "punish" themselves for eating. Similarly, girls who exercise a lot because they participate in sports will not eat because they want to improve their sports performance. You need to eat more when you are active to keep your body fueled. **The BEST REASON to exercise is to STAY HEALTHY.** Exercise because you love your body and you want to care for it, not because you are trying to be thin.

Exercise at least 30 minutes a day for 3 days. Keep a log of how you felt and ate.

Day 1
My reason for exercising:_____
How I felt after I exercised:_____
Did I eat well and drink water after I exercised?_____

Day 2
My reason for exercising:_____
How I felt after I exercised:_____
Did I eat well and drink water after I exercised?_____

Day 3
My reason for exercising:_____
How I felt after I exercised:_____
Did I eat well and drink water after I exercised?_____

I can benefit from balanced exercise.

Handout 59

"Go Green" Hulk Smoothie Recipe

GO GREEN: The Famous Hulk Smoothie

You're a living, growing being.
You need living, fresh food every day.
Empty calories leave you feeling empty emotionally.
EAT YOUR GREENS!

The Famous "HULK" Smoothie

Makes 2 "Hulk-Size" Servings

1 6-8 oz. carton (1 c.) yogurt
1 cup milk or orange juice
½ c. fruit, fresh or frozen (bananas, strawberries)
½ to 1 c. fresh spinach
2 t. honey (optional)
5 ice cubes

BLEND until SMOOTH

I can make a green smoothie every day.

Handout 60
Take the Food Mood Challenge

Take the FOOD MOOD Challenge

Have you ever "pigged out" on pizza and thought: "Ugh, I feel sluggish." Or ate tons of candy at Halloween and noticed: "Wow! I feel hyper and irritable." When you eat a healthy salad or drink a big glass of cold water, do you feel refreshed and energized?

Maybe you just haven't taken time to notice how your food affects your mood. Now is a great time to hear what your body has to say.

Hint: Try starting your day with a HULK SMOOTHIE. Do you feel energized? If you miss a day, your body says: "Hey, I want a Hulk Smoothie. I work better when you feed me something nutritious!"

THE FOOD MOOD CHALLENGE
Write down everything you eat for three days. Pay attention to your emotions. Make a note anytime you notice a change in your emotions after eating. If you skip a meal, notice how you feel. Rate your overall mood at the end of each day.

I can support my emotions by eating healthy.

www.healthytransitionsforgirls.com

Handout 61
Take the Food Mood Challenge Food Log

Take the FOOD MOOD Challenge

THE FOOD MOOD CHALLENGE
Write down everything you eat for three days. Pay attention to your emotions. Make a note anytime you notice a change in your emotions after eating. If you skip a meal, notice how you feel. Rate your overall mood at the end of each day.

DAY 1

Breakfast	Snack	Lunch	Snack	Dinner	Notes:

DAY 2

Breakfast	Snack	Lunch	Snack	Dinner	Notes:

DAY 3

Breakfast	Snack	Lunch	Snack	Dinner	Notes:

I can support my emotions by eating healthy.

Healthy Transitions for Girls Healthy Snacks

Ants on a Log or Ants in the Grass

Celery sticks
Peanut butter

Sunflower seeds
Alfalfa sprouts

Spread peanut butter on celery sticks. Top with sunflower seeds and sprouts.

Fruit Planet

1 head of purple cabbage, halved
Toothpicks
Chunk pineapple

Bananas (dip into pineapple juice)
Mandarin oranges

Poke toothpicks through fruit pieces and secure onto cabbage head.

Honey Kettle Corn

8 cups popped corn
1/3 c. honey

¼ c. butter or coconut oil
dash of salt

Boil the butter and honey to about 240º F. This is called the "soft ball" stage in candy making. To test, drop some of the cooking honey/butter mixture into cold water. If it forms a soft, pliable ball that flattens after a few moments in your hand, then it is done. Removed from heat and immediately pour onto popped corn. Add a dash of salt and stir thoroughly.

Carmel Apple Dippers

1 package (8 oz.) cream cheese
1/4 c. honey
¼ c. peanut butter (optional)
Apple slices, such as Granny Smith and Red Delicious

Mix together cream cheese, sugar, and peanut butter. Serve with apple slices.

I can care for my body and mind by choosing healthy snacks.

Handout 63
Turn Over a New Leaf

Turn over a New Leaf

Turn over a new leaf. *Idiom.*
Means to replace a negative habit with a positive habit.

Whether you call it going "GREEN" or turning over a new "LEAF" (pun intended), when you realize how many miraculous things your body does for you each day, you are ready to begin to start some healthier eating habits. How we eat is a reflection of how much respect we have for our bodies. Say "THANKS" to your body each day by giving it good food and eliminating habits that make your body work harder with less fuel.

PICK A NEW HABIT FROM THE LIST. DO IT FOR ONE WEEK.
HAVE A FAMILY MEMBER OR FRIEND PICK A HABIT, TOO.
CHALLENGE EACH OTHER TO MAKE A NEW HABIT.

1. Eat something fresh and green every day.
2. Replace soda with juice (no sugar added) or water.
3. Give up deep fried food.
4. Eat wheat bread instead of white.
5. Follow My Plate guidelines for each day's meals.
6. Munch on baby carrots instead of cookies.
7. Eat two palm-size meat portions each day.
8. Drink six to eight glasses of water each day.
9. Eat consciously. Ask, "Am I really feeding my body?"
10. Use dark green lettuce instead of iceberg lettuce.
11. Eat 5 small meals instead of 2 or 3 huge meals.
12. Do not skip breakfast.
13. Eat light butter popcorn instead of potato chips.
14. Give up sugar and candy.
15. Give up caffeine drinks.
16. Eat a second helping of salad.
17. Cut dessert in half or avoid it altogether.
18. Eat brown rice instead of white rice.
19. Eat an apple each day.
20. Eat a whole grain cereal instead of a sweetened cereal.

THE NUMBER I CHOOSE IS: _____

I can choose to eat healthy every day.

 www.healthytransitionsforgirls.com

Handout 64

Don't Dump on Your Body

Don't DUMP on Your Body

Your body holds your beliefs and emotions. Awareness of stress and worry in your body can help you avoid "junk food." Take out the "trash." Care for your body and your emotions instead of stuffing your body with "junk."

1. **What are you aware of inside?** (How full is your trash can? Are you overflowing with stress and worries?

2. **What do you want?** (Instead of junk food, what are you really longing for? What do you need right now, in the moment?)

3. **What can you do to care for yourself in a healthy way?**
(Use these tools from this workbook when you are stressed: *Healthy Transitions for Girls Healthy Snacks, Be Your Own "Cheerleader," "Palace of Possibilities Affirmations,"* The Butterfly Hug Self-Soothing Technique, EFT Tapping Steps, *"Blowing Balloons" Relaxation Activity, What to Do When I'm Blue Card File.*)

I can avoid junk food and care for negative emotions I feel in my body.

Handout 65

I Am Thankful for All My Body Does for Me

\ Am Thankful for ALL My Body Does for Me

> Have you thanked your body today? It works hard every day. Give your body a "pat on the back." Your body loves to hear positive messages from you!

Dear Body:

I can't believe everything you've done for me today. I take you for granted a lot! You accomplish miraculous things every day. Here is a list of things you have done for me today:

1.

2.

3.

4.

5.

6.

7.

8.

9.

10.

Wow! You're amazing! Thanks for being such a great friend.

With love,

_____

I can send a message of appreciation to my body every day.

Handout 66
My Body Is a Miraculous Creation

My Body Is a Miraculous Creation

(That's why I WILL promise to take care of it!)

I WILL treat my body with respect and
    kindness.

I WILL listen to my body's need
    for good food and rest.

I WILL thank my body for all it does
    for me every day.

I WILL not harm my body with drugs.

I WILL not allow others (except doctors)
    to touch the private parts of my body.

I WILL remember that my body
    can carry me to my dreams.

My Full Name: _____

My Signature: _____

Date I Made This Promise: _____

I can commit to care for my body every day.

Figure 1
Palace of Possibilities Display Board

Materials Needed.

1. A tri-fold presentation board.
2. Scrapbook paper and glue.
3. Markers or printed text.
4. A mirror.

Activity Steps.

1. Glue scrapbook paper to the face of the display board. You want the background to look like painted walls. Be creative!
2. The right side of the tri-fold board contains positive affirmations. Suggestions are given in Handout 8, *Palace of Possibilities Affirmations*, but feel free to add your own. The left side of the board lists common negative self-statements. The middle of the display board explains the Palace of Possibilities metaphor.
3. The diagram on the following page shows how to place the Palace of Possibilities display text. You may either write the text directly on the scrapbook paper with a marker, or you may print the text on plain paper and glue it to the board.
4. Glue a mirror on the right side of the tri-fold and have girls look in the mirror or obtain a picture of the wicked witch from the movie *Snow White* or *Maleficent* to represent the negative self-talk of Activity 6, *Mirror, Mirror Activity*.
5. Keep your board on display during *Healthy Transitions for Girls* workshops and activities.

Figure 1
Palace of Possibilities Display Board Template

Right Side	Middle	Left Side
What is written on your walls?	**YOU are a PALACE OF POSSIBILITIES.**	**"Mirror, mirror, on the wall..."** (Wicked Witch Picture Or MIRROR)
• Beauty comes in all shapes and sizes.	Your life is like a palace with many rooms yet to be explored. Some rooms you visit often. You are constantly consulting what is "written on your walls." These messages influence how you feel, what you say, and ultimately, the choices you make.	• I hate my body.
• My body is a miraculous creation.		• I hate being so ugly.
• I am responsible, strong, and true to myself.		• If I just had a boyfriend...
• I am changing in wonderful ways.	The messages on your walls come from family, peers, and from the media. Some messages are negative and some are positive. You can discover and then choose what is written on your walls. You can replace negative messages with positive ones.	• I'm so fat.
• I am a wonderful mixture of talents and challenges.		• I'm so stupid.
• My challenges are opportunities for growth.		• If I was just pretty, thin, or sexy, I would be popular.
• I am gentle when I notice my shortcomings.		• Nobody likes me.
• I am looking for friends who bring out my best.		• I can never measure up.
• I am responsible for the life I create.		• I hate my... nose/legs/thigh/skin/breasts/height/weight/emotions/smile/teeth/hair.
		• I can't do anything right.
Negative self-talk hurts your confidence and your mood.	**"I can shut the door on media that says I am not good enough just the way I am."**	**What you say in the mirror is CRITICAL.**

Figure 2
Promotional Parent Flyer

Help girls navigate the minefield of negative media messages

The answer is: POSITIVE BODY IMAGE

What one factor helps build strength to resist:
- Eating disorders
- Substance abuse
- Depression and mood disorders
- Unhealthy dating behaviors
- Risky sexual behaviors
- Low self-esteem
- Girl bullying and "drama"

Healthy Transitions for Girls
An *Essential* Prevention Tool
~ For Girls ages 8 to 14 ~

Addresses All Factors Shown By Research to Promote
POSITIVE BODY IMAGE
- Supports parent and peer relationships
- Supports global and physical self-esteem
- Encourage healthy concepts of femininity (gender role)
- Teaches coping skills and media literacy
- Creates awareness of negative belief systems

Please attend a *Healthy Transitions for Girls* Workshop
For Parents (Mentors, Grandparents) & Daughters
Where:
When:
Presented By:

Figure 3

Healthy Transitions for Girls Parent Consent Form

_____ will be presenting a series of workshops for girls designed to support positive body image. Having a positive body image builds strength to resist substance abuse, depression, unhealthy dating relationships, girl bullying, and eating disorders. Activities from the *Healthy Transitions for Girls* Curriculum by Peggy A McFarland, MS, LPC, will be used. Workshop sessions will be held

Dates & Time:_____

Location: _____

Please initial each area of this consent form and sign below if you wish your daughter to participate.

_____*Healthy Transitions for Girls* is a skills group, not a therapy group, and may not be appropriate for girls who have experienced serious mental illness or trauma. The parent agrees to consult with their child's mental health provider before consenting for participation. The parent agrees to inform the workshop presenter of any health or behavior issues before consenting for their child's participation.

_____ You are invited to review workshop materials which are available upon request. Please initial to show that you are satisfied with the content of the curriculum. Skills learned in *Healthy Transitions for Girls* groups include:

- How to replace negative beliefs with positive beliefs.
- How to develop a healthy mind-body connection.
- How to develop strong parent and peer relationships.
- How to challenge unhealthy pop culture media messages.
- How to recognize what is so special about being a girl and to develop healthy femininity.
- How to care for their bodies as a valuable partner they will have for life.
- How to increase coping skills and problem-solving skills.

_____*Healthy Transitions for Girls* is not a "sexual education" program, but the physical development that occurs during puberty will be discussed. A focus of *Healthy Transitions for Girls* is to help girls develop positive belief systems regarding the changes occurring in their reproductive systems.

_____It is not the intention of the program to get girls to disclose information that is highly sensitive or embarrassing. The nature of adolescents is, however, that they tend to be very open about their emotions and experiences. The girls will be asked to respect the confidentiality of what their peers share during the workshop activities; however, confidentiality cannot be guaranteed.

_____*Healthy Transitions for Girls* is voluntary, and each girl's participation in any of the workshop activities is voluntary; however, girls are expected to attend each workshop session. The parent agrees to help their daughter attend each group and to assist her in the parent/child homework assignments.

----------You agree to the fees and financial terms specified by the presenter (when applicable). You also understand that refunds will not be given after the 3rd week of the program and that no refund is given for groups which your daughter has been unable to attend.

If you have any questions regarding this program please contact:

Name/Phone:_____

By signing this form, I consent to have my daughter _____/_____
(Child's Name/Birthdate)

participate in a Healthy Transitions for Girls for Girls Workshop Series.

Parent Signature/Relationship to Child/Date:_____

Figure 4

Healthy Transition for Girls Evaluation Form

1. How did you find out about this *Healthy Transitions for Girls* group?

2. What is your overall opinion of *Healthy Transitions for Girls*?
(Check one.)

_____I wouldn't participate in this group again.

_____It was okay. I can take it or leave it.

_____I thought it was interesting most of the time.

_____I looked forward to coming each week.

_____This was a really great experience that has helped me feel better about growing up.

3. What activity will you remember most? (Check one.)

_____Learning how to be a media detective.

_____Role-playing how to solve problems.

_____Learning about the messages that are written on the "walls of my castle."

_____Learning how to recognize how my "body talks" about my emotions.

_____Learning how to calm anxiety by "blowing balloons" or the "Butterfly Hug."

_____ Designing my own special dress.

_____Making green smoothies and learning how eating affects my emotions.

_____Making the "What to Do When I'm Blue" Card File.

_____Other _____

4. In the group we discussed that the media wants you to feel distressed. Write the media messages and tricks that you remember. (Write 2 or 3).

Figure 4, continued

Healthy Transitions for Girls Evaluation Form

6. I felt comfortable sharing my thoughts and feelings in this group. (Circle one.)

Never   Once in a while   Sometimes   Most of the time   Always

7. I felt like the workshop leader(s) understood my feelings and experiences. (Circle one.)

Never   Once in a while   Sometimes   Most of the time   Always

8. What is the most helpful thing you learned in this group?

_____

9. Share something you learned to help you deal with "girl drama."

_____

10. How have your feelings about your body changed from the beginning of this group?

_____

11. How have your feelings about growing up changed from the beginning of this group?

_____

12. How often did you come to the group? (Circle one.)

Once or twice   Three or Four Times   Most of the Time   Every time

13. I discussed the things we talked about in group with my mother, grandmother, teacher, or another woman who is a close friend. (Circle one.)

Never   Once in a while   Sometimes   Most of the time   Always

14. Is there anything you would like to share about this group? (Your answers will not be shared with anyone else.)

Figure 5

Healthy Transitions for Girls Comprehensive Materials List

Items that Need to be Ordered or Prepared in Advance

- *Healthy Transitions for Girls Handout Pages* Workbook for each girl.
- *Killing Us Softly* Handout Photos from http://www.mediaed.org/assets/products/206/studyguidehandout_206.pdf. (See Chapter 8, Activity 25 and Chapter 12, Activity 45).
- 12 to 15 advertisements featuring females from magazines.
- "Fold and Go Castle"castle for $49.99, plus shipping, through www.melissaanddoug.com.
- Palace of Possibilities Display Board (See directions Figure 1).
- White board and dry erase pens and eraser.
- Essential oils and spray mister.
- Large quilt, carpet squares, or blanket.
- Long table and chairs.
- A long piece of butcher paper or newsprint (approximately 5 ft long), for the icebreaker activity described in Chapter 12, Activity 47.
- Mailbox with a lid that opens (optional).
- Villainess black hat and cape, life size.
- Princess tiara and wand.
- CD or MP3 player and relaxing music with no words.
- Eye patches (Optional, See Footnote, Chapter 2, Activity 2).
- *Cinder Edna*, written by by Ellen Jackson and Kevin O'Malley, available at www.amazon.com
- *Princess Academy, written* by Shannon Hale, available at www.amazon.com
- *National Geographic Incredible Human Machine* (DVD) available at www.amazon.com
- *104 Activities that Build: Self-Esteem, Teamwork, Communication, Anger Management, Self-Discovery, Coping Skills* by Alanna Jones, available at www.amazon.com
- Food items for Healthy Snacks (See Chapter 11, Handout 62).
- Orange or raisins for each girls (See Chapter 3, Activity 9).
- Broomstick or Yardstick (See Chapter 12, Activity 45).
- (2) Full length mirrors (See Chapter 2, Activity 6).
- Blender
- Utensils and dishes for making snacks
- Lunch tray with divided sections
- Lima beans or other sortable objects

Figure 5, continued

Healthy Transitions for Girls Comprehensive Materials List

Office or Dollar Store Supplies

- Post-it Notes.
- Name tags (Chapter 12, Activity 45).
- Regular sized poster board (for group rules, See Chapter 12, Activity 46).
- Glue stick for each girl.
- Scissors for each girl.
- Yarn, at least 36 inch piece for each girl.
- Ruler for each girl (See Chapter 3, Activity 11).
- Envelopes, 1 for each girl.
- Crayons, markers, pens, pencils.
- Scrapbook paper.
- Plain white drawing paper.
- Index cards, 25 for each girl.
- Ribbon.
- "O" rings, 1 for each girl.
- Hole Punch.
- Napkins and paper goods for serving snacks
- Small mirror for each girl (optional).
- Princess stickers and other stickers (Please don't use Disney Princess stickers).
- Art supply tote to bring basic art supplies each week.

References

Alaimo, K., Olson, D. M., & Frongillo, E. A. (2000). Family food insufficiency, but not low family income, is positively associated with dysthymia and suicide symptoms in adolescents. *The Journal of Nutrition, 132*(4), 719-25.

Amen, D. (2010). *Change Your Brain, Change Your Body.* New York: Harmony Books.

American Psychological Association. (2007). Sexualization of Girls Executive Summary. Retrieved from http://www.apa.org/pi/women/programs/girls/report.aspx

Bandura, A. (1977). *Social Learning Theory.* Englewood Cliffs, NJ: Prentice Hall.

Bandura, A. (1992). Self-efficacy in cognitive development. *Educational Psychologist, 28*(2), 118.

Brady, S. (2011, April 20). Life-size Barbie sparks body image debate. Retrieved from http://www.brandchannel.com/home/post/2011/04/20/Life-Size-Barbie.aspx

Busby, D., Carroll, J. & Willoughby, B. (2010). Compatibility or restraints? The effects of sexual timing on marriage relationships. *Journal of Family Psychology, 24*(6), 766-774.

Casey, K. (2007). *Be Who You Want to Be: Dealing with Life's Ups & Downs.* San Francisco, CA: Conari Press.

Cash, T. (2008). *The Body Image Workbook* (2nd ed.). Oakland, CA: New Harbinger Publishers, Inc.

Center for Media Literacy. (2011). Media literacy: A definition and more. Retrieved from http://www.medialit.org/media-literacy-definition-and-more

Charen, M. (2009, October 10). Repeat after me: Mothers belong at work. *National Review Online.* Retrieved from http://article.nationalreview.com/print/?q=MTljM2MxNTVlYTAxMmVmODkyYTNiMzBlYmEwMmE0OTA=

Choate, L. (2007). Counseling adolescent girls for body image resilience: Strategies for school counselors. *Professional School Counseling, 10*(3), 317-326.

Choate, L. (2008). *Girls' and Women's Wellness: Contemporary Counseling Issues and Interventions.* Alexandria, VA: American Counseling Association.

Choate, L. (2014). *Adolescent Girls in Distress: A Guide for Mental Health Treatment and Prevention.* New York, NY: Springer Publishing Company, LLC.

Choquette, S. (1999). *The Wise Child.* New York: Three Rivers Press.

Cikara, M., Eberhardt, J. L., & Fiske, S. T. (2010). From agents to objects: Sexist attitudes and neural responses to sexualized targets. *Journal of Cognitive Neuroscience. 23*(3) 540-551.

Cloninger, C.R. (2006). The science of well-being: An integrated approach to mental health and its disorders. *World Psychiatry, 5*(2), 74.

Collins, M.E. (1991). Body figure and preferences among pre-adolescent children. *International Journal of Eating Disorders, 10*, 199-208.

Craig, G. (n.d.) Used by permission. *Palace of Possibilities: Utilizing Emotional Freedom Technique with the Law of Attraction.* Nancy Gnecco, (Ed.). Retrieved from http://www.nancygnecco.com/pdf/PALACE%20WORKBOOK.pdf

Dimeff, L. & Linehan, M. (2001). Dialectical behavior in a nutshell. *The California Psychologist, 34*, 10-13.

Dove Self-Esteem Fund. (2008). Real girls, real pressure: A national report on the state of self-esteem. Retrieved from http://content.dove.us/makeadiff/pdf/SelfEsteem_Report.pdf.

Dowd, E. T. (2005). Cognitive behavioral therapy: Evidence and new directions. *Journal of Cognitive Behavioral Psychotherapies, 5*(1), 103.

Ellis, A. (1962). *Reason and Emotion in Psychotherapy.* New York: Stuart.

Ellsworth, S. (2002). *How Did I Get This Way?* Orem, UT: Massai.

Faer, L.M., Hendriks, A., Abed., R.T., & Figueredo, A.J. (2005). The evolutionary psychology of eating

disorders: Female competition for mates or for status? *Psychology and Psychotherapy: Theory,*

Research and Practice, 78, 406.

Feinstein, D. (2004). *Energy Psychology Interactive: Rapid Interventions for Lasting Change.* Ashland, OR:

Innersource.

Ferron, C. (1997) Body image and adolescence: Cross-cultural research results of the preliminary phase

of a quantitative survey. *Adolescence, 32*(127), 735-45.

Fowler, J. (2004). Identity, intimacy, and "hooking up." *Ethics News & Views,* 13(1).

Gordon, T. (2000). *Parent Effectiveness Training: The Proven Program for Raising Responsible Children.* New York,

NY: Three Rivers Press.

Grossman, M. (2007). *Unprotected: A Campus Psychiatrist Reveals How Political Correctness in Her Profession*

Endangers Every Student. New York: Penguin Group.

Grossman, M. (2008). *Sense and Sexuality: The College Girl's Guide to Real Protection in a Hooked-Up World.*

Herndon, VA: Clare Boothe Luce Policy Institute. Retrieved from

http://www.miriamgrossmanmd.com/wp-content/uploads/2012/11/SNSbooklet.pdf

Grossman, M. (2009). *You're Teaching My Child What? A Physician Exposes the Lies of Sex Ed and How*

They Harm Your Child. Washington, D.C.: Regnery Publishing.

Hale, Shannon. (2007). Princess Academy. New York: Bloomsbury USA Childrens.

Harris, A.H.S., Thoresen, C., & Lopez, S. (2007). Integrating positive psychology into counseling: Why and (when appropriate) how. *Journal of Counseling & Development, 85*, 3-13.

Hewlett, S. A. (2002). *Creating a Life: Professional Women and the Quest for Children.* New York: Hyperion.

Holland, J. (2015, February 28). Medicating women's feelings. *New York Times.* Retrieved from http://www.nytimes.com

Jacobs, E., Masson, R., & Harvill, R. (2006). *Group Counseling Strategies & Skills* (5th ed.). Belmont, CA: Thomson Brooks/Cole.

Jhally, S. (Producer), & Kilbourne, J. (Director). (2000). *Killing Us Softly III* [Motion Picture].   Northampton, MA: Media Education Foundation.

Jones, A. (1998). *104 Activities That Build: Self-Esteem, Teamwork, Communication, Anger Management, Self-Discovery, Coping Skills.* Richland, WA: Rec Room Publishing.

Jones, D. (2001). Social comparisons and body image: Comparisons to models and peers among adolescent girls and boys. *Sex Roles, 45*(9/10), 645-664.

Kingston, T., Dooley, B., Bates, A., Lawlor, E., & Malone, K. (2007). Mindfulness-based cognitive therapy for residual depressive symptoms. *Psychology and Psychotherapy: Theory, Research and Practice, 80*(2), 201.

Kostanski, M., & Gullone, E. (1998). Adolescent body image dissatisfaction: Relationships with self-esteem, anxiety, and depression controlling for body mass. *Journal of Child Psychology and Psychiatry, 29*, 255-262.

Kupelian, D. (2005). *The Marketing of Evil.* Nashville, TN: Cumberland House Publishing, Inc.

Kuther, T. (2004). Early adolescents' experiences with and views of Barbie. *Adolescence, 39*(153), 44.

LeCroy, C.W., & Daley, J. (2001). *Empowering Adolescent Girls: Examining the Present, Building Skills for the Future with the Go Grrrls Program*. New York: W. W. Norton & Company.

LeCroy, C.W., & Daley, J. (2001). *The Go Grrrls Workbook*. New York: W. W. Norton & Company.

Lipton, B. (2005). *The Biology of Belief*. Felton, CA: Mountains of Love Productions, Inc.

Linehan, M. (1993). Interpersonal effectiveness handout 5: Cheerleading statements for interpersonal effectiveness. In *Skills Training Manual for Treating Borderline Personality Disorder* (p. 119). New York: Guilford Press.

Linehan, M. (1993*). Skills Manual for Treating Borderline Personality Disorder*. New York: Guilford Press.

McGoldrick, M. (2005) Women through the life cycle. In B.Carter & & M. McGoldrick (Eds.), *The Expanded Family Life Cycle: Individual, Family, and Social Perspectives* (3rd ed.). Boston: Allyn and Bacon.

McKinley, N. (1999). Women and objectified body consciousness: Mothers' and daughters' body experience in cultural, developmental and familial context. *Developmental Psychology, 35*(3), 767.

Media Education Foundation. (n.d.) *Killing Us Softly* 3 study guide handouts. Retrieved from http://www.mediaed.org/assets/products/206/studyguidehandout_206.pdf

Moore, C. (2014). *The Resilience Breakthrough: 27 Tools for Turning Adversity into Action*. Austin, TX: Greenleaf Book Group Press.

Moynihan, R. (1998). Motherhood in corporate culture. *The American Feminist, 5*(2), 13. Retrieved from http://www.feministsforlife.org/taf/1998/summer/Summer98.pdf

Muth, J. L., & Cash, T.F. (1997). Body-image attitudes: What difference does gender make? *Journal of Applied Social Psychology, 27,* 1438.

Myers, J., & Sweeney, T. (2005). Introduction to wellness theory. In J. Myers & T. Sweeney (Eds.), *Counseling for Wellness: Theory, Research, and Practice* (pp. 7-14). Alexandria, VA: American Counseling Association.

Myers, J., & Sweeney, T. J., (2005). *Counseling for Wellness: Theory, Research, and Practice.* Alexandria, VA: American Counseling Association.

Myers, J., & Sweeney, T.J., (2005b). The indivisible self: An evidence-based model of wellness. *The Journal of Individual Psychology,* 61(1), 269-279.

National Center for Chronic Disease Prevention and Health Promotion, Division of Adolescent and School Health. (2010). Nutrition and the health of young people. Retrieved from http://www.cdc.gov/HealthyYouth/nutrition/facts.htm

Nilsson, K., Abrahamsson, E., Torbiornsson, A., & Hagglof, B. (2007). Causes of adolescent onset anorexia nervosa: Patient perspectives. *Eating Disorders,* 15(125), 125-133.

Papazoglou, O. (1992). Despising our mothers, despising ourselves. *First Things, 16,* 11. Retrieved from http://www.firstthings.com/article/2007/12/001-despising-our-mothers-despising-ourselves-24

Pardeck, J. T. (1994). Using literature to help adolescents cope with problems. *Adolescence,* 29(114), 421.

Pert, C. (1999). *Molecules of Emotion.* New York: Simon & Schuster.

Peter, J. & Valkenburg, P. (2007). Adolescents' exposure to a sexualized media environment and their notions of women as sex objects. *Sex Roles, 56,* 381-395.

Pipher, M.B. & Media Education Foundation. (1998). *Reviving Ophelia: Saving the Selves of Adolescent Girls.* Northampton, MA: Media Education Foundation.

Rink, E., & Tricker, R. (2003). Resiliency-based research and adolescent health behaviors. *The Prevention Researcher,* 10(1), 1-4.

Rogers, P. J. (2000). A healthy body, a healthy mind: Long-term impact of diet on mood and cognitive function. *The Proceedings of the Nutrition Society, 60*(1), 135-43.

Rushkoff, D. Goodman, B. Fanning, D. Tabor, K., & Banker, L. (Producers) & Goodman, B. (Director). (2001). *Frontline: The Merchants of Cool.* [Motion Picture]. United States: Public Broadcasting Service (PBS).

Seidah, A., & Bouffard, T. (2007). Being proud of oneself as a person or being proud of one's physical appearance: What matters for feeling well in adolescence? *Social Behavior and Personality*, 2007, 35(2), 255-268.

Sapiro, V. (1999). *Women in Society: An Introduction to Women's Studies* (4th ed.). Mountain View, CA: Mayfield Publishers.

Smith, J. (2008). *Unsteady: What Every Parent Absolutely Must Know About Teenage Romance.* American Fork, UT: Covenant Communications.

Strouse, J., & Buerkel-Rothfuss, N. (1995). Gender and family as moderators of the relationship between music video exposure and adolescent sexual permissiveness. *Adolescence, 30*(119), 505.

Summers, A. (1994). *Damned Whores and God's Police: The Colonization of Women in Australia.* Ringwood, Victoria, Australia: Penguin Books.

Todd, T. (2000). Solution focused strategic parenting for challenging teens: A class for parents. *Family Relations, 49*(2). 165-168.

Tufts University. (2002). Special report: Is sugar really addictive? *Tufts University Health and Nutrition Letter, 20*(8), 1-3.

Tuttle, C. (2003). *Remembering Wholeness: A Handbook for Thriving in the 21ˢᵗ Century* (2nd ed.). Seattle, WA: Elton-Wolf Publishing.

Vander Zanden, J., Crandell, T., & Crandell, C. (2007). *Human Development* (8th ed.). New York, NY: McGraw Hill.

Verkuyten, M. (1990). Self-esteem and the evaluation of ethnic identity among Turkish and Dutch adolescents in the Netherlands. *The Journal of Social Psychology, 130*(3), 285-297.

Vernon, A. (2006). *Thinking, Feeling, Behaving: An Emotional Education Curriculum for Adolescents (Grades 7-12).* Retrieved from http://www.researchpress.com

Waller, M.W., Hallfors, D.D., Halpern, C.T., Iritani, B., Ford, C.A., & Guo, G. (2006). Gender differences in associations between depressive symptoms and patterns of substance use and risky sexual behavior among a nationally representative sample of U.S. adolescents. *Archives of Women's Mental Health, 9*(3), 139-150. Retrieved from http://www.nih.gov/news/pr/may2006/nida-15.htm

Weir, K. (2015). Teens, identity, and intimacy. *LDS Living Magazine,* March/April 2015, 25-26.

Wood, K., Becker, J., & Thompson, J. (1996). Body image dissatisfaction in preadolescent children. *Journal of Applied Developmental Psychology, 17,* 85-100.

Index

Made in the USA
Columbia, SC
12 September 2017